PLUM WARNER

PLUM
WARNER

GERALD HOWAT

UNWIN HYMAN
London   Sydney

First published in Great Britain by Unwin Hyman, an imprint of
Unwin Hyman Limited, 1987.

UNWIN HYMAN LIMITED
Denmark House, 37–39 Queen Elizabeth Street, London SE1 2QB
and
40 Museum Street, London WC1A 1LU

Allen & Unwin Australia Pty Ltd
8 Napier Street, North Sydney, NSW 2060, Australia

Allen & Unwin with the Port Nicholson Press
60 Cambridge Terrace, Wellington, New Zealand

British Library Cataloguing in Publication Data

Howat, Gerald
  Plum Warner.
1. Warner, *Sir* Pelham Francis   2. Cricket
players —— England —— Biography
3. Marylebone Cricket Club —— Biography
I. Title
796.35'8'0924   GV915.W35
ISBN 0–04–440023–3

Set in 11 on 12½ point Garamond by
Nene Phototypesetters, Northampton
and printed and bound in Great Britain by
Biddles Ltd, Guildford and King's Lynn

For Sue White

Contents

Illustrations

Acknowledgements

An invitation from my publishers to fill an important gap in the biographies of major cricket figures by writing on Sir Pelham Warner is the occasion of this book. As any contemporary biography does, it owes a great deal to the co-operation of those who made archival material and personal memories so freely available.

The book also provided both the excuse and the opportunity to visit Australia. For permission to consult the Gowrie Papers in the National Library, Canberra, ACT, I am grateful to the Director, the curator of the Gowrie Papers (Miss Catherine Santamaria) and to the Hon. Malise Hore-Ruthven who gave me permission on behalf of himself and his brother, the present Lord Gowrie. For permission to consult the Menzies Papers in the same source, I have to thank the Director and the trustees of Sir Robert Menzies' estate. For much help in finding my way around archives in Melbourne, I am in debt to Rex Harcourt, curator of the Melbourne CC Library. And for the overall hospitality of Melbourne CC, who made me their guest while working there, I acknowledge the generosity of the secretary, Dr John Lill and his wife, Rosemary. My travels through Australia were made the more pleasurable by the kindness and help of Dr Richard Cashman at whose University of New South Wales I was delighted to be asked to talk on the technical aspects involved in writing the biographies of sportsmen. To Christopher Harte and Percy Samara-Wickrama, I have a particular debt. They made it possible for me to have interviews with Sir Donald Bradman and H. L. Hendry, respectively.

The epicentre of Sir Pelham's universe was Lord's and among those who assisted me at the Marylebone Cricket Club were J. G. W. Davies, president in the year I concluded the book, Sir George Allen, past president and past treasurer and, in E. W. Swanton's phrase, 'Man of Cricket', Stephen Green, the curator and the then secretary, J. A. Bailey.

Those engaged in research are always made most welcome at the BBC Written Archives Centre in Caversham, Reading where Amanda Mares guided my way through the sources.

Having used the Bodleian Library, Oxford and the Newspaper section of the British Museum for over a quarter of a century does not stop me continuing to thank their staffs for assistance and aid.

The Librarian at Rugby School, Jennifer Macrory, produced the manuscript records of Warner's time there and arranged for me to use the portrait of him in the James Pavilion on the jacket of this book.

Sir Pelham Warner died in 1963. It was therefore possible to discuss his influence on the world of cricket with a substantial number of people of whose conversation and correspondence I was the beneficiary: the late Ronald Aird; Sir George Allen, CBE; Rex Alston; L. E. G. Ames, CBE; W. E. Bowes; Sir Donald Bradman, AC; F. R. Brown; J. G. W. Davies, OBE, D.Litt; Lady Dickson; Marshal of the RAF Sir William Dickson, KCB, KBE, DSO, AFC; the late W. J. Edrich, DFC; the late P. G. H. Fender; R. T. Gaby; A. R. Gover; Canon Bryan Green, DD; S. C. Griffith, CBE, DFC, TD; Mrs Pamela Hampton (née Langford); Peter S. Hargreaves; H. L. Hendry; Mrs E. R. T. Holmes (née Leveson Gower); Lord Home of the Hirsel, KT, PC; Sir Leonard Hutton; Earl Jellicoe, DSO, MC, PC; H. Larwood; A. L. Le Quesne; Sydney Levey; the late P. H. B. Lyon, MC; Roger Mann; P. B. H. May, CBE; T. B. Mitchell, Gerald Pawle; Albert Pellett (of Bearsted); Miss Netta Rheinberg, MBE; R. G. Sinfield; Miss B. Smart; Miss Doris Smith; P. A. Snow, OBE; W. Stupple (of Leeds Castle); E. W. Swanton, OBE; the late W. Voce; Marcus Williams; Mrs Mollie Wyatt; R. E. S. Wyatt.

Whatever claim to originality this book may have comes from the generosity of the Warner family in giving me unrestricted access to the papers of Sir Pelham. Marina Warner, his granddaughter, and a distinguished writer, broadcaster and critic in her own right, understands the problems of a biographer, even if her *Joan of Arc* can have little in common with my *Plum Warner*. Mrs Emilia Warner, Sir Pelham's daughter-in-law, let me draw upon her memories of him in the last 20 years of his life. For recollections from *c.* 1914 onwards, I was indebted to his daughter, Mrs Elizabeth Henderson, while his younger son, John, selected 1926 as the date at which I might begin to probe his prodigious memory. Other relatives answered small points and contributed reminiscences. For the fourth time, as a biographer, I have forced my attentions on a family and yet again been welcomed and accepted. It is an intrusion on their time and on their privacy. I thank the Warners most warmly for permitting it and giving all the appearance of enjoying it.

The Warner papers proved an immense collection and the initial collation of them was undertaken by Susan White in intervals between working at the Ashmolean, Oxford. When the calls of duty took her to Africa with her husband, I had occasion over and over again to be grateful for the orderly way in which she had prepared everything for my attention. Without her, I doubt if

I could have found time to complete the book on schedule and so it is to her that I dedicate it in gratitude and appreciation.

Brian Croudy of the Association of Cricket Statisticians provided the details of Warner's first-class career and Norman Lilley of the Queensway Studio, Thame assisted me in the preparation of photographs. There remain three people, who, in different ways, are invaluable to me in my writing. Max Reese reads my manuscripts with the authority of a sports writer, the scholarship of an historian, the perception of an examiner in English and the candidness of an old friend. The solecisms remain my own and have not eluded his keen eye. Carole Gilbert has typed more words for me over the past 17 years than either of us care to count. Her complete willingness to act as general factotum in the production of my books far outweighs her reluctance to be converted to word-processing. Finally, my thanks go to my wife, Dr Anne Howat, who undertook the demanding task of compiling the index.

North Moreton
Oxfordshire
1987

GERALD HOWAT

1

Childhood in Trinidad, 1873–87

Admiral Nelson, on board HMS *Victory* in the east Atlantic off Cadiz, sent out the signal, 'the enemy's fleet is at sea'. Far to the west and two days before Trafalgar Catherine Warner, on board a 500-tonner West Indiaman, gave birth to her first child, Charles, whose own son, Pelham, would find in naval history an abiding hobby and be the friend of Admiral Jellicoe, commander of the Grand Fleet at Jutland. In cricket he would find the passion of a lifetime and span an era from Grace to Cowdrey.

Pelham Warner was proud of his father, proud that the historian J. A. Froude had written, 'to have seen and talked with Charles Warner was worth a voyage round the globe', proud that he was one of the greatest names in Trinidadian history and proud of his own West Indian origins.

The business which took Catherine Warner to the West Indies in 1805 was very properly that of joining her husband, Edward, who had been appointed aide-de-camp to his father-in-law, General Charles Shipley, in the West Indian theatre of the Napoleonic Wars. During the truce of 1802–3, Edward had met Napoleon but now he was as committed, in a more modest role, to defeating him as was Nelson on the eve of Trafalgar. He accompanied General Shipley in the capture of Martinique and Guadeloupe from the French in 1809, being awarded a medal and a clasp 'for conspicuous gallant conduct', and when the wars ended in 1815 he settled in Trinidad, continuing a tradition of Warners in the West Indies which went back to his great-great-great-great-grandfather, Sir Thomas Warner, in the seventeenth century.

Trinidad had been captured from the Spanish in 1797 and in the peace settlement of 1815 it was retained by the British. There had been little active plantation under the Spanish, and it was Britain's policy to develop a sugar economy, as she had done in her other islands. Edward Warner bought 640 acres of land and combined estate-ownership with soldiering. He was appointed commander of the island garrison, became a colonel, and won the nickname of 'Warming-Pan' Warner for choosing a vessel of that nature as a wedding present from his regiment of Hussars to the Prince Regent. When he died in 1849 he had lived long enough to see his son Charles become a person of distinction in the island's history.

Charles Warner was sent to England to school at Eton. His arrival there was during the headmastership of the famous John Keate who brought some order and discipline into an institution notable for rioting and violence. The battle was not won in Charles Warner's time and he experienced the stern endeavours of Keate to control 170 rioters in one room. But amidst all this drama, he was able to benefit from Keate's distinguished classical teaching and acquire a love of the classics, particularly Pindar and Thucydides, which remained with him all his days.

After leaving Eton he entered legal chambers in London, married Isabella Carmichael at the age of 24 and took his bride back to Trinidad. His cousin, Ashton, was Chief Justice and provided the introductions which led Charles to become licensed as an advocate. He returned briefly to England to be called to the English Bar by Lincoln's Inn and then settled to his life's work as a lawyer in Trinidad. In 1841, he became Solicitor-General and three years later Attorney-General, a post which he held for over a quarter of a century. He was also involved in two areas of the island's development – immigration and education.

In 1833, slavery had been abolished throughout the British Empire and its abolition meant the loss of the labour force on the sugar plantations as the newly freed negro society created its own peasant communities and established cocoa and coffee estates. Charles Warner first saw the possibilities of bringing immigrants from the Indian subcontinent and from China to work as indentured servants on the plantations. It was he who drafted the Ordinances outlining the regulations for such immigration and laid down the guidelines governing the scheme until its closure in 1917. His work, said the *Port of Spain Gazette* in 1887, 'not only saved the colony from absolute collapse and ruin but was the chief factor in its rapid progress and development'. By far the greater number of Indians and Chinese chose to stay in Trinidad and their descendants can be found in the varied composition of Trinidad cricket sides.

Warner was also instrumental in the implementation of the island's education policy. He was involved in the setting up of elementary education and of a teacher training college, and it was he, said the *Port of Spain Gazette* again in 1887, who laid the foundations of 'our present great and extended educational advantages'. His delight in the classics led him to encourage such learning in the island's main government secondary school, Queen's Royal College, to which he sent some of his sons.

However, his main work was as a lawyer and as the member of the government responsible for the administration of justice. His contribution here lay in introducing the principles of British judicial procedure to an island where no such sustained tradition existed.

When he died the *Port of Spain Gazette* described him as

The central figure in the history of the island during more than thirty years of the most anxious and critical period in its existence as a British Colony. He was pre-eminently the most distinguished lawyer, the ablest and ripest scholar, the most astute politician and the most gifted and polished gentleman of his time.

For his services in connection with Immigration alone, the name of Charles Warner deserves to be gratefully remembered by every one interested in the Colony.

A more detached view of Warner may be found in Fraser's *History of Trinidad*:

Governor will succeed Governor and each will play his part more or less skillfully, but he, the real Governor, the master mind, will be there, like Warwick, or Wolsey, or Richelieu, nominally the adviser, really the ruler. For five-and-twenty years he held absolute sway.

Yet there were those of his friends who felt that he could have taken his talents to London. Shortly before his death, one of them wrote that 'he had deserved the larger area of English public life and his brilliant abilities would assuredly have carried him to the highest places of the Bar and the Bench'. Consolation lay in the fact that he had helped, said an obituary, 'to make Trinidad what it was and within the island limits in which his lot has been cast his work was well done'.

Charles Warner's first wife died in 1841. She had borne him six children. Of those who survived to adulthood, Shipley served as an ensign in India, dying in 1849, and Edward became Attorney-General of the North-Western Provinces of India in the 1870s.

In 1848, at the age of 43, he married again. Ellen Rosa Cadiz was not quite 18. Her father, John Joseph Cadiz, was the stipendiary magistrate of Port of Spain and her grandfather, another lawyer, had left Venezuela during the bitter independence struggles early in the century. The Cadiz family claimed descent from a Spanish officer, wrecked on the Irish coast after the Spanish Armada, who had married an Irish girl.

John Joseph Cadiz, three centuries later, had also married an Irish girl called Eliza Galwey. Charles Warner's child bride was thus, in two respects, of Spanish–Irish stock. She was, to say the least, an unlikely mother for a future England cricket captain. Her son, Pelham Francis, was born at The Hall, Port of Spain, on 2 October 1873, the youngest of Charles Warner's 18 children. Many of them had already left home and some had died. Pelham was 43 years younger than his eldest step-brother. Years later, his grandchildren would gently tease him by asking him to recite the names of as many of his full and half-brothers and sisters as he could.

His father had retired from public office three years before Pelham was born. He had been made a Commander of the Bath but had declined the offer of a knighthood. That decision was not as significant as was his refusal of a Colonial Office pension because it was less than he regarded as his due. That self-destructive decision meant that his family were ill-provided for in his declining years and it caused trouble and anxiety for his second wife. When the chance of some financial compensation came just before he died, a friend begged him not to refuse 'that which the Colonial Office are ready to give because it falls short of what they might give. That is a luxury of resentment not to be indulged.'

Yet despite the hazards of the family circumstances, of which he was only dimly aware, Pelham's childhood in Trinidad was a good one. His earliest recollections were of his elder brothers playing cricket. There was a large garden at The Hall and there was also a marble gallery where he would play in the dawn with Killebree, a negro lad employed by his parents. Windows were broken without upsetting his tolerant, elderly father who would murmur 'there's that wretched boy again'.

Charles Warner had played the game only a little. He had been born in the year of the first Eton v. Harrow match and cricket was one of the few diversions in the harsh Eton of his day. The playing-fields of Eton may have helped to win Waterloo,[1] as the Duke of Wellington observed, but the wickets were crude and rough and they were the only ones Charles ever played on. By the time cricket had been first introduced to Trinidad in 1842, Warner was a busy lawyer and family man. But the game itself was encouraged by his friend the third Lord Harris, Governor of the colony from 1846 to 1854.

For the few years of Harris's governorship, the two families were closely linked. Both Lord Harris and Charles Warner had Trinidadian wives of similar age and both would have sons born there who would grow up to become future England captains. The fourth Lord Harris was 20 years older than Pelham. Pelham first met him when a schoolboy in England and got to know him when Lord Harris returned from being Governor of Bombay. Throughout his life the younger man held the older one in considerable awe.

Warner also ensured that his youngest son learnt to read in what some biased observers might think was the best of all possible ways. He had had *Wisden's Cricketers' Almanack* sent out to him from its beginning in 1864, and by the time Pelham was 5 the first 14 volumes (even their facsimiles are collectors' pieces today) awaited his attention in the schoolroom. According to Pelham's own testimony, he set about the task with relish and could quote the names of all the players in the earliest Anglo-Australian encounters before even the days of Test matches.

Aucher and Raymond, Pelham's immediate elder brothers, had both been sent to Queen's Royal College, Port of Spain, where cricket, and indeed the whole apparatus of the nineteenth-century English public school ethos, had been enthusiastically adopted. From the same nursery, a generation later, came the writer and thinker C. L. R. James. Both Warner brothers played much of their cricket on the vast expanse of the Savannah where visiting naval squadrons would play sides which they had raised. The sailors, Prince Louis Battenberg among them, would be billeted at The Hall and the impressionable Pelham would acquire, from a very early age, that interest in people which never left him.

One day, some time in the 1880s, the brothers took him the 40 miles by ship to San Fernando in the south to watch them play. Afterwards, the town band escorted everyone to the harbour and the small boy was carried shoulder-high on board.

His two elder brothers did much to encourage cricket among the negro and Indian population from the 1880s onwards. C. L. R. James, in his *Beyond the Boundary*, has paid tribute to the way in which they and other white families, such as the Austins, made it possible for cricketers from a peasant society to play at colony level and eventually come to England, in 1900, under Aucher

Warner's captaincy. The patronage extended beyond an encouragement of skills, especially those of fast bowlers, to the
supplying of boots and clothes. It was patronage, also, which made
it possible for one of the first negro batsmen, Lebrun Constantine,
to accompany the 1906 side to England when, even as the ship had
left port, he stood disconsolate because he could not afford to
leave his family. But money for their support and a fast launch
were quickly found and he caught the vessel in the Gulf of Paria.

Pelham, who had played so often with young negro cricketers,
grew up with a much more balanced approach to racial issues than
many of his English contemporaries and throughout his life the
colour of a man's skin played no part in his likes and dislikes.
'My young life was all happiness,' he wrote later, but it was not
necessarily all cricket. He learnt to swim, rode his snow-white
donkey and went for fishing trips and picnics in the five islands.
Lessons, of course, intruded on his leisure, first with a governess,
then at Queen's Royal College, and in 1883, at the age of 10, he was
sent to Harrison College, Barbados.

One can only guess at the reasons: there may have been a
decision to put a boy with an ageing father and grown-up brothers
into a residential atmosphere of boys of his own age. Harrison
College is nowadays an important West Indian public school. Then
it 'was a pretty rough place with a good deal of bullying and we
were not overfed', and he was often homesick. But the school gave
him plenty of cricket and his companions in the 4th XI, to which he
aspired as soon as he got there, included E. L. Challenor, brother
of George Challenor, the first great West Indian batsman. The
headmaster, 'a stern, bearded and terrifying figure', had a love and
encouragement of cricket in his favour.

By the time he was 13, Pelham had reached the 1st XI, a
remarkable achievement for a boy in a school whose upper age
was 18. Against the Army Garrison XI he played his first important
innings of 31 runs, which made him for a time 'a small hero'. The
three years he was a boarder at Harrison College gave him a
memory of the Barbados cricket scene he never forgot. There
were matches against the rival school, the Lodge; visitors to
Barbadian families such as the Challenors for 'boarders''
weekends, and cricket to be watched at the Pickwick Club in
Bridgetown.

Meanwhile, back in Trinidad, Charles Warner's long life was
drawing to a close, and Ellen was pursuing with some determination her husband's pension rights. Among those whom she wrote
to in London were the historian Froude (who would befriend the
family when they came to England) and the son of her old friend,

Lady Harris. George Harris had succeeded his father to the title and had become, in 1886, a member of the government. Before her husband's death she had secured a lump sum of £3000 and in 1894 the Colonial Office provided a further £1500. In the end, these sums almost represented the total of the annual pension between 1870 and 1887 which would have been paid to Warner had he so wished. Nevertheless, reduced circumstances forced them to move, in the last year of Charles Warner's life, to a smaller house in Brunswick Square in Port of Spain.

Pelham was informed of his father's death in February 1887 by his sister Dorothy. She was 19 and he was 13 at the time. She was devoted to her young brother and the many pages of her letter contained both the warmth of deep affection and the poignancy of tragic grief. It was essentially the letter of a Victorian in mourning even in that far-flung sector of the Queen's empire. The schoolboy receiving the letter in Barbados read every detail of his father's last hours. Even at this distance of time the biographer feels a sense of intrusion in reading Dorothy's letter but the final page declares the family intentions for the future:

> We shall be leaving this house a month today and we shall go to England and live there. Trinidad without Papa would be very strange and miserable so it is better that we make an entire change and do what is only right and fair to you younger ones.

And so Pelham bade farewell to Harrison College and made the short voyage back to Trinidad. Just two months after his father's death Ellen and the younger children set sail from Port of Spain. The older ones remained with ties of occupation and marriage to continue the association of the Warners with nineteenth-century Trinidad. But Pelham's future would be no part of that tradition. On a grey May day in 1887 he first saw the shores of England, a small, slightly built lad whose frailty was offset only by the tan of the West Indian sun. That would fade when the memories of a Trinidadian childhood still lingered.

2
Rugby and Oxford, 1887–96

The afternoon of Friday 20 May 1887 was cold and wet, relieved only by occasional shafts of sun. Hail and rain had swept over Lord's on and off for two days and the match between MCC and Sussex was stuttering between the showers to some sort of conclusion. Just before lunch, W. G. Grace had been dismissed for 18 and the MCC batsmen at the wicket were F. E. Lacey, a future secretary of the Club, and 'Parson' Thornton who had played a bit for Kent and made a lot of runs. The Sussex bowling was in the hands of James Hide, not long back from Australia, and C. A. Smith, the future Hollywood actor.

Huddled in front of the tennis court, the small boy who had just come through the turnstiles watched every ball with excitement. No matter that he was shivering with cold and the crowd, such as it was, was sparsely scattered around. Mr Bowen had brought him to Lord's almost as soon as he had arrived in London. Pelham Warner had made the first of countless entrances and Lord's would become his kingdom and his cathedral.

The next trip to Lord's came in June when he was taken to see the centenary match between the MCC Club and Ground and England. This was the grand occasion. WG passed quite close to the small boy 'and I gazed with undisguised admiration, not to say awe, on the most dominating personality the cricket world had ever seen'. Arthur Shrewsbury and A. E. Stoddart put on 266 for England. Men who would become his friends and associates, such as Hawke and A. J. Webbe, made a contribution. The couple, forever immortalised in Francis Thompson's haunting lines, 'O my Hornby and my Barlow long ago,' were there.

There was a banquet during the match at which nearly all the great players of late nineteenth-century English cricket gathered.

The small boy went home in a brake to dream dreams, with the poet Thompson, of a ghostly batsman playing to the bowling of a ghost. Fifty years later, in 1937, he would join Hawke and Webbe at the one hundred and fiftieth anniversary dinner.

Warner's family having got their priorities right – the visits to Lord's – the next most serious business of the day was to get him into a public school in the autumn. During the summer term he was a weekly boarder at Mr Turner's preparatory school at 10 Collingham Road, in south-west London, which took the long view of things: there was a cricket match between those pupils destined for Oxford and those destined for Cambridge in which Warner made his first-ever century. He presented himself to the scholarship examiners at Winchester who found many gaps in his Latin prose, a judgement endorsed by those at Rugby but who nevertheless offered him an ordinary place.

Meanwhile, his cricket education was taken south of the Embankment in August when he joined the crowd of 24,000 to see the Bank Holiday match at The Oval between Surrey and Nottinghamshire. So great was the crush that 'I had to be handed over the turnstile to avoid being trampled on'. All these heady delights had to be put behind him a month later when he boarded the train at Euston for Rugby and presented himself at Mr Whitelaw's house.

He was lucky in both his housemaster and his headmaster. Robert Whitelaw, his housemaster, realised the loneliness and frailty of the small boy facing his first English winter and not strong enough to play football. Pelham had to settle in as quickly as he could to a routine of cold baths, chapel before breakfast, fagging and the classics, but Whitelaw kept an eye on him. While the rest of the house played football, Mrs Whitelaw, his housemaster's wife, took Pelham for nature walks.

A new headmaster had arrived at Rugby. John Percival, a former headmaster of Clifton, had taken the unusual step of giving up the presidency of Trinity College, Oxford to return to schoolmastering. Quite apart from what he was to do for Rugby (which had declined since the great days of Thomas Arnold, a generation earlier), he liked cricket and used his influence to have standards and facilities raised at Rugby.

Pelham initially had little with which to commend himself to other boys, some of whom were surprised that 'I was not black, coming from Trinidad'. Nor did he win social esteem by receiving a prize at the end of his first term for being the neatest boy in the form. 'Warner always has his hair nicely brushed and his collar clean,' ran the citation. He was forming the fastidious habits of a lifetime but on the face of it might be seen as a target for bullies. Whitelaw, however, would tolerate no such behaviour in his house and Pelham got through those first two winter terms with nothing worse to fear than bouts of homesickness. Indeed, he has left on record his view that Rugby was not a school where bullying was tolerated.

As soon as the summer arrived he was able to make his mark by scoring 46 in a junior house match and going on to be awarded his School 'XXII'. This privilege allowed him to take advantage of a motion passed at Bigside Levée that in future only members of the XI and XXII might keep their brown shoes in the pavilion.

Membership of the XXII put him in the 2nd XI against the Old Rugbeians on OR Day. Arrangements seem to have been delightfully casual. By eleven o'clock 22 men had turned up and two games were begun. By midday a further 11 ORs led to a 3rd XI being composed by the boys. 'This did not stem the stream of new arrivals and so after luncheon a 4th XI was got together,' reported the *Meteor*, the school magazine. Warner scored 19 in his particular game and ended the season with a half-century for Whitelaw's in the house match final. A member of the OR 1st XI, R. A. Wilson, wandered across to the 2nd XI and 'saw a small and delicate-looking slip of a boy bowling the OR's out with more pace than could have been expected from so small a frame'. Odds had been laid by his friends on his getting into the 1st XI but his size and age were against him. So small was he still when his second year began that Whitelaw felt that he should, despite his XXII, continue to wear his Eton collar, hallmark of the smaller brethren. But compensation came in his appointment to be head of toast fags. By now, he had acquired the nickname which would be his for life: '"Plum", a mumbled contraction of Pelham, I suppose, given me first, I fancy, by a boy called George Blair, in Whitelaw's, with whom I shared a study. Blair was a typical Scotsman who despised cricket.'[2]

His second summer at Rugby marked the arrival of Tom Emmett whom Warner recalled as a coach encouraging boys 'to develop on natural lines'. He had a friendliness which won their support, matched by the experience which gave them confidence. The *Meteor* began the term with the plea, 'if only fellows would learn to field while they are still small' and reported that a Bigside Levée had defeated by one vote a motion that cricket, as football, should be compulsory. Warner, with 46 not out against Oriel College, Oxford, 3 wickets for 17 against Trinity College, and 28 against Rugby Town established himself in the side and was awarded his 1st XI colours in June, 'provided that you play in our match at

Lord's', by A. W. Dixon whose written invitation was delivered by a fag at seven o'clock before first lesson. Between breakfast and second lesson Warner had got to the school shop and bought the light blue ribbon to adorn his straw hat.

The school fixture list in those days makes strange reading. There were no matches in term against other schools and the few fixtures were confined to games against club sides and various Oxford colleges, all of whom travelled by train to Rugby. The term ended with the only away match, and the only school match, the contest at Lord's against Marlborough. This was Warner's first appearance at Lord's and his contribution was 3 and 16, including a boundary he would savour for the rest of his life and which would mark the site of the Warner Stand 70 years later. He ended his first year in the XI having made 222 runs for an average of 14.12 in a side, said *Wisden's Cricketers' Almanack*, which bowled better than it batted. Warner took 14 wickets at a cost of 22.70, *Lillywhite's Cricketers' Annual* calling him a 'useful all-round player'.

He was still only 15 but the summer holidays brought the first introduction to country-house cricket and his first acquaint-anceship with young men such as Stanley Jackson and A. C. MacLaren who would become his friends. There were 'weeks' at Althorp Park, the Spencer family home, and at Eastbourne where he found himself fielding out an MCC total of nearly five hundred.

In 1890 he made his first century for the school, 177 not out against the Free Foresters, batting through the entire 303 runs the school scored. 'Keep a straight bat and a modest mind,' said F. B. Westcott to him after the match, a man whom Warner remembered not just for his advice but because he, like Warner's housemaster, Whitelaw, and W. G. Michell, represented a trend towards friendliness to the boys and the breaking down of barriers.

Michell, who had been in the Cambridge XI, was an important influence on Warner both as a coach and as a teacher. Warner never reached the sixth form, though his cricket status gave him sixth form 'power'. Much of the classics, history and English literature he learnt came from being in Michell's form in a day when the form master was responsible for most of the teaching of his pupils.

The highlight of the season was the match against Marlborough at Lord's. Despite a Marlborough victory, he was the outstanding batsman on either side, his 38 and 85 providing, said the *Morning Post* (of its future cricket correspondent), 'the best cricket in the match. He showed remarkable knowledge for so young a cricketer, great skill, commendable steadiness and hitting power of no mean order'. He was presented by the school 'with several bats for his score', recorded the Whitelaw House notes. There followed another summer of country-house cricket which led to an invitation to play for Kent against Warwickshire (who were then second class) but officialdom ruled that he had neither birth nor residential qualification. For the same reason, an invitation to join Essex in 1892 fell through. But he was being noticed and on a Devon tour with the Ishmaelites found himself playing at Taunton against most of the Somerset side.

His third year in the XI, 1891, was handicapped by a lingering injury from football. He had made a start the previous winter, describing himself as 'a very light forward and a very bad one', and then injury ended his playing of a game for which he was physically unsuited. Yet he headed the school averages and made top score in a rain-ruined match against Marlborough. *Lillywhite* called him a thorough cricketer who could bat in almost faultless style. Term was followed by an invitation to return to Rugby to play in Michell's cricket week, 'a great compliment for a boy still in the school'. Designated in the batting order as δ παῖς (the boy), he scored 56 not out against Old Reptonians and made another friend in C. B. Fry who 'watched this small boy with his correctness, his aplomb and his dry-wicket driving on a wet turf; worthy of his coach, Tom Emmett'. 'This future champion dawned on my admiring vision,' wrote Fry later, though he himself would be far the better cricketer of the two. A few days later came a century against the Gentlemen of Surrey with Fry again playing against him.

In 1892 he captained a poor Rugby side, weak in batting and saved only by a reasonable attack from several defeats. The captain had to 'carry' the batting, making twice as many runs for twice the average of anyone else. Among his principal scores were 69 (v. New College, Oxford), 58 not out (v. the Old Rugbeians) and 37 against Balliol College, whose opening batsman was M. R. Jardine. Forty years on, M.R.'s son, D.R., would be linked with Warner in the events of 1932–33. His school career ended sadly with 1 and 0 at Lord's but over the years his record had been:

Innings	Runs	Times Not Out	Highest Score	Average
64	1499	7	177*	26.29

He had taken 31 wickets for 700 runs.

Warner has recorded that Rugby cricket in his day reached no great heights. The impact of Emmett as coach was not felt until the mid-1890s and the wickets on which all boys except those on Bigside played were 'decidedly rough'. Yet only Bigside players were allowed to wear two pads! A plea in the 1891 edition of *Meteor* came for indoor nets and this, and related matters such as the coaching of juniors, was tackled in the immediate years after Warner had left.

R. A. Wilson, the OR who had watched Warner in the 2nd XI, joined the staff soon afterwards and recalled him in 1892: 'His batting soon went ahead of his bowling and, as captain, no judge could look more serious than he when the cares of captaincy were upon him.' Wilson added that though Warner 'wasn't in the sixth he was a very fair performer in school'. Wilson could 'recall prose which was Latin and not culled from *Wisden* or *Lillywhite*'.

In the tradition of the day, Warner received primarily a classical education but he was at a school which had pioneered the teaching of modern (as opposed to ancient) history. This had been one of the important contributions of Thomas Arnold, who believed that the study of modern history was a relevant pursuit for pupils entering the world of British nineteenth-century imperialism and industrialisation. Arnold, who died in 1842, took a long, not to say a prophetic, view of Britain's future role in the second half of the nineteenth century.

Warner was the beneficiary of this. He gave up Latin Verse to join the Special History class and acquired a love of the subject, particularly military and naval history, which remained with him throughout his life. Sailors and soldiers would be among his friends. They might press him 'to talk cricket' while he would encourage them to talk about wars and battles. Towards the end of his life, he wrote to me answering some questions about his education at Rugby and he recalled that British history from Marlborough onwards had been a particular study. 'The history I was taught was very interesting and I enjoyed it very much – lots of great men, of course, and lots of not so great. I was very well taught.' He was encouraged to read Macaulay, the eloquent narrator of Britain's role and progress.

All this has added relevance for Warner in another direction. Not only would the concept of Britain and Empire mean so much to him as he travelled the world playing cricket, but he would also become a distinguished cricket historian writing in the descriptive tradition of Macaulay and narrating cricket's story and its role in the Empire from which he himself had sprung.

Apart from his cricket, Warner made no formal impact on Rugby. His name only once appeared in prize lists (and when it did, 'the school roared with laughter'), he did not figure in debates nor perform as an athlete or footballer. But he left 'with many happy memories' of a time when schoolboys were 'simple and unsophisticated'. 'We never read the papers and my years were a placid time in the Victorian age.' Informally, though, Rugby did much for him. He made friendships, learnt the art of captaincy and prepared for the next step, Oriel College, Oxford.

As we have seen, he had never got higher than the fifth at Rugby and three months with a 'crammer' were necessary for him to satisfy Oxford's Responsions requirements. In January 1893 he went up to Oriel, a small college of some eighty men, which had been at the heart of some of Oxford's great intellectual and religious debates a generation or two earlier but was now, in common with much of the Oxford of the 1890s, a place of conscientious tutoring for the rigorous demands of the various 'Schools'. It was also a great sporting college with more than its share of Blues in various sports. In a warm February senior men in the college had him in the nets. But 'flu struck twice and he appeared in the Freshmen's match in poor health and with no practice, contributing 17 and 34. It was nothing beside the 230 and 70 not out of F. G. H. Clayton and the 113 and 24 not out of G. O. Smith, both of whom, like Warner, failed to secure their Blues as freshmen. All three men totalled 19 between them in five innings when picked for the Next XV against the University. Runs were indeed there to be got, as the final trial revealed with 1093 being scored for the loss of 22 wickets, but few of them came Warner's way.

Yet he was not despondent. In the first summer term Schools still seemed far away and he would join the young men crowding into brakes in the High every afternoon to go off and play college cricket at Cowley. Before term ended he had scored 151 against Exeter and 103 against Trinity, and had gone back to play against Rugby. During the long vacation he played in two country-house cricket weeks, made a lot of runs and showed the talents as a dancer which made him so much in demand by hostesses in the next few years.

He was a young man who dressed well, usually in a stiff-fronted, high-collared shirt with a broad bow in his tie. He would wear a cut-away coat, a straw hat or a bowler and carry a stick. His hair, already beginning to recede, revealed a broad forehead and his face had the freshness and youthfulness which it retained throughout his life. His most striking features were his eyes, piercing black and commanding. He could not be called a handsome man by comparison with, say, Fry, but his ease of manner and his ability to converse gave him qualities which both men and women found attractive.

Country-house cricket, to whose ranks he was now being admitted, had been part of the social activity of the nobility and landed gentry throughout the nineteenth century. By the 1890s it was at its zenith. Wealth, leisure, space and mobility had combined to make it possible for cricketers of reasonable talent, assured behaviour and acceptable pedigree to be brought together at some great house to play a week's cricket while enjoying their host's wines, appreciating their hostess's menus and dancing with the wives and daughters of their fellow-guests.

During the day, the game itself might attract some thirty or forty spectators, all part of the assembled house-party, who would watch with varying degrees of interest until the close of play was marked by the long shadows of stately oaks and elegant colonnades creeping over the ground and everyone flocking indoors to change for dinner. It is an image true but incomplete. For the cricket which they had witnessed would have been good. The country-house cricketers provided the amateurs of the county championship sides, especially teams such as Kent, where Warner would live after his marriage, and Middlesex, for whom he would play.

Warner, in joining the ranks of such cricketers, improved his game, established his reputation, saved his pocket and enjoyed himself. He was laying with great care the foundations on which the edifice of his life would be created. Through the portals of the building would come fame, happiness and marriage.

His second summer at Oxford was marred by regular pain, the beginnings of the duodenal ulcer which would plague him for so many years. A fifty in the Seniors' match, three catches and two wickets, was a not unimpressive performance but the competition for batting places was severe and his only other chance came when he played for MCC (to which he had been elected on 15 March 1892 while still at school) against the University. Ironically, he was dismissed twice cheaply by the two Freshmen who won Blues that year. This was Warner's debut in first-class cricket and was followed, after the University match was over, by his first appearance for the University in a match against Essex. He opened the batting with Fry, the University captain, and made 50 off the bowling of C. J. Kortright. Warner, at the end of his career, thought him the fastest bowler he had ever faced.

Shortly afterwards he made his first century at Lord's, 163 for Middlesex 2nd XI against Kent 2nd XI, a performance which led to a letter from A. J. Webbe, the Middlesex captain:

Dear Warner,
Will you play for Middlesex against Somersetshire and

Gloucestershire beginning at Taunton on the Bank Holiday. You might send me a wire here. There is a 10.00 a.m. train on Sunday morning. Murdoch at Lord's will send you a railway ticket.

Warner always remembered the warmth with which Webbe greeted 'a very shy and strange boy' and he later extended the same kindness to those who under his captaincy made their Middlesex debuts. His first appearance for the county 1st XI was not spectacular – he scored 6 and 4 – but he did rather better against Gloucestershire at Clifton College with 14 not out and 29 not out. There he played against WG for the first time, describing him as a 'jolly old bear, full of fun and good humour'. From these heights he went by train and dog-cart to Hartley Wintney in Hampshire, to play for the Free Foresters on one of the oldest village greens in England. His score of 39 was the top score, for the visitors, who escaped with the worst of a draw.

Warner had settled very easily into the life of an undergraduate of the 1890s. On his first Sunday in January 1893 he had been asked to breakfast by V. T. Hill, already a Blue, and at once was accepted in the circle of men who played games or who rowed. He presented essays to his tutor, A. G. Butler, who took a sympathetic view of other claims on a young man's time in the summer term, and he attended Sir William Anson's lectures on the Law of Contract. He made occasional visits to the Union to hear men discussing Ireland and listened to Cosmo Lang, the future Archbishop of Canterbury, preaching in St Mary's. He dined at Vincent's for 2/6 and became president of the Ran Dan Wine Club. He developed his interest in military history and was able to discuss the Franco-Prussian War with Hilaire Belloc. He learnt to ride a bicycle in Norham Gardens and went for his first ride in a car.

Towards the end of his time, he was asked to breakfast by the Provost of Oriel to meet Cecil Rhodes and Dr Jameson. Rhodes had been for some time Prime Minister of the Cape and the great protagonist of British imperial interests in South Africa. One year after this breakfast occasion, both he and Jameson would temporarily fall from power and influence over Jameson's 'Raid' into Boer territory. The young man was drawn into conversation on colour and declared to Rhodes his own readiness to accept people on their merits.

Throughout his time at Oxford, he had had £200 a year from his mother and he kept within it. The more expensive side of Oxford life, belonging to the Bullingdon, hunting thrice a week, dining and wining extravagantly, were no part of him. His mother, as we have seen, had acted with more prudence than his father over money. She had leased a house at 7 Leonard Terrace in south-west London and made a home for herself, Pelham, Dorothy and Audrey. Ellen Rosa Warner would live until 1913, enjoy her son's triumphs and be remembered by him with great devotion.

Warner would spend part of his vacations at his mother's home. He visited France, Switzerland and Jersey, stayed with the Palairets and went to country-house parties to play cricket. Each March found him back at Oxford busy in the nets.

The summer of 1895 saw the fulfilment of his University ambitions. He was in good health, made a century in the Seniors' match, and half-centuries successively against Somerset, the Gentlemen of England and Yorkshire. In the Yorkshire game he wore a Harlequin cap for the first time. Like D. R. Jardine, this would be the cap he wore throughout his career. In the last home match, against MCC, he was awarded his Blue. In the University match itself he did little, Cambridge winning unexpectedly by 134 runs. Among his contemporaries in the side were Fry, H. K. Foster and H. D. G. Leveson Gower. Playing against him was W. G. Grace junior who made 40 and 28. It was the year of Grace's father's tremendous triumph when, at the age of 47, he scored over a thousand in May and averaged over fifty in the season. Warner himself had seven matches for Middlesex that summer but did very little and *Wisden* noticed that he had confined his best performances to Oxford.

His final year at Oxford was under the captaincy of Leveson Gower, the tributes to whose leadership at the time suggest that he might have been seen as a future England leader. Warner's achievements were scarcely adequate for an opening batsman and he finished well down in the averages, but his appearance against Cambridge (in which he was run out twice) was made memorable by the decision of the Cambridge captain, Frank Mitchell, to give Oxford runs so that he should not have to enforce the (compulsory) follow-on. The incident brought demonstrations against Cambridge, 'many members in the pavilion hooting and hissing', Warner noted, but the law was changed soon afterwards.

He had more on his mind than cricket that summer. 'Roman Law and Real Property were not conducive to run-getting', and the demands of Final Schools became more persistent. Finally the aid of a 'crammer' was enlisted whose skill at spotting likely questions was renowned. After four feverish days of examinations and a stiff *viva* he emerged with a Third in Jurisprudence. Work was not over, however, and that Christmas he successfully presented himself to the Bar examiners in Torts and Criminal Law.

Oxford and cricket had introduced him to the company of men who would be his friends and associates for a lifetime. He would never question very seriously social values and standpoints, least of all in the halcyon years which immediately lay ahead. Rugby and Oxford together had prepared the young West Indian for the English upper middle-class milieu in which he would move with ease.

3
Colonial Enterprises, 1897–1904

'Cricket, with death and matrimony, is one of the few things that give all classes a common interest,' reported the *Daily Argosy* of British Guiana in April 1897. The writer continued:

> How far England's immunity from the revolutionary upheavals which have shaken Continental countries as moral earthquakes is due to the catholicity of cricket is a subject worth the investigation of the social historian. What is of even more interest to colonists, however, is Cricket as an imperial factor. Even more than the tie of language the tie of cricket helps to hold together the units which compose the vast British Empire.
>
> A striking instance of cricket in both the aspects of which we have been speaking occurred on the cricket ground on the 29th ult., when Lord Hawke was clean bowled by a black boy in the employ of the Club, and the significance of the incident was not lost upon the crowd. Here was a practical example of cricket both as a social and an imperial factor, and in that small event the philosopher might read a large part of the secret of the loyalty and affection of what are known as the native races to the Mother Country.

The occasion for this essay on social cohesion and imperialism was the departure of Lord Hawke's team from the West Indies. The tour had begun in January 1897 and it was the first of many occasions on which Warner would play overseas. The invitation had come just after he had finished his Bar examinations and it took him back after ten years to the island of Trinidad, where his appearance at Port of Spain against the Queen's Park club was all he could have wished for. He was, reported the *Trinidad Guardian*, accorded 'a hero's return':

There was record cricket and a century unprecedented in the history of Trinidad cricket, the Englishmen compiling 428. The century was made by a Trinidadian, Pelham Warner whose 119 was put together in a fine exhibition of free batting all round the wicket. There must have been 3000 present and they included the wealth and fashion and youth and beauty of Port of Spain.

Warner wrote:

Scores of black men rushed across the ground shouting out: 'I taught you, Mr. Pelham. You play well, Sir; we are proud of you.' – 'I tell your farder when you were so high – 'Mr. Pelham, he make a batsman, Sir.' I can never forget it, nor when my old black nurse, Kitsey, embraced me in front of the hotel to the huge delight and amusement of the rest of the team. 'Oh – Puggie darling, you not so pretty as you were – you pretty little boy; still you not bad!'

Only 60 years earlier, Trinidad had still been an island with negro slavery. The scars had healed surprisingly quickly and the master and slave relationship had been replaced by a paternalism of white towards black that would last until after the Second World War. Pelham Warner, son of an Anglo-West-Indian family, was the beneficiary that January day in 1897.

The second match was against Trinidad, and it was the bowling of two negro cricketers, A. Cumberbatch and J. Woods, which secured the colony a victory by 137 runs. Both were fast and their dismissal of Hawke's side in the second innings for 58 pointed the way West Indian cricket would one day go. The two men took between them 19 wickets for 191 runs. In the return match the same two bowlers took between them 18 for 158 and Trinidad won by 5 wickets. Two other players in the Trinidad side were Warner's brother, Aucher, and Lebrun Constantine, the father of Learie.

The *Port of Spain Gazette* hoped that the cricket victories would bring 'political benefit to the colony in this, its centenary year under British rule'. 'Lord Hawke's team are men of influence' and the writer hoped that they might persuade the British Government to keep European Government-subsidised beet sugar out of Britain in the interests of West Indian cane sugar. Five years later

Joseph Chamberlain's plans for colonial development helped to restore sugar prosperity.[3]

Warner himself was presented by the Governor with the island centenary medal and took his colleagues to visit the family estates before sailing for Grenada. The tour itself has some importance in that cricket was played in so many of the islands, distant Jamaica being alone excluded. For Warner, it helped towards his establishment as an up-and-coming English cricketer, even if we accept the note of local pride in the St Vincent newspaper which reported his 156 as follows: 'If ever there has been a better display of batting in St. Vincent, it has not been our privilege to see it. The most magnificent score in the annals of the island was made by a batsman who is "one of us".'

He was also successful in Barbados where another century (and the winning hit against the colony) led the *Barbados Advocate* to report that the troops of the King's Liverpool Regiment lifted the old Harrison College pupil on their shoulders and 'deposited the idol of the moment within the pavilion. It is impossible to overpraise his magnificent batting'. The tourists also went to Antigua and St Kitts where, cricket aside, Warner visited the tomb of his ancestor Sir Thomas.

He finished easily top of the batting averages, having scored four centuries, and made almost a thousand runs for an average of 51.15. *Wisden* called him 'undoubtedly the success of the tour'. He had begun to write reports for the *Sportsman* and his own judgement on West Indian cricket was contained in his final 'bulletin':

The future of West Indian cricket is a good prospect, with an excellent climate and good grounds. The visit of a West Indian team to England is by no means improbable. Four or five natives should be included and the side would prove a good attraction.

In later years, Warner was to say that West Indian cricket had not advanced as quickly as he had believed it would in 1897. On his own last visit to the West Indies in 1948, accompanying G. O. Allen's team, he found it had advanced with a vengeance, and Len Hutton had to be flown out as a reinforcement!

A few weeks later, the early season fixture between MCC and Yorkshire brought Warner his first century in first-class cricket. The press were complimentary though some commentators a little surprised. *Sporting Life* remarked that he had at last gratified those who were certain of his capacities while *Wisden* commented that 'no one was prepared for his splendid batting'. But another century a month later for Middlesex against Nottinghamshire led the *Morning Post* to write of, 'this finished batsman of whom great things have always been expected: a batsman now clearly in the front rank. His strokes were made as elegantly as Nottingham girls make lace.'

That summer he became an established member of the Middlesex side, 'one of the mainstays', wrote *The Times*. He was selected for The Oval Gentlemen v. Players match and opened the innings with W. G. Grace – both their names would one day be given to the artifex at Lord's. He played in all 16 Middlesex matches and in club and country-house cricket and a typical week in July found him appearing for Linton Park, Harlequins and Teddington.

In the autumn he captained a side to the United States, playing in New York and Philadelphia. His own performance was relatively modest – with a top score of 56 – but the tour demonstrated his qualities as a leader, first displayed at Rugby. The Philadelphia *Cricket Club Life* wrote:

What shall we say of the captain? It was no effort in Captain Warner to do or say the right thing at the right time. This faculty showed itself all the while, it bubbled up like a never-failing spring. His courtesy knew no bounds; the public, the committees, the ladies, the opposing team, and his own men, all knew that he was captain, and yet they were made to feel that his first thought was in their individual interest.

The tour received wide coverage in the Philadelphian press, typical headlines being, 'Waterloo for Englishmen: beaten at their own game'; 'the beast of John Bull having fun with the sedate bird of Freedom'. The one acknowledged a Philadelphia victory by four wickets, the other a defeat by seven wickets.

By 1897 Warner had 'arrived' as far as the game at first-class level was concerned, though his place in the averages was only forty-ninth. *Vanity Fair* invited young cricketers to emulate his fielding. In all games at every level that year he had the following record:

Innings	Runs	Times Not Out	Highest Score	Average
79	2676	5	176	36.12

He had also continued his efforts as a writer. His contributions to the *Sportsman* (which described itself as 'the oldest, largest and leading daily sporting paper in the world') helped to finance him, and the editor of *Wisden* invited him to write an article on the West

Indies and American tour of 1897. He saw a future for West Indian tours to England, on the other hand, he believed American cricket would not prosper until more attention was paid to the wickets.

At the conclusion of the 1897 American tour one newspaper there had remarked: 'Mr. Warner has selected the law as his profession, and as we think of the many sterling qualities he exhibited here, we cannot fail to prophesy for him an eminent career in the ranks of England's foremost counsellors.'

The first step towards such 'an eminent career' was taken early in 1898, when he became a pupil of Alfred Lyttelton whose chambers were at Paper Buildings, The Temple. Lyttelton was at that point a man of 40 with a distinguished cricket career behind and a distinguished political career before him. He had played for England in a famous Test match in 1884 at The Oval when Australia amassed 551. Lyttelton, despite being the wicket-keeper, had two spells of bowling and his lobs secured the last 4 Australian wickets for 19 runs.

Prior to this appearance, virtually his last in first-class cricket, Lyttelton had been a member of the famous Cambridge side of 1878 which defeated the Australians by an innings, and a Middlesex player. He had also played football for England.

Warner's entry into Lyttelton's chambers brought him into contact with some of the most distinguished men at the Bar. He sat in court to hear cases in which Lyttelton, as junior and not yet a KC, was 'led' by H. H. Asquith, the future Prime Minister. He watched great lawyers such as Isaacs, Marshall Hall and Carson and he was praised, during his pupilage, for his work on a complicated company case and given another similar brief to prepare.

Yet he never became an industrious pupil. In the Easter vacation of 1898 he went on a brief cricket tour in Portugal. Summer came, and so did the call of Middlesex! He played in almost every match and in September he again took a side to the United States (and to Canada).

The Portuguese tour was primarily a social occasion in which the visitors competed against the English community at Oporto in golf and tennis as well as cricket. Every night there was a dance at the English Club and the local press in bravely attempting to report the victory of 'Inglaterra' over 'Porto' compared Grace and MacLaren (though neither was playing) to the great Spanish bullfighters of the day.

Warner's return to the American continent in the autumn of 1898 was a more extended one with matches being played as far apart as Montreal, Toronto, New York and Chicago. In a series of low-scoring encounters, he only averaged 16. Before the match against eastern Canada at Montreal, he received a letter from an admirer whose loyal support was duly rewarded by an English victory!:

Dear Sir, You will never know my name (sounds rather mysterious, doesn't it?) or else I could not thus write to an utter stranger but I am an English girl and *do* want you to win, for the glory of the old home and the honor of English cricket. They say, out here, that your bowling is poor and, except for one or two, your bats not very good therefore your fielding is the only part they fear much. I am not going to turn spy or I might tell you their weak points but even should I do so I know that you, as a gentlemen, would not like it. At Philadelphia be on your guard as they say you are almost sure to be defeated there. It seems laughable to go on writing like this when we will never be other than strangers but I thought you would like to know that there were eyes (not mine only by *any* means) eagerly and anxiously watching your campaign which will be brightened or saddened by your victory or defeat although I, for one, do not much fear the latter. I shall be there (D.V.) either today or tomorrow to watch you play and rejoice at your victory. Remember, my gallant unknown knight, that there are the bright eyes of unknown fair ladies intent on your actions. Go on and win! Now I will close this anonymous letter with a hearty cheer for dear old England. Hip! Hip! Hurrah! and again *Hurrah*!

A Lady Friend

The tour included contrasts such as a military band playing at one match and a Southern dance band at another while crowds of over ten thousand watched. He was given a gold watch chain by his team 'in memory of a great time, an unbroken record, perils by sea, ditto by fair women, a few broken hearts and other adventures'. These were uncomplicated young men from the upper middle classes of English society who happened to be reasonably good at cricket. Their world, in the closing years of the old century, still seemed certain and secure. They accepted Warner indisputably as a leader, this young man who less than a dozen years earlier had arrived in England as an unknown West Indian. He might not ever lead in court but he bade fair to be a leader of men.

Each successive cricket enterprise had taken him further away from his Bar studies. Only days after his return from America, he accepted an invitation to tour South Africa and it seemed the die was cast. The law had lost a lawyer and cricket had gained a cricketer. His motives may be explored. His master in chambers, Lyttelton, who had become the president of MCC in 1898, was aware of his pupil's qualities as a leader, his competence as a cricketer and his immense enthusiasm for the game. Warner believed that he would never make a career for himself at the Bar in the face of the brilliant men around him. Lyttelton was ready to support that decision and he remained a confidante until his comparatively early death in 1913 after having held office as Conservative Colonial Secretary. When he died, his old friend (but political opponent) Asquith said of him, 'he perhaps of all men of his generation came closest to the mould and ideal of manhood which every English father would like to see his son aspire to, and if possible, attain'. Among the mentors of the young (and early middle-aged) Warner, Lyttelton was a quietly guiding and effective figure.

Another influential friend was Lord Hawke himself. He was 13 years Warner's senior and had already captained Yorkshire for many seasons with distinct success. His belief in the virtues of good captaincy by amateurs was well known. Sydney Pardon was to write of him, 'he has won the affection and regard of his professionals without for a moment losing his authority'. Hawke saw in Warner the qualities of leadership which he recognised in himself. Like Lyttelton, he played a part in influencing Warner's decision to commit himself to cricket rather than the Bar. Over many years the two men remained close friends.

Less distinctly, we may notice a third influence in Warner's career at this stage. As we have seen, his mother and the mother of Lord Harris had been friends, contemporaries and Trinidadians. Lord Harris, by 1898, had already captained England, been president of MCC, served as a member of the government and been Governor of Bombay. He had just begun a long tenure in the powerful role of treasurer of MCC. He was a generation older than Warner, who regarded him with respect and some fear. They would be associated through cricket for over forty years but there was never a close relationship. Harris's support for Warner was based on his judgement of him as a captain and as a player rather than through family links. The few letters between them, which survive, lack the warmth of much of Warner's other correspondence. Nevertheless, it was better to have Harris as an ally rather than a foe, as others discovered.

Yet, despite all this patronage, the question of Warner's finances has to be remembered. There is some evidence to suggest that Hawke helped him in connection with the tours of the West Indies and South Africa but not to any extent and certainly not to embarrass a blossoming friendship. Warner's mother continued the small allowance she had provided for him at Oxford but the basis of his income – such as it was – came from journalism. He was commissioned to report the forthcoming South African tour for the *Sportsman* and a generous editor allowed him to contribute, in those spacious days, column after column.

On the eve of his departure for South Africa, *Sporting Sketches* published a long article by Fry on Warner. It offers, as this extract suggests, a contemporary assessment of his abilities as a batsman by one of the outstanding batsmen of the day:

He is about the most correct batsman playing. His style is not hackneyed or common, but he plays literally by the book. While waiting for the ball he stands up his full height, one foot just inside the other just outside the crease – a picture of all that is correct. After a quick survey of the arrangement of the fieldsmen, he grounds an absolutely perpendicular bat, and is ready for any ball that can be bowled. He stands a model of uprightness and alert concentration.

The most noticeable point about his strokes is the straightness of his bat. Back or forward, it is the same, straight as a rush. Yet he has so far overcome nature that there is no trace of unnaturalness in any position he assumes.

His back-play is severely simple. Unlike most strong back-players, he does not move his right foot towards his wicket; he stands stock-still, watching the ball closely and meeting it just as it passes the crease.

His aggressive strokes, again, are classically correct, but they are also extremely brilliant. In playing forward he advances the left leg to within an inch or two of the ball's line of flight, and consequently leaves no room inside his bat for the ball to pass. He is quite free from the commonest fault in forward play – a tendency to make the stroke too soon. He plays forward at the last possible moment, and very quickly. So his stroke is lively and full of sting, and can be carried right through without fear of disaster. With a strong wrist and a faculty for exact timing, he can compass a hard hit and yet appear to use little force.

Hawke's team arrived in Johannesburg in the heart of 'Boer' country in February 1899, and within six months of the Anglo-Boer War Warner made his first appearance for an England XI. What *Wisden* called 'the English Team' were 106 runs behind on the first innings. Warner's 132 not out was the main feature of the second innings and helped to secure victory over 'South Africa' (as designated) by 32 runs.[4]

In his reports for the *Sportsman* he presented his readers with a graphic picture of a vast continent in which transport by train (Rhodes' dream of the Cape to Cairo) made communication possible while other forms of transport left the would-be cricketer struggling to get to the crease on time. The team pioneered new ground for an English side when they journeyed to Rhodesia to play two matches at Bulawayo. This is Warner's account of the journey north from Kimberley:

All day Friday we were travelling through British Bechuanaland, the monotony of the journey being broken occasionally when stopping for a few minutes at a small station. Then everyone bustled off the train for a walk along the platform to have a look at the natives, who were a very diminutive-looking lot, very different from the other tribes as regards physique. On Saturday the scenery all day was a sight for sore eyes, the country assuming a rich pastoral aspect. This was appreciated by everyone, after the strain of being blinded the last few weeks in the Transvaal and Kimberley by a bright sun blazing down on the dried-up wilderness. The mineral districts are the rich places and the mainstay of South Africa; but to travel through hundreds of miles of rich grass and undergrowth was a most welcome change to us. At about 4 o'clock the engine began to show signs of caving in, and an hour's halt was made at a station while the machinery was cooled down and overhauled, enabling us to converse for a few minutes with the natives, just to learn the language. An indaba was held by Lord Hawke outside the saloon with a group in full dress, waist-band and a few bracelets.

Those of their opponents who had come from Salisbury had an even tougher journey, so he was told:

When only twelve miles from Salisbury, a river was encountered, the heavy rains having converted it into a torrent about 30 feet deep and 100 yards wide. The difficulty in crossing it was at last overcome by Taberer, who is a good thrower, succeeding, after several attempts, in throwing a cricket ball over with string attached to someone on the other side. Next a rope was drawn over by the string, and then a wire hawser. After the men had got safely over, a span of thirty oxen dragged the coach bodily through the river. For four successive nights no-one had a wink of sleep, as they travelled night and day, and arrived in Bulawayo the day before the match in the best of spirits, none the worse for their wonderful trip – looking black as tinkers, smothered in dust and mud – and after a good day and night in bed they turned up at the ground on Saturday, looking fresh as paint and laughing at their week spent on the roads.

Their efforts were not entirely unrewarded as one of the Salisbury contingent, H. M. Taberer, a former Essex player, took five English wickets although XV of Rhodesia lost by an innings and 65 runs.

Warner's comment on Bulawayo itself offers a contemporary picture of the pioneering colonial:

At present there is an air of depression about Bulawayo, very little business being done, a lot of strapping young fellows walking about booted and spurred, dressed in riding breeches, flannel shirt, minus jacket or waistcoat, and a wide-awake hat, a sort of high-class cowboy of Texas costume being the correct thing. Everyone has heaps of time and no money, and don't seem to worry much, as all are waiting for something to turn up. The something is I believe in the shape of gold mines, which at present are waiting for proper machinery, etc., to be developed. No doubt there is a brilliant future before Rhodesia, and a boom may come at any time, but at present it is decidedly slow, and we've not heard a single lion roar.

Finally, he captured the sense of the remoteness of it all in his description of the send-off the Englishmen received on their departure for 'home':

By 8.30 the station platform at Bulawayo was taxed to its utmost with a most enthusiastic crowd who had come to say 'Good-bye', and, although we were all very glad to be getting through the town, it was with feelings of the utmost regret that we listened to all the well wishes for a successful time and a good run home. It was the most solid English crowd we have as yet encountered. The fierce way in which they wrung our hands and the 'Good-byes' came straight from their hearts, and not a few of them got very quiet and thoughtful before the finish, and would have given anything to have been coming away with us.

After their adventures, the team made the long journey south to the Cape where they played the second 'Test' on the beautiful

Newlands ground at Cape Town. Here they were all out for 92 just after lunch on the first day (Warner 31) but their dismissal of South Africa for 35 in the second innings secured them a victory by 210 runs. Warner, despite a lean spell at the start, had scored nearly eight hundred runs and topped the averages for the tour and had played against cricketers of the calibre of J. H. Sinclair and G. C. B. Llewellyn.

But he was nowhere near selection at home in the forthcoming 1899 series against Australia. Without decrying his performance in South Africa, he had nevertheless been the man available at short notice to go there. Indeed, the story of Warner's bachelor years, between leaving Oxford and his marriage in 1904, is of the young man, 'have bat, will play'; in the context of the demands of a social hostess, the spare man who could always be asked but was nevertheless very good value. Since Warner was an excellent dancer, the parallel has a certain aptness. He had two-stepped in Philadelphia and waltzed in Oporto.

A curious feature of the *Wisden* of 1900 was the provision of the averages of all Englishmen who appeared in any game against Joe Darling's 1899 Australians. Warner, who batted against them six times, had an average of 15 while the figures were headed by players such as Tom Hayward, Ranjitsinhji, Fry and MacLaren, all of whom had appeared in the Tests (in which Australia won the rubber). Warner's season was chiefly noticeable for a strong contribution of nearly a thousand runs (no one scored more) to Middlesex's runner-up position in the Championship. His 69 against Sussex at Hastings on a difficult wicket won praise from the critics. His 'duck' against Kent at Lord's was only consoled by watching the Middlesex last pair (one of whom, R. W. Nicholls, had been in the Rugby XI with him in 1892) put on 230 for the tenth wicket, a record which survived until two Kent men themselves, F. E. Woolley and Arthur Fielder, put on 235 in 1909.[5]

The winter of 1899–1900 found his energies rather differently deployed. The Anglo-Boer War had broken out in October and there had been three British defeats in 'Black Week' in December. Lord Roberts and Lord Kitchener sailed for South Africa with reinforcements and young men all over England volunteered for military service. Warner joined the part-time regiment of his Inn of Court known as 'The Devil's Own'. He had not totally abandoned the idea of being called to the Bar and his winter days were passed in working in chambers and in drilling. The Easter of 1900 saw him billeted in Winchester College with some eight hundred other men and in the spring he was promoted to lance corporal after a field day on Wimbledon Common. As we have seen, things military appealed to him and he would always number naval and military men among his friends and make as much of a contribution as bad health permitted when the time came in 1914.

Meanwhile, the summer of 1900 beckoned and his season began with 83 and 69 against Yorkshire, 114 against Sussex and 146 against Lancashire. These performances coincided with the publication by Heinemann of his first book, *Cricket in Many Climes*, an account of his tours based on his articles. It was very favourably received, the *Westminster Gazette* writing:

> Mr. Pelham F. Warner is not only a great batsman but a great traveller and a successful organiser. His descriptions of men and grounds, of cricket crowds, and his numerous anecdotes are written not only with keen observation but with abundant humour. If every tour is to produce an equally interesting book Mr. Warner should be encouraged to continue his wanderings in search of sport.

The *St James' Gazette* declared, 'he has a keen faculty for observation, and in some of his brief descriptions of the scenery in the West Indies and South Africa he uses it to excellent advantage'.

The summer also brought the first visit of the West Indians to England under the captaincy of his brother, Aucher. Pelham was asked to comment on their prospects and he wrote:

> On the whole, I feel pretty confident that the team will attract favourable attention all round, and my view is, I know, shared by many sound judges. The visit of any new team to England is always an experiment, attended with more or less possibilities of failure; but that they will be a failure I do not for a moment think, and in any case West Indian cricket will be greatly improved.

Their tour opened at the Crystal Palace against W. G. Grace's London County. Grace himself made 71 and the side included two other distinguished players in J. R. Mason and the Australian W. L. Murdoch. Although the West Indians lost by an innings, Pelham had the satisfaction of watching his brother make 49 in the match for once out. After five defeats in the first six matches, Pelham offered to help them during a spell in early July when Middlesex were without a match. In his debut for the West Indians against Leicestershire, he helped C. A. Olliviere put on 238 for the first wicket, both men making a century. The tourists achieved a victory by an innings, a result matched by their defeat of Surrey in two days later in the month.

Pelham reported on the tour for *Wisden*. He regarded it as a success especially as 'the team had never played together before and were quite unaccustomed to the strain of three-day cricket'. He was critical of the fielding (an unusual judgement in the view of later West Indian achievements) and he believed the English would be 'right glad to welcome another West Indian XI'.

Warner had, by playing for the first West Indian tourists, made his own small contribution to history. Exactly 50 years later, as president of MCC, he would welcome the side which would overwhelm England in the Test series. Once again, as in 1900, the Leicestershire fixture would give the tourists an innings victory, with double-centuries from Frank Worrell and Everton Weekes and 17 wickets by Sonny Ramadhin and Alf Valentine. Throughout his life, Warner was conscious of his West Indian origins and delighted in the achievements of his 'fellow-countrymen'. There was a genuine affection for the islands of his ancestors.

The year 1900 continued to be a good summer for him and he finished second in the Middlesex averages. Although he was formally called to the Bar in the autumn, it may be regarded as the year in which he finally turned his back on the law as a career. All his instincts were to continue to let cricket dictate the course of his life. He was writing sufficiently to make a modest living, he was a frequent cricketing guest at country-house parties, he was in demand at dinners (as a huge collection of menus bears testimony) and he scarcely ever played less than fifty innings a summer. Between 1897 and 1900 he had the following record at all levels of cricket:

Innings	Runs	Times Not Out	Highest Score	Average
264	9080	24	176	37.83

The new century (strictly, 1901) brought the vice-captaincy of Middlesex and a first appearance for Gentlemen v. Players in the Lord's match. He shared in a century opening partnership with Fry only to see the side subsequently lose 9 wickets for 42 runs. Against Somerset at Lord's he made his then highest score of 197 not out, carrying his bat. *The Daily Telegraph* correspondent wrote:

He appeared to score with almost equal facility from all bowlers brought against him. At one time his cutting would be particularly noticeable, at another his placing on the on-side appeared the feature of his play, and then came a period during which onlookers had to wonder how a man of such comparatively slight physique could get so much power into his drives. Yesterday he got most of his runs by cuts, but he brought off some very big drives.

Curiously, this match, played at Whitsun in the last week of May, was Middlesex's first game of the season. There were only three professionals on the playing staff, whose employment hitherto had been bowling to MCC and Middlesex members in the nets. Middlesex was comparatively unusual for those days in that the amateurs did a substantial amount of the side's bowling.

With the Bar firmly behind him and with no tour in which to play and write upon, Warner spent the winter of 1901–2 in France, staying with a family in Paris and gradually beginning 'to think in French'. He visited the Louvre, Versailles and Fontainebleau but enjoyed most of all the theatre and seeing the great actress Sarah Bernhardt. To his love of history, he was gradually adding a love of the theatre. In the earlier part of his life he saw most of the famous names on the English stage and he liked to follow a day at Lord's with an evening in the theatre.

In 1902, the Australians returned and the England XI which faced them in the first Test was one of the greatest of all time. Indeed, every member would score a century in first-class cricket. There was no place for Warner throughout the series so that he missed playing in the famous match at Old Trafford which Australia won by three runs. It was a wet summer and the slow wickets were against him, a man of his slight physique finding it difficult to force his game but he was the only man in the Middlesex side to make two centuries.

In the autumn, Lord Hawke asked him to join his side going to New Zealand and then Australia. At the last moment, Hawke found himself unable to go and he invited Warner to take over the captaincy. Hawke, as we have seen, had long ago summed up Warner's qualities as a leader but even he could not have anticipated the implications of this tour for the young man's career. There is, of course, a point where we can no longer call Warner a young man. But, as he set off for New Zealand, wise in the experience of touring, he was still under 30 and looked it.

The main purpose was to give stimulus to the game in a country which, as a nation, was itself only 60 years old and whose national Cricket Council had been formed in 1894. Warner's side (or Hawke's as it was officially known) was the first to make an extended tour though George Parr's All England XI had gone on from Australia for a brief visit in 1864.

The captain set a fine example, making runs in virtually every match, several of which were against odds of 22. In the eleven-a-side match v. Otago he scored a double-century. The tour ended with two 'representative' matches against New Zealand which the visitors, not surprisingly, won comfortably.

The umpire in the first of these games was Charles Bannerman, who had faced the first ball bowled in Test cricket at Melbourne in March 1877 and gone on to make the first Test century. Warner, with his sense of history, offered an attentive ear to Bannerman's reminiscences, especially of the game in which the Australians had dismissed MCC for 19 in 1878.

The tour was followed by three matches in Australia, against the Australian States. The third of these, against South Australia, revealed the absurdity of the compulsory follow-on which still applied in Australia.[6] Hawke's side made 553 and dismissed South Australia for 304. They had no option but to accept South Australia batting again and field out a further 454 runs. In a high Adelaide temperature, the tourists were in the field from after lunch on the Saturday until after lunch of the following Wednesday. As a consequence, they were a jaded set of men who set about getting 206 to win, and they were well beaten.

Warner topped the batting averages for the New Zealand part of the tour. More important were the qualities of leadership which he continued to display. He had led a party of 19 men on a world trip of some thirty thousand miles who were away from home for six months. No manager accompanied them, and he was responsible for everything on and off the field.

The possibility of his bringing out a side to Australia in the following domestic season had been mentioned to him during the match between Hawke's XI and Victoria at Melbourne in March 1903. Behind the suggestion lay a prolonged correspondence between the secretary of the Melbourne CC, B. J. Wardill and the 'reigning' England captain, MacLaren. Wardill had been secretary of the Melbourne club for a quarter of a century. He had raised its membership from 400 to several thousand and he was a powerful figure in Victorian cricket circles. Furthermore, he had managed three Australian sides to England. MacLaren had led England at home in 1899 and in 1902 and he had taken out, in 1901–2, as was the custom, a private side to Australia. But he had declined Wardill's invitation to do so again in 1903–4, offering to do so instead a year later. Wardill was not prepared to wait and he asked Warner to bring out an XI.

Warner, in his third spell as a touring captain, suggested that the time had come to ask MCC to take official responsibility and send out a team in their name. In making a recommendation which was accepted he helped to initiate a policy that lasted throughout his own lifetime. One can only guess at his reasons. His remark that 'MCC was the proper body' had some basis in that Wardill had first approached them with the idea in 1899. It may be that he felt he lacked both the financial acumen and the authority to take on such a large enterprise. MacLaren was the businessman, which Warner never was, and he had negotiated terms and expenses suitable to both professionals and amateurs for his 1901–2 side.

So much for Warner being the bearer of the invitation to London. Three months later he had just lost his wicket in Middlesex's match v. Yorkshire at Lord's when he was summoned to the Committee room, 'feeling a bit nervous and wondering what I had done!' What followed was a request to captain the first official MCC team to play overseas and even if he were not the Committee's first choice, he was assuredly their second. F. S. Jackson had already been asked but was unavailable.

The public furore which followed centred on two points: the rejection of MacLaren and the selection of Warner. MacLaren had, of course, a record as a player with which Warner could not compare and he had led England in the previous 14 encounters against Australia – ever since Grace's last match at Nottingham in 1899. Admittedly, England had only won twice under his leadership but the major reason for his rejection was a clash of personalities between him and Lord Hawke, the chairman of the selectors. The wonder was that he he survived so long because they had disagreed strongly over selection policy (notably at Old Trafford in 1902). Hawke also felt, with reason on his side, that MacLaren's status as an amateur could not stand the closest examination.

Warner was, of course, Hawke's protégé in the same way that Gubby Allen would be Warner's 30 years later. The chairman of selectors admired his leadership. Like Hawke's own captaincy of Yorkshire, this was more important than the runs Warner might get, especially on an overseas tour. Warner was also to learn from Hawke that the Australians, and in particular Wardill, wanted him. But he had, in the contemporary view of things, never played in a Test and certainly never played against Australia.

The press took sides, with the more 'popular' papers siding with MacLaren and the 'establishment' ones arguing for Warner. *The Times* challenged MacLaren's 'prescriptive right to command' and C. W. Alcock in *Cricket* felt Warner to be the 'most abused man of the day'. The flames of dispute were fuelled by the news that MacLaren was hesitating whether or not to go as a player under Warner. In the end he declared himself unavailable as a matter of etiquette but not before Warner had had to issue a statement to the press denying that he was willing to give up the captaincy to MacLaren. Finally, MCC publicly declared their support for Warner. Between the two themselves, there was no antipathy. MacLaren returned as England captain in 1909 and Warner played once under him. In his *Cricket* (1920), Warner assessed him as a fine tactician but 'a man of moods'. Their exchange of letters in the 1940s had the warmth and affection of two old men remembering the happy days.

An unusual assessment of Warner's standing at the time may be estimated by examining the prices attracted at an auction of bats conducted by the *Daily Express* in aid of the Cricketers' Benevolent Fund Society. Bidding was high for that donated by WG, with telegrams and telephone calls pouring in before the highest bidder secured it for £50. That of Victor Trumper realised £42. In descending order, followed 'Ranji', 13 guineas, Jessop, £8; Lord Hawke, £5 10s; Fuller Pilch (of nineteenth-century single-wicket fame) £5 10s; MacLaren, 5 guineas; Fry and Hayward each, £4; W. L. Murdoch, £3 10s; Warner, £3 (bought by someone in Ostend!); S. E. Gregory, £2 10s; M. A. Noble, £2 5s; and C. I. Thornton, £1 17s.

The auction apart, Warner found all the publicity embarrassing, especially for one who had become used to the plaudits of the press and, as we shall come to realise, needed them. But the very public discussion of his suitability to be captain of MCC coincided with the very private question of his suitability to be the husband of a quite wealthy young lady.

Agnes Blyth was the daughter of Henry Blyth who, until his death, was a partner in the firm of Gilbey, the gin distillers. He had been a successful, self-made Victorian businessman who, by his own efforts, had risen to the top of a firm with which he had no family connections, declined a peerage and died, a wealthy man, at the comparatively early age of 49. Agnes lived with her mother at 45 Portland Place and they had a country house at Stansted in Essex. Within the society circles in which she moved, Pelham Warner was no great 'catch'. He was a young man without money and without a career whose main claim to fame was his controversial selection as captain of the MCC touring party.

The romance blossomed quickly. In July he was playing at Old Trafford (and having the conversations with MacLaren which would lead to his press statement). He wrote to her, 'My dear Miss Blyth' and signed 'Yours sincerely, P. F. Warner.' She was given an account of the Lancashire match, a summary of the criticism in the provincial northern evening papers of his selection as captain and an invitation to watch him play at Leyton a week later. He did not, however, play and was kept indoors with a chill but, on hearing the result, sent her a telegram, 'Middlesex won. Seven wickets. Warner.' Telegrams announcing the results of cricket matches were often used by him as a mark of favour to his friends and Miss Blyth can have been left in no doubt where both his and her future interests might lie.

At the end of August, back in the pavilion at The Oval after making three he wrote her a four-page love-letter on Surrey County Cricket Club notepaper, of which one sentence is all we need intrude on, 'if I had the eloquence of Demosthenes, I could not tell you how much I love you'.

Clearly the time had come to approach her mother and her uncle, Sir James Blyth. Middlesex had become county champions and were again playing at The Oval, against the Rest of England. On the evening of the first day's play Warner wrote to Agnes asking her to lunch at The Oval the next day[7] to meet 'one of my best pals, Martin Hawke, who won't tell a soul and is terribly keen to meet you'. The letter also asked for Sir James Blyth's address so that Warner could inform him of his honourable intentions:

> He should know everything, my position as far as this world's goods are concerned. As you know, I am dependent on my own brains for my livelihood. When my mother dies I shall have a little but not much by any means. I hate writing this but I want to be straight as a die and as 'out' it must come at some time or other, the sooner the better.

The lunch duly took place and Warner obliged her afterwards with 73 not out (which became a century on the following morning, as Agnes was informed by telegram) while Lord Hawke fielded for the Rest. That evening the two men dined out and Hawke agreed to be his best man, if all went well with the Blyth family. Thus the chairman of the selectors became a very personal link between Warner's public and private life.

Events now moved even more rapidly, for Warner not only won his fair lady but secured approval from her family and from MCC for her to accompany him to Australia less than a fortnight later, with one of the passengers acting as chaperone.

Warner had all this time been involved with the selection committee choosing the side for Australia. None of the leading amateurs of the day was available though Fry tried hard to get some work as a journalist in Australia to make it possible for him to go. But Warner secured R. E. Foster of Worcestershire and B. J. T. Bosanquet of Middlesex whose selection he encouraged. No problem existed in gathering together the best of the English professionals, one of whom was chosen only after Warner undertook to guarantee he would have him on the field punctual and sober. The guarantee was fulfilled.

The captain wrote in the *Sportsman* just before the party left, 'The team is far from representing our best amateur strength but I very much doubt if the professional element could have been strengthened.' Among the names which remain part of the folk history of the game, besides his own, were Tyldesley (J. T.) of Lancashire, Tom Hayward of Surrey, George Hirst and Wilfred Rhodes and A. A. Lilley and Herbert Strudwick the wicket-keepers.

Gradually, as the time for departure approached, all sections of the press swung round to support Warner. Fry, in the *Daily Express*, sent him off with some encouragement:

This is a bigger job than you've had as yet, this captaincy of an English side in test matches. But with your knowledge of the game, your accommodating temper, your tactful touch, and your sanguine view of things, you should do very well in this job, too. Then, too, Pelham, they say you have luck – that you are a lucky Captain. They say that of Lord Roberts, also. It is difficult to find the dividing-line between luck and management in war and cricket.

And now, Pelham, farewell for a season. I shall think of you as I dig with my niblick in the furze bushes, and, likely enough, regret I am not with you hitting at a bigger ball with a simpler instrument. If you win your first test match every hand at home will stretch out to you across the sea; and, if you do not, every real cricketers's hand will stretch out all the same.

Warner had expected only 'a few of the general public to give us a good word' at St Pancras. Instead, the whole station was crammed with people, among whom was the Surrey poet Craig (a famous figure in his day), doing immense business with his doggerel:

> We'll stand by Warner as we ought,
> The honour was by him unsought,
> We've faith in him, and nothing shall remove it.
> We English love fair play,
> At least, that's what we say,
> If 'tis so, by our actions let us prove it.

Warner therefore became the first man to lead an official MCC tour abroad. 'It is probable,' said a contemporary comment, 'that the day of private adventures in international cricket is past.' Later events in the century have shown this not to be so, both politics and economics creating sides that may be so styled. Nevertheless, teams under the auspices of MCC would tour overseas until the formation of the Test and County Cricket Board in 1968 changed the structure of authority and administration. After 1977 England XIs rather than MCC toured overseas.

Once aboard the *Orantes* at Tilbury, Warner, his fellow cricketers, and his fiancée could relax.

During the voyage out, the editor of *Wisden* was drafting his piece on Warner for the 'Five Cricketers of the Year' feature in the 1904 edition. Without knowing the eventual result of the tour, he wrote that the honour was deserved not only because Warner was MCC captain in Australia but also as 'he had fairly won his place among the representative batsmen of his day'. No one could match him in enthusiasm and what he had achieved had been 'won by strenuous and persistent effort'. His slightness of figure was against him so that he did not 'fill the eye as a great batsman but once having seen him get a hundred runs one is no longer in doubt as to his qualities', while his personal qualities made him 'the most popular of cricketers'. This was the man who landed at Adelaide and promptly addressed 2000 people in the Town Hall. On his own captaincy, so much criticised, he commented, 'I have been captaining XIs since I was 15 years old and I am not aware that a great deal of fault has been found with me.' His speech was modest without being self-effacing and confident without being arrogant. It was warmly received by the Australian press.

MCC came to the first Test at Sydney having easily beaten Victoria and New South Wales and had the best of a draw with South Australia, but recent history was not on England's side. In the last four series between England and Australia, the Australians had been successful.

Warner regarded himself, in his own words written a year later, as playing in his 'very first Test match and at the same time in the onerous position of captain'. Despite the use of 'Test' match by some papers in describing the 1898–9 South African tour, clearly the contemporary view was that the Anglo-Australian games were the only encounters to have official status. Not until 1921 did Warner write of himself as having made a century on his Test debut in 1899.

That first Test of 1903 is remembered for Foster's 287 which easily eclipsed Murdoch's 211 at The Oval, for Australia. England led on the first innings by nearly three hundred but a fierce Australian reply which included 185 not out by Trumper, left them 194 to win – achieved with five wickets to spare but not without its anxious moments. Warner himself believed the match was won in the first three overs of the first day when three splendid catches were held to dismiss R. A. Duff, Trumper and Clem Hill with the Australian total at nine. The captain had his first exercise in diplomacy when the Australian crowd (including those in the members' seats in the pavilion) booed an umpiring decision. Warner went across and spoke to the members and got hissed for his pains. The *Daily Mail* correspondent reported to his paper that he was at fault in speaking to them rather than ignoring them. At all events, he kept his men on the field in a continuing atmosphere 'of yelling and hissing up to the drawing of stumps'. It was his first experience of crowd reaction and he wrote sardonically of the incident: 'Yes; they are a lovely crowd at Sydney, and anyone who has taken part in a test match there may consider himself thoroughly salted and fit to play before an audience from the infernal regions.'

England went two up after the second Test whose result was largely determined by the weather. The 221 for 2 on the first day was made in fine batting conditions. Thereafter the two sides lost 38 wickets between them for 430 runs (an average of 11.31 per wicket) on a wicket badly affected by torrential rain. Rhodes took 15 Australian wickets and Lilley did not concede a bye. Warner himself made runs, sharing in an opening partnership of 122 to which he contributed 68.

Between the second and third Tests, MCC played XVIII of Ballarat. Warner found these matches against odds 'a weariness of the flesh'. The travel was irksome, the cricket undistinguished and his temper not improved by the barracking of small boys. He wrote:

> These youths should be put down with a rod of good birch for, if they are not suppressed now, in eight or ten years' time, they will grow up into the type of man who 'barracked' so disgracefully at Sydney. But they are apparently encouraged in their behaviour by many of their elders. Players should not have to stand up before a running fire of noisy impertinence.

The only consolation for him was his first wicket in Australia ('off a long hop: a ball I not infrequently bowl').

The third Test at Adelaide brought an Australian victory by 216 runs. England were always outplayed though the captain contributed the highest aggregate for his side. Warner had made 48 in the first innings, and he and Hayward set about the gargantuan task of making 495 runs to win by putting on 148. After they had gone (Warner 79, Hayward 67) no one stayed with Hirst, and Australia had, he conceded, 'a thoroughly well-deserved victory'.

Between the third and fourth Tests, MCC visited Tasmania and then beat both Victoria and New South Wales. The Tasmanian trip got off to a bad start with a rough crossing, a crowded hotel with an 'exceedingly badly mannered female who ran the show' (wrote Warner) but ended more propitiously with two enjoyable games and a day at the races ('at which I won ten shillings'). The Victoria match produced the sensation of the tour when Rhodes and E. Arnold dismissed the home side for 15, still (in 1987) the lowest total in Australian first-class cricket. The New South Wales game was won thanks to the batting and bowling of Bosanquet whose century, half-century and 8 for 96 dominated the match.

Before the fourth Test Warner was involved in correspondence with the New South Wales Cricket Association on the subject of its umpires. Hitherto, the two captains had chosen the umpires and they were prepared to do so for the fourth Test. The Association overruled Warner's choice and he wrote a firm, but polite letter insisting that the two men chosen by him and Noble should stand and offering to meet any extra expense from MCC resources.

To his annoyance, his letter was released to the press and described by its recipients as 'highly discourteous, in very bad form, impolitic and impertinent'. In the end, he got his way. Thirty years later history would repeat itself when a telegram from him, as manager of the MCC 1932–33 party, was released to the press.

All Warner's tact was required again when he and the Australian captain were in dispute during the fourth Test about rolling the wicket. The circumstances are not now important but they arose because of an inadequacy of definition. Warner won his point but made a plea on his return to England for exact rulings to be established. England led by over a hundred on the first innings and went on to win the match by 157 runs. Bosanquet took 6 for 51 in the Australian second innings and, as England's second best bowler in the series, vindicated Warner's advocacy of him. Among Warner's attributes was the ability to 'spot' a cricketer and this quality later made him invaluable as a Test selector for so many years.

The victory meant that England had regained the Ashes. There were many 'great days' in Warner's long love-affair with cricket, but 3 March 1904, he wrote (a few months afterwards), was the greatest one so far. England's defeat in the fifth Test, as much the victim of the weather as Australia had been in the second one, scarcely mattered. Warner believed it was the England bowlers who won the rubber, with 'a man for every type of wicket'.

His own performance as a batsman was modest with an average of 27.66 and a highest score of 79. But his qualities as a leader of men had been confirmed. A vast crowd saw MCC off from Melbourne with a display of goodwill and good humour which they would show again in 1912 but which would contrast sadly with his departure from Australia in 1933.

The Australian press also treated him most generously. 'No reasonable ground existed for the attack made on him in the old country when he was chosen,' wrote *The Australasian*. 'How Warner can smile at his critics now!' The Melbourne *Truth* devoted a whole column to his qualities of leadership, of welding together 'fourteen men of varying temperaments and social qualities for thousands of miles . . . without jealousies, frictions and heartburnings'. This was leadership in the truest sense of the word, 'such men are rare in any sport'.

Yet all this was accomplished by a man who was so much in love that he could scarcely be parted from his fiancée for a moment. When they were, as for example during the team's visit to Tasmania, he wrote her love-letters of great eloquence, if in some ways as old as the hills, 'I could not possibly say how much I miss you. I am just living for Tuesday;' 'In my love for you I am a millionaire for there my wealth is untold.'

Warner was far from being a millionaire, as we have seen. In another letter, written from Launceston to Agnes in Melbourne, he wrote, 'When this tour is over, as I hope successfully, I have done my duty to England and English cricket and I would like to give up the game and get some billet and work hard for you.' As a start, he told her he had just written two articles for the *Westminster Gazette* and two for the *Sportsman* 'just to make some money for my darling'.

Warner did not, of course 'give up the game'. His approach both to work and to money will call for comment from time to time in the chapters which follow.

The MCC gave a dinner to the successful tourists. Speeches on such occasions are of necessity eulogistic but the tribute of Lord Alverstone, the president, to Warner was a warm one, 'a man of infinite tact and discretion who entered into the life and happiness of the team off as well as on and made friends wherever he went.'

Cricket had become the business of Warner's life as other men became soldiers or bankers. The image of the general leading his men in campaign often came easily to his mind and he had seen himself in that role on the tour. In his reply he said:

> I tried to convert that strip of twenty-two yards into a battlefield on which no quarter was to be given; and, if we were to go down, we were to do so fighting to the very last ball.
>
> I am proud – very proud indeed – but with my pride there is a feeling of great humbleness, for I could have done nothing myself without the loyalty and support of my Team. Lord Roberts has said of the South African Army that they were heroes on the field of battle and gentlemen off it – and I can say the same of this Team.
>
> I shall never forget the unswerving pluck with which you fought every inch of the way; I shall never forget the pride of being your leader. I have led great men into battle, and we have come out of the fray victorious. And now I lay down the staff of office with gratitude and pride.

Tribute to Warner's captaincy also came from the players. For the first time professionals and amateurs all stayed in the same hotels on tour and although the social distinctions of the times remained, they were minimised. Bosanquet's tribute to him would have found complete acceptance:

> The important factor in our success was the personality of our captain. The keenest of enthusiasts, and, as he would say 'a cheerful optimist' he infected the whole team with his own spirit, and in addition never spared himself if he could do anything for the comfort, or pleasure, of the men under him. His sole thought was for us, and no-one of us can ever properly appreciate, or be sufficiently grateful for, all he did for us. A wise, and most successful captain on the field, his tact and kindly influence in less strenuous moments had even more to do with his final triumph.
>
> Most of the hard work of the tour, and most of the troubles and worries incidental to such a trip, fell on his shoulders. He never shirked and never complained, and herein performed the greater proportion of a captain's duty.

Three weeks later, he led his successful team against the Rest of England at Lord's. In bleak, cheerless and bitterly cold conditions, 8000 people came to watch a match in which the MCC Australian XI achieved a first-innings lead of 53 in a drawn game. The captain himself made 27 and 22 not out and the Rest XI included both

Jackson and MacLaren. In the early weeks of the season Warner appeared regularly for Middlesex without accomplishing anything of note, except being the principal batsman in Middlesex's victory against Yorkshire and running out Lord Hawke four days before the Yorkshire captain appeared with Warner 'on the same side' as his best man.

On 7 June 1904 Warner was married to Agnes Blyth. What had been the engagement of a young woman in London society to a man of Anglo-West Indian origins with no particular claims upon that society became marriage with a figure of national importance. The *Daily Chronicle* reported that 'less than a year ago Pelham Warner was a mere cricketer among cricketers whose private affairs were no concern of the general public. Now he is become a national treasure. England won and the importance of Warner was hinted by the public interest in his wedding.' The *Daily Mail* wrote, 'if anyone doubted the hold cricket had on the public imagination, the sight of the enthusiastic reception accorded to Mr P. F. Warner and his bride would have dispelled any such idea.' One provincial paper went so far as to call it 'the wedding of the year', while another evaluated the social nuances in saying that 'the aristocrats of the West End are but *parvenus* compared with the aristocrats of cricket'.

To cricketers, the substantial reporting at great length through England and Scotland provides a measure of the contemporary view of cricket as a national pastime and of the importance attached to defeating the Australians, which two previous captains, Stoddart and MacLaren, had failed to do. The occasion was a testimony to Warner's personal popularity. The press called him 'famous', 'the most popular cricketer in England', 'celebrated' and 'a man of thorough sportsmanlike qualities'. From *The Australasian* came the comment, ''till last year a gentleman of comparatively little weight in the world of sport, now he is a great personality'.

Vast crowds thronged the streets around Marylebone Parish Church and groundsmen and spectators poured out of Lord's to join them when play was stopped so that those participating in the match between the Gentlemen of England and the I Zingari might attend the wedding, including the best man, Lord Hawke. Cricketers, of course, were there and their names would be a banner roll of the leading players of the day. All the Middlesex side, amateurs and professionals, were invited. The date had been set, like many another cricketer's wedding, when the team had no fixture. From other walks of life came Lord Roberts, commander-in-chief in the Anglo-Boer War, Sir Henry Irving the actor, and noblemen and MPs. Seven hundred people packed the church, the larger number of whom were ladies 'millinered and gowned and wearing a multitude of hats which no man could price' (wrote the *Morning Leader*). Among the officiating clergy was Bishop Welldon who would, four years later, officiate at the wedding of Winston Churchill. The wedding presents ranged from a diamond tiara to a 'Life of Stonewall Jackson'. Tom Hayward sent one on behalf of the professionals who had been on the MCC tour. The reception took place at the bride's home and the couple spent their honeymoon at Cookham.

It was all a very long time ago and the splendour of the occasion belongs to a vanished age. The sun, in every sense, shone on Pelham Warner. The society which had now become his world rejoiced with him. Cricketers of every ilk wished him well. Those on the perimeters of luck and fortune in the many-sided scene which was Edwardian Britain shared for a moment the colour and gaiety of this romance. Warner might be forgiven if he felt that many concentric circles revolved around him.

Small wonder that Lord Hawke took the opportunity a little later to whisper, 'Is it quite the same Plum who left us last September?' Plum, in his own words, 'took the hint' and avoided the indignity of having to order a larger size in Harlequin caps. Instead, he set about establishing a home for himself and Agnes at 15 Tedworth Square where once had lived Charles Dickens' son, Sir Henry. The couple bought it from Mrs Lily Langtry.

4
The Golden Years, 1904–14

'The title is a mistake as the word ashes is, at the best, slang and has only a very temporary significance,' wrote a reviewer of Warner's *How We Recovered the Ashes* which Chapman and Hall published at 18/6. He was not alone in his opinion. Another remarked that 'the ashes was a rather undignified borrowing from the Yellow press'. But the Ashes had come to stay and to remain the hallmark of Anglo-Australian contests, a prize of mythical substance and elusive value forever kept at Lord's.

Ashes swept aside, the book won high praise for, as the *Westminster Gazette* put it, 'its bright and manly narrative, genuinely worth writing and written genuinely well'. It earned its author about £300 which was a reasonable contribution to the first year of married life and represented many a professional man's salary for a year.

While Warner was in no way able to earn with any regularity an income of (say) £300 from his writing, there would be two or three more books in the next ten years and a modest income from journalism. As we shall see, thanks to his wife's financial circumstances, he and Agnes would lead a life of somewhere between affluence and comfort.

For Warner himself, the ten years between his marriage and 1914 saw him combine his writing with playing for (and leading) Middlesex, with touring abroad (and occasionally appearing for England at home) and with establishing a family home in the country. It was a decade to which the romantics have given a rosy hue and the cricket historians a golden furbish. The fortunes of Warner certainly find a place in that romantic view of the pre-1914 era and in the 'Golden Age' of cricket.

In his career as a county cricketer, he was among the leading batsmen in the country between 1904 and 1914. He finished in the top 12 in the national averages on six occasions and only really fell from grace in 1914 when he followed behind some one hundred and fifty others and failed to make a century. Apart from that year, he was top or near enough of the Middlesex county averages. From some two hundred appearances for Middlesex or MCC some examples may be drawn. In 1904 he scored 166 not out in sharing in an opening partnership of 306 with J. Douglas against Notting-hamshire and, in the following year made 204 for Middlesex v. Sussex at Lord's. He followed this double-century by two 'ducks' in the next match and, on going to church the Sunday after, was surprised to hear himself the subject of Prebendary Carlile's sermon on the general theme of pride coming before a fall. On greeting the departing congregation, Carlile remarked to Warner, 'I seem to know your face,' to which he replied: 'You have just been preaching about me!'

The years 1907 and 1908 were times of great achievement. Only by a decimal point did he not come top of the national averages in 1907 and he adapted himself to making runs in a summer of wet wickets which lent themselves less to his style of play. He made two centuries in the match between the Rest of England and the champion county, Nottinghamshire. *Wisden* commented that 'his 149 at The Oval was perhaps the most brilliant display he has ever given. All through the summer Warner was a model of consistency, scarcely knowing what it was to fail.'

His ability on sticky wickets was again demonstrated in 1908 when he batted right through an MCC innings for 64 not out in a total of 95 against Yorkshire, repeating the performance with another 64 not out (out of 124) against Kent. Only one other player, out of 22 innings, made double figures. For being undismissed all week from Tuesday onwards at Lord's, MCC gave him two bats!

After a summer of indifferent health in 1909, he had another outstanding year in 1910, lying third in the national averages, scoring a century in each of his last three matches at Lord's and (wrote *Wisden*) standing 'ahead of all other batsmen except Tyldesley'. But the season contained one curiosity which he was to recall 40 years later when the Lord's scoreboard was floodlit for his eightieth birthday. 'There have been times when that Lord's scoreboard needed black crepe instead of floodlighting so far as Warner went. I remember how in 1910 I went in to bat against Kent at 12.45 p.m. I got a duck. My goodness, I was in again before tea, and I got another duck.'

In 1911 he made over two thousand runs in the season for the first time. His county performances were as consistent as ever and his average was 43.09.

That summer, the England selectors were seeking a captain to take MCC to Australia and he was invited to captain an XI bearing his name against Jessop's in a trial match. He scored 60 not out and 28 and, in a second trial, he made 32 and 53 as captain of the Rest v. England. Fry was offered the MCC captaincy first but declined for business reasons and Warner was then appointed. He led the MCC Australian XI in the Scarborough Festival but, with a foreboding of things to come, had to bat last through a severe recurrence of his old stomach pains.

Nevertheless, he finished the season in grand style for the Rest of England v. Warwickshire, the champions. Batting at no. 4, he found himself in the unusual position of not going to the wicket until the total was almost two hundred. There he stayed for 5½ hours, driving with great power and scoring 244, the highest innings of his career. Among the spectators was the future West Indian Test player, C. R. Browne,[8] then a young man of 19. 'It was the greatest innings I have ever seen,' he wrote years later to Warner. 'You attacked and kept on attacking Frank Foster, Field, Santall and Quaife during the whole of your innings. That will always remain a classic in my mind's eye.' Even if one makes some allowance for an old man remembering the hero of his youth – and delighting in having come to know that hero – the judgement rings true. Never again would Warner play an innings of such sustained mastery though he confessed that only brandy and soda at the intervals had kept him going. Sadly, the ill and reluctant no. 11 at Scarborough, rather than the high-scoring no. 4 at The Oval, was the harbinger of his fortunes in Australia.

His selection as captain of MCC in 1911–12 brings us back to those gifts of leadership which were the mainspring of his cricketing ability. He had been deputy captain of Middlesex for some years before he succeeded George MacGregor as captain in 1908. His assumption of the Middlesex captaincy coincided with the departure of some of the more regular amateurs such as his predecessor MacGregor and the pioneer of cricket photography, G. W. Beldam. He chose also to reduce the number of amateurs making occasional appearances. In 1904, for example, 23 of them had appeared for Middlesex. Warner kept the figure well under twenty most of the time. Nevertheless, there remained those good amateurs essential to a county side and Warner drew in particular on the services of four such men. Bosanquet, whose selection for Australia in 1903–4 he had secured, appeared infrequently and virtually only as a batsman. The schoolmasters, C. M. Wells and

Douglas were important acquisitions principally in August, as was E. L. Kidd, the Cambridge captain of 1912.

He came to depend on a solid core of seven professionals, men whose contribution to Middlesex cricket (besides his own) ensured that the county never fell below sixth in his years as captain. Nearly all of them made their mark in the game over a long period and, with one possible exception, belie the image of the humble professional cricketer plying his lowly trade of bowling among the amateur batsmen of the 'Golden Age'.

J. T. Hearne was an outstanding bowler, a man of immense energy of whom a great deal was demanded both by Middlesex and by MCC, and the first in England to take 3000 wickets. He was essentially a medium-paced bowler whose occasional fast ball could catch a batsman unawares. He had first played for Middlesex in 1888 and was in his twenty-first year with the county when Warner became captain. By then he had played in Australia (in a Test series), in South Africa (on a tour) and in India (as a coach). Hearne was a man of wisdom and judgement, some six years older than Warner, and he would become, at Warner's instigation, the first professional elected to the Middlesex committee.

The other senior professional was Albert Trott, one of two Australians in the side. He had played with distinction for Australia against England in 1894–95 and in 1898 had qualified for Middlesex. By the time Warner became captain, Trott's greatest days were over. The man who had been the most popular professional at Lord's had declined to the extent that his contract was ended in 1910.

The other Australian was Frank Tarrant whom Warner had seen as a ground staff bowler at the Melbourne Club during his 1902–3 visit. They had discussed the idea of his coming to Middlesex and Tarrant came to Lord's, where he qualified in 1905. His all-round contribution to Middlesex cricket in the years before 1914 was enormous, accomplishing the double eight times and having a highest score of 250 not out against Essex in 1914. Warner was known to have encouraged him to come and there was some criticism at this importation of an overseas player until he displayed his talents. Tarrant was an individualist and a man who knew his worth. Warner had spotted the potential and as captain was able to get the best out of him. After the First World War Tarrant, back in his native Australia, abandoned cricket as a regular activity for the more lucrative enterprise of buying and selling racehorses, and his final excursion onto the cricket field was to manage an Australian team in India in 1935–36 and play himself at the age of 55.

The Middlesex wicket-keeper was Harry (or 'Joe') Murrell who came from Kent and remained until 1926. Like many another wicket-keeper who failed to achieve international recognition simply because a contemporary was a little better or more established, Murrell remained in the wings while E. J. ('Tiger') Smith and Strudwick held the stage. Warner consulted Murrell a great deal and it was Murrell who nicknamed him 'general'.

Edward Mignon had come into the county side while Warner was deputy captain as a fast bowler. He served Middlesex loyally enough for some reasons but in 1913 his engagement was ended because he was not 'the fast bowler of real class' the county wanted. He was to serve in the First World War and his early death from pneumonia in 1925 was a consequence of that service.

Warner brought into his side two new professionals who would achieve great distinction. J. W. Hearne was the cousin of J. T. Hearne. He was on the ground staff at Lord's when Warner selected him in 1909 as an all-rounder destined to perform the 'double' five times and still to be playing for Middlesex as late as 1936. Warner, with that judgement of the young cricketer which was so acute, successfully pressed his claims, in the face of considerable opposition, for the 1911–12 tour of Australia under his own captaincy. At Melbourne Hearne hit his only century in a Test but his overall talents as a hard driver of the ball and as a leg-break bowler won him selection in most of the Tests played up to 1926. Hearne would remain, when his playing career ended, a popular figure at Lord's as a coach and, after 1949, as a life member of MCC.

Finally, there was 'Patsy' Hendren – like J. T. Hearne a future member of the Middlesex committee and like J.W., a future life member of MCC. Warner brought Hendren into the Middlesex side in 1909, and there he stayed until 1937, accumulating for England, MCC and for the county over 57,000 runs and compiling 170 centuries. In the years between the wars he was the mainstay of Middlesex. In the period of Warner's pre-1914 captaincy, he was quietly consolidating his position in a side distinguished for its batting if, by 1914, distinctly thin in bowling.

These, then, were the seven professional cricketers whom, day in and day out, for some seven seasons, Warner captained. Quite apart from their exceptional talents as cricketers, they were men of great loyalty and service. Their station in life might have been different from Warner's but it was a situation tacitly accepted without embarrassment in pre-1914 England. The game they played was a bond of unity, and cricket to its credit in later years drew upon the wisdom and rewarded the commitment of several of them.

Warner's relations with them were conducted within the conventions of the day. He had learnt from Lord Hawke the qualities of what a later age would call 'man-management' so that he combined firmness with a readiness to concern himself with a player's personal problems, sometimes domestic ones. But one incident of which Warner himself is the source jars a later age. Trott, as the senior professional, was instructed to administer 'six of the best' with a hair brush to the errant Mignon in the players' dressing room after play for a lapse in the field. One is left with an image of Warner meanwhile striding off to the amateurs' dressing room leaving his 'senior prefect' to act as disciplinarian.

That Warner, as a whole, won the respect and admiration of the professional cricketer of his day cannot be seriously challenged. Some of them, such as Hendren and the Hearnes, were visitors, as we shall see below, to the pre-season coaching occasions at his country home in Kent. The letters he had received at the time of his wedding were further testimony. From men more used to wielding a bat than a pen their calligraphy was a credit to the elementary education of those days quite apart from the sentiments they expressed. Many years later, Hendren would describe Warner 'as the greatest leader I ever knew', while a contemporary tribute came from Trott, writing in 1907 in the sporting paper, *The Winning Post*: 'his own personal popularity is shown by the fact that we paid players almost worship him, and he is exceedingly kind and generous to the side, winning or losing'.

Trott's generous praise of Warner in 1907 was scarcely reciprocated by the comment in *The Times* 18 months later, 'Albert Trott is very seldom effective these days and scarcely worth his place in the eleven'. Warner was by now writing regularly for *The Times* as its 'special correspondent' and all his contributions, such as this one, were anonymous. Over several years, before 1914, he wrote a pre-season review of the counties. His piece in 1908 branched out with the opening sentence, 'This is the Age of Progress. Cricket is now more scientifically played and has advanced in popularity.' He then wrote over a column on the techniques of batting. Usually, this annual article would review the counties and it was in this context that he had commented upon Trott in 1909, adding 'if Tarrant and Mr Warner can produce their previous season's form, all will be well'.

During the summer, he would write upon games he played in himself. As an example, when Middlesex played Nottinghamshire at Lord's in 1910, he wrote, 'the Middlesex openers rendered their side great service'. *Wisden*'s report reads, 'Warner and Tarrant gave the home side a splendid start.'

Overall, one cannot take exception to the objectivity of his reporting, and when 'Mr Warner played a faultless innings of 150' it was probably true! Only the confidential files of *The Times* contained the name of the paper's special correspondent and Middlesex reporter. Warner was employed in 1919 by the same paper to write a series of Reminiscences 'From a Correspondent' which appeared in book-form a year later. To some extent, therefore, by 1920, his cover was 'blown'.

We must now turn to Warner's role as a tourist and as an England player in this period. Despite the high drama of the MCC tour of 1903–4, he was not invited to play in any of the Tests against Australia in 1905. Instead, he was asked by Hawke to contribute his youthful experience as an England selector and to share in the choice of such front rank batsmen as Jackson, Fry, R. H. Spooner, MacLaren, Tyldesley and Hayward, all of whom made substantial scores. By the autumn Warner was once again the England captain, chosen to lead the MCC side to South Africa. Curiously, J. R. Mason of Kent was also offered the captaincy by Lacey, the MCC secretary, after the earlier invitation to Warner. Aware of Warner's appointment, Mason tactfully declined and maintained a discreet silence.

The side, as Warner admitted, was 'not by any means representative of the strength of England' although the party contained players such as J. N. Crawford, a prolific all-rounder at Repton who had left school a few months earlier but was already well established in the Surrey side. David Denton was halfway through his great career for Yorkshire (which would include 61 centuries for the county). Colin Blythe, the Kent left-arm slow bowler, would take exactly one hundred Test wickets before 1914.

The press were critical of the team but not of Warner whose overall record as a touring captain and whose personal popularity in South Africa rendered him the right man for a tour which was both a good-will mission and an occasion to assess the current strength of South African cricket.

The Anglo-Boer War lay between the last visit of an English side and this one. While the visitors might look with confidence towards their welcome in Cape Town there was some apprehension about their possible reception in Johannesburg. The *Cape Times* in an open letter to Warner on their arrival sought to put them at their ease:

Precisely what happened subsequent to your departure in 1899 is not recorded in the sporting columns of the papers. There was trouble and a lot of it and some of the best on both sides went under. Many good men whom you met in your last visit have paid for their opinions with their lives. Today, however, it is with a unanimity of opinion that you are welcomed, and you will be sure of the heartiest of greetings wherever you go. In the world of cricket it is a United South Africa – one in thought and mind, and one indeed in the welcome that is extended to the MCC.

One of the MCC party, J. C. Hartley, had served with the Royal Fusiliers and took part in the assault of Pieter's Hill, a bitterly fought English success in 1900, when the West Province cricketer Pieter de Villiers, a Boer commandant, was captured. De Villiers was sent as a prisoner to Ceylon and had been allowed parole there to talk to MacLaren's team when they stopped on their way to Australia. Hartley and de Villiers played against each other when MCC met a Country Districts XVIII at Worcester, de Villiers taking 6 MCC wickets for 76.

Warner reported the tour for the *Westminster Gazette* and, from time to time, his articles would include comments upon the evidence and scenes of the war such as the following:

> On Thursday we reached De Aar, and from that moment we were on historic ground, passing Orange River, Belmont, Graspan, Modder River, and Magersfontein. Lord Methuen's advance was parallel to the railway, and as the battlefields spread out before us one could not but think of the many gallant fellows who came up this line never to return. Here was the kopje which the Guards took at the bayonet's point; there the scene of the Naval Brigade's charge at Enslin, while away in the distance stretched the flat, with little or no cover beyond an occasional ant-heap, where Lord Methuen's infantry lay the whole day under a fierce fire in the broiling sun.

The fixtures for the tour were arranged by Mitchell, who had played for England v. South Africa in 1898–99 and would play for South Africa v. England in 1912. The programme minimised the travel as far as possible in a huge country but produced an uneven balance. There was a lot of matches against odds, some of whose sides Warner felt were so weak that they should not have been played at all, while four of the five Test matches were embraced within the final five matches of the tour in the last three weeks.

After three wins in the Cape, MCC played two games at Kimberley against Griqualand West XVs. The team were taken to see the diamond mines and Warner described what he saw to his English readers:

The compound of the Kimberley mine is supposed to be one of the sights of the town, but it did not appeal to some of us, who thought the whole thing rather unedifying and the kind of spectacle that one does not care to see twice. The scene below ground in the galleries is very unlike the popular notion of a diamond-mine. All was dirt and grime, and half-naked men bathed in perspiration were hammering, shovelling and picking. And all this strenuous labour, organisation, and expenditure just for a few stones to deck my lady's finger!

It was an occasion when Warner's comments stood a little apart from the simple theme of a Dutch and English white society in South Africa seeking reconciliation and drew attention instead to the huge black community in the country. He was by nature a man of manners, and his politeness would be extended to the underdog, be he a black in South Africa or in his own native West Indies or a poor man in London. He took the world as he found it and, if from time to time he cast his eye on misfortune, he was sad. But we must not expect to find in him a social campaigner.

South Africa was an issue in the General Election being fought in Britain in January 1906, and the 'Union' was one of the platforms on which the Liberals fought and won. As the MCC party approached Johannesburg, Warner reported: 'We knew we would encounter cricketers well worthy of our steel while you in England are busy at the hustings and deciding more important questions than the supremacy of MCC or South Africa at a mere game.'

The first opponents 'worthy of our steel' were Transvaal who defeated MCC by 60 runs on the Wanderers' ground at Johannesburg, despite 134 not out by Denton. Warner, who had done little as a batsman so far, then made a century against XVIII of Potchesfroom urged on by the military band which accompanied the match.

The first Test match followed. It proved to be a game of fluctuating fortunes. England lost 3 wickets for 15 and barely recovered to reach 184 but their bowlers dismissed South Africa for 91. The crowd of 10,000 had awaited the arrival of Sinclair with the same sort of expectancy later accorded by Australians to Sir Donald Bradman. Alas! He was out first ball and with him went a large part of South African hopes.

England, 93 ahead, lost three early wickets but Warner himself made his only half-century of the series. The score of 160 for 5 became 190 all out and South Africa were left the not inconsiderable target of 284. The game went England's way as South Africa fell to 105 for 6 and even more so, at 239 for 9. P. W. Sherwell, the captain and wicket-keeper joined A. D. Nourse. He hit a four off his first ball and in the last session of play the remaining 40 runs became a feasibility. With the scores level a full-pitch on the leg-side presented Sherwell with the winning four, leaving Nourse 93 not out. South Africa had beaten England for the first time and Warner reported the achievement:

> Never have I witnessed anything like the scene at the finish. Men were shrieking hysterically, some even were crying, and hats and sticks were flying everywhere. When the winning hit had been made the crowd simply flung themselves at Nourse and Sherwell and carried them into the pavilion. So ended a match which deserves to rank amongst the classic contests of cricket, and one which I shall remember to my dying day. It is a game like this that tries a captain. He has to think, think, think, and must never for a second take his mind off the business in hand, and if in the end his side loses he is apt to reproach himself, or at any rate to wonder whether Smith instead of Jones would not have been a better change.

South Africa went on to win the series 4–1, only losing at Newlands in the fourth Test. Their other three victories were all by substantial margins and England were outplayed by a team unique in being unchanged, splendidly led by Sherwell, equipped with batsmen such as G. C. White and Nourse and with a bowling attack led by S. J. Snooke, R. O. Schwarz and G. A. Faulkner. Warner analysed their success:

> It would be hard, indeed, to name a side which could boast of so many good batsmen. In the history of the game there must be few elevens who can boast of better batsmen at 9, 10, and 11.
>
> But if the batting was powerful the bowling was almost equally so. There was such variety, ranging from the fast medium Snooke to the leg-breaking White, while sandwiched between these two were the Bosanquet-like Faulkner, the fast medium break-backs of the left-handed Nourse, the deceptive flight of Sinclair, the huge off-break of Schwarz, and the quick leg-break of Vogler. No two bowlers were alike, and every change was a real change. And then finger-spin bowlers like Schwarz, Faulkner, and Vogler were suited exactly by the matting wickets on which it is so difficult to jump out to drive, and on which the ball not only turns twice as much and twice as quickly as on grass, but occasionally gets up a little.
>
> The fielding of the South Africans was admirable. And thus we

had for opponents an eleven which was splendidly armed at every point, and which had the additional advantage of playing under conditions with which they were familiar; and I do not think that I am exaggerating when I say that it would require an eleven as strong as the one MCC sent to Australia to defeat the present South African team in their own country.

So Warner, the victor of the Ashes two years earlier, met defeat, but he was generous in his plaudits to South African cricket and ready, in his own words, to describe himself as 'Disappointment No. 1' of the tour. He had averaged 8.90 in the Tests and 16.70 in the eleven-a-side games. He was unable to find a place in the Test side when substantially the same South Africans appeared against England in 1907. Indeed, only two of his 1905–6 party, Crawford and Blythe, did so.

His absence from an England side at home can be understood. He was not quite good enough to command a place and his particular qualities of leadership of a touring party were not needed. All those who captained England in England in this period had a considerably better Test record (measured at the end of their careers) than he. But *Wisden* believed that only 'a doubt about his fielding' kept him out of the series against South Africa in 1907.

Less easily explained is his absence from the party to go to Australia in 1907–8. Albert Trott leapt to his defence in *The Winning Post*:

Those who have all along urged his inclusion in the Australian side have had abundant justification this season, for he has played innings after innings of great merit. He stands with an average of 46 at the head of his county, but in other contests he has done even better. No information has been vouchsafed to the public, and he has been too loyal to say a word on the matter himself, but he has crowned the plodding work of many years by a triumph which only a select few have equalled.

Trott's comment implies that Warner was not asked. Warner himself is silent on the subject. If he were not asked, he was in good company because neither was Fry. At this distance of time the vagaries of selection seem curious since Fry *was* asked in 1911–12 and had to decline. Another, much more plausible reason, is that Warner by now had a daughter, Elizabeth (Betty), born in 1905, and another child due to be born about the time the party would sail for Australia. It would not have been easy, even for such a dedicated tourist as Warner, to have accepted the captaincy and left Agnes at a time when she most needed him. It might be possible in 1987 when nowhere in the world is much more than 24 hours away from Britain: not so 80 years ago. So A. O. Jones became the second man to lead an MCC side abroad though he was to relinquish the Ashes.[9]

It was the series of 1909 against Australia which brought the first of Warner's three appearances in 'home' Test matches, redeeming him a little from the charge that his Test career only existed because he was so often available to tour. But an opening partnership with Spooner of 78 when the fourth Test at Old Trafford had lost all point was not enough to give him another chance that summer.

We have noted that he had been invited to captain MCC to Australia in 1911–12 after Fry had declined the offer. None of those who had gone to South Africa with him six years earlier was included and his side, with the exception of Fry and Spooner, was about the strongest available. Warner had urged that some younger players be included to build for the future and the choice had fallen on Foster, the Warwick all-rounder, Woolley, and, as we have seen, his own county colleague J. W. Hearne.

Just before he left for Australia Warner completed editing a lavishly produced volume entitled *Imperial Cricket*. Contributors from all over the Empire wrote pieces on their particular country and as a source-book for pre-1914 cricket it has its own value, a value, indeed, that made its 900 subscribed copies command a dealer's price of over £300 each in 1987. It was the most glamorous of all Warner's books and enhanced his reputation but it made him little money. He conducted all the correspondence with his contributors, arranged the photographs (including some in colour) and edited the copy. Work such as this, though he obviously enjoyed it, dispels the lingering notion that he was lazy – simply because he did not keep 'office-hours'.

The tour began at Adelaide against Western Australia with an overwhelming victory by an innings and 194 runs which set the tone. Warner made 151 out of the MCC total of 563, an innings on which Jack Hobbs wrote, 'he had played an innings which seemed just what should come from a country's captain; one that was sound in every way, and was sure to inspire confidence in every man jack of the team'.

After a hot and dusty night journey to Melbourne in which very few of the players were able to sleep, Warner excused himself next morning from a reception given by the Lord Mayor and effectively bowed out of the tour. His recurrent ulcer troubles had assumed serious proportions and he was to spend the next few months either in a nursing home or convalescing. He was taken by sea from Melbourne to Sydney and Hobbs visited him during the match between MCC and New South Wales.

It was very touching to see him lying there almost helpless. I got my first insight into his wonderful keenness for cricket. I would like to pay a tribute to his ability as a captain, for as I conversed with him I began to realise what his absence from the side might do for us, so popular was he with every man and able to get the best out of his eleven. A fine captain, a great cricketer, and a charming friend to those with whom he comes in contact.

Hobbs was not then the senior professional of later years. He was still a young man and his comment serves once again to indicate the attitude of his generation of professionals to Warner.

Warner believed he owed his life to the surgeon Sir Charles Blackburn whom he was to meet again in Australia 20 years later. Part of his convalescence was spent in Government House, Sydney while his wife and children, who had accompanied the party, were looked after by friends.

He chose J. W. H. T. Douglas to be captain in his place and, under Douglas, the Ashes were resoundingly won by four games to one. Hobbs wrote at the end of the tour that Douglas's splendid captaincy was supported by the continuing influence of Warner.

We saw, in Chapter 3, how generous had been Australian opinion of Warner's qualities of leadership. Despite his virtual non-appearance, the Australian press felt that England's victory owed a great deal to him. The *Melbourne Herald* wrote on 16 February 1912:

In the face of public opinion, the judgement of one man never faltered. From the very commencement Warner felt tolerably certain that he had a great side. To him England very largely owes her success, for he practically picked the team.

Ill-health prevented him from actually participating in the games, but his advice and influence were ever present. Douglas, who captained the team, tells us that he invariably sought Warner's advice and acted upon it. Thus it is that Warner will ever be remembered in Australia as one of the greatest leaders that has visited our shores.

Warner in his autobiography offered his own evaluation of a team which Lord Harris thought the best touring side ever:

Looking back, I believe that (Harris) was right, and I rank it with the great England Eleven of 1902, Chapman's M.C.C. Australia side of 1928, and Jardine's of 1932. At all events, I would be prepared to back them against any team of my experience, chiefly for the reasons that in Barnes and Foster we had an almost incomparable pair of bowlers, and that Hobbs – there has never been a greater batsman on all wickets – was in his finest form.

He returned from Australia believing, with some justification, that, as a man of 39, his best days were over. But the Triangular Tournament of 1912 brought him two final Test matches, both of them at Lord's. Against the South Africans he went in when England had made 183 for 3. He contributed 39, receiving (said *Wisden*) a 'very warm welcome from the crowd'. Lord's, of all places, knew how ill he had been a few months earlier. Two weeks later against the Australians, again going in when England had made a similar start (193 for 3), he made only four. Of the 65 Test matches played by England between Warner's first appearance in 1899 and 1914, he had participated in 15, 12 of them overseas.

His record in the earlier years was much the more impressive as compared with those covered by this chapter. He was not, it has to be accepted, a player of Test match calibre after his triumphal return from Australia in 1904. His overall record reads as follows:

	Tests	Innings	Runs	Times Not Out	Highest Score	Average
1898–99 to 1903–4	7	14	456	2	132*	38.00
1904 to 1914	8	14	166	0	51	11.86
Total	15	18	622	2	132*	23.92

The ten years between 1904 and 1914 also saw his influence increasing in the cricket world in directions other than the field of play. He was, we remind ourselves, an established writer combining the dual role of player and reporter on tour and he was also a sound judge of a cricketer's abilities. In 1911, he was invited by the editor of *Wisden* to select the best young cricketers of the day and discuss their potential. He selected 14, nine of whom subsequently played for England.

All this makes it less surprising than at first sight that he became a member of the MCC Committee as early as 1904. He would for the next half-century be close to the corridors of power though, as an incident showed, not so close that everything immediately came his way. The centenary of the existing Lord's ground, the second MCC playing area after Dorset Square, was celebrated in 1914. Warner received a letter from his friend Lord Hawke, the president of MCC, inviting him to captain the Rest of England against the MCC South African tourists of 1913–14 in a centenary celebration match. But the sides were announced and he was not even selected, let alone as captain. Indeed, in the context of the time, the proportion of amateurs selected for the two teams was very small. The confusion turned on the fact that the Rest of England team was picked on its merits and (in Australian fashion) the captain chosen from within. Warner had not been chosen by the selectors and Hawke had prejudged events but Warner, as a member of the committee, had an honoured place at the Centenary Dinner. The match itself was the last great occasion at Lord's before war broke out six weeks later.

By 1914, Pelham and Agnes Warner had been married for ten years. At first they had lived the life of an upper middle-class couple in Edwardian England in their town house at Tedworth Square, Chelsea. They kept a staff and entertained. Warner made no further effort to pursue a formal career in Law or business as he had once promised his fiancée he would, but had settled for such rewards – financial and otherwise – which writing on cricket might bring him. Through writing, for instance, he became friendly with J. A. Spender, the editor of the *Westminster Gazette* and this led to invitations to meet Spender's friends, many of whom were Liberal politicians. He thus met Lloyd George, Reginald McKenna and Winston Churchill. Throughout his life, Warner took more than a passing interest in politics and, in the 1950s, became a frequent attender at debates in the House of Lords. His own politics, influenced by his views on Empire, were Conservative rather than Liberal. Perhaps surprisingly, he found much to admire, after initial anxiety, in the Labour Government which held office from 1945 to 1951.

When the Warners themselves entertained, their guests usually came from either the world of cricket or the Services. During these years of gathering international crisis, Warner would translate his theoretical interest in things military into practical military training while his associations with the Navy blossomed. But they did not live long in Tedworth Square. The house, he wrote, 'was difficult to run for it meant having a good many servants'. They had taken it with 46 years of its lease to run but from 1907 onwards it was let to Mrs Patrick Campbell, the actress, and they only briefly lived there again.[10]

In the autumn of 1906 the Warners took a long lease on Caring

House, near Maidstone, close to the villages of Bearsted and Leeds. This was to be their country home until 1920 with a small flat at 136 Ashley Gardens meeting their needs in London. Here their first two children, Betty and Esmond, would spend their childhood.

Caring House is Elizabethan in origin and one of the largest examples of a hall house in Kent. Cromwell's troops had used it in the Civil War. Among its features were Druid panels with Latin scripts, beamed ceilings and a Jacobean oak overmantel. A walled garden led to an orchard where Warner established a grass tennis court and a practice wicket. He and his family had moved to a country house of distinction[11] set amidst the rolling pastureland and fruit farms south of the North Downs.

The Warners employed a cook, parlour-maid, housemaid, nanny, two gardeners and Bill Stupple, the houseboy. He would come in the mornings, after feeding his father's pigs and before going off to school, and then return in the evenings. 'For sixpence a week I cut the grass, did the odd jobs and cleaned Mrs Warner's car.' For, indeed, it was Agnes's car (and she drove it) and not Pelham's. Mr Stupple was quite aware of this as he was aware of the extra sixpence which was his if he could 'bowl out Mr Warner in the nets'. 'I did so sometimes but I always had to chase him for my sixpence.' Life was extra busy for the domestic staff when 'the cricketers came at Easter'. For Warner would bring both the Middlesex amateurs and professionals such as the Hearnes and 'Patsy' Hendren for some serious net-practice. Other visitors from further afield were Lord Hawke, Jessop, Spooner and F. L. Fane.

Promising schoolboys were also invited, among them Geoffrey Hopley who, as a 15-year-old, wrote in his diary on 10 April 1907, 'played at the nets. I batted better than I could ever have hoped and much better than yesterday' and, a few days later, 'played in the nets in the morning and afternoon, Mr. Warner bowling'. Later in the month he was back at Harrow recording in his diary that Warner sent him a telegram with the result of a match against Bearsted. Warner, as we have seen, sent telegrams with results as a mark of his favour! A few months before the outbreak of war in 1914 Hopley, by now a Cambridge cricket and boxing Blue, was again at Caring for pre-Easter coaching, writing to his father abroad of 'the usual delightfully healthy and pleasant life that one has here'.

Geoffrey Hopley has left us a picture of those days at Caring House, expressed in some six pages of doggerel verse written in the spring of 1914. Somehow it links Warner's devotion to cricket with his concern that the political crisis required fit and able men ready to fight:

The training is hard and earnest
but the troops are getting fit.
If the Germans land tomorrow
we shouldn't mind a bit.

Agnes is around, supervising the household, bandaging wounded cricket heroes, planning the social events of the evening, playing Auction Bridge. Esmond is being an annoying but engaging small boy escaping from his governess 'the practices to see'. Betty has gone to stay with friends. Jim, the fox-terrier, is the best fielder of them all. As for Warner himself, he is 'the camp commandant', engaged in battle with his landlord about the drains, looking after the pig, marshalling a church parade, quoting 'his *Wisden* from end to end' and 'out in the camp among the boys from daylight unto dark'. There is J. T. Hearne partnering an Old Etonian oarsman at tennis and a West Indian, Cumberbatch,[12] 'striking a cherry branch with an impact like a bomb'. Such were 'those strenuous happy hours, the sunny days we spent at the Caring Camp'. Just a year later, 2nd Lieutenant Hopley, Grenadier Guards, died of his wounds in Flanders. Warner wrote laconically, 'the spring of 1914 saw the last of the training camps'.

Caring House itself is in the hamlet of Caring but it was with cricket in nearby Bearsted that Warner involved himself. Bearsted has one of the oldest and most attractive village cricket grounds in England. A sloping square is surrounded by Tudor, Georgian and Victorian houses set amidst oak trees. All must have been witness of the great days of the 1840s when Alfred Mynn, 'the Lion of Kent' and Pilch played there. And in old age Pilch umpired when the young WG played for a local XXII there against William Clarke's All-England XI. It was a game which a young lad called Bill Fryer had watched and he, as an old man, welcomed the arrival of Warner in their community, 'a lucky event for Bearsted as he at once began to take an interest in sport in the village'.

Warner organised work on the ground in the spring of 1907 so that the centre was returfed and some levelling done at a cost of £50. He gave a talk in the village hall, promising to bring a side to play the village to launch the new season. He was, of course, too busy in the game at county level to play regularly at Bearsted but he had shown that his sympathies were in the right direction and he fulfilled his promise by bringing an XI to play on 20 April.

The game itself was somewhat one-sided as Warner's team made 206 and dismissed the village for 61 and 82. The local press commented, 'possibly the thought of meeting Bosanquet, the googly man who diddled out the Australians may have had

something to do with it'. The occasion was also an early ex-
periment in cricket market research for the firm of Billenness and
Weeks were allowed to try out their automatic wickets. The *Kent
Messenger* reported:

> These wickets are a device by which the stumps fall out of the
> perpendicular without leaving the socket into which they are
> fixed. Whether they will be perfected to such an extent as to
> render them suitable for first-class matches remains to be seen.

Warner was sent a complimentary set which duly went up in his
garden and he replied that he felt they had a future 'for practice
purposes'. Later in the summer, when Middlesex did not have a
game for a month, he played occasionally for Bearsted, scoring 66
against Sutton Valence and he also played for W. T. Fremlin, a local
brewer who had his own ground.

On Saturday 8 May 1909, he captained Bearsted, with a side
composed of both first-class and village players against HMS
Dominion, then in dock at Chatham. Three future Admirals of the
Fleet turned out, including his friend John Jellicoe. Crowds
encircled the ground, the naval band played and Warner himself
made 73. Two days later, on the Monday, he opened the batting for
MCC at Lord's with MacLaren against Nottinghamshire, and ended
the week playing for MCC v. Kent before the serious business of
Middlesex cricket began the week after.

Some letters to Agnes while she was away in Paris give us
another glimpse of matches at Bearsted. 'Spectators came in their
hundreds and Mrs. Whitehead organised our tea in a huge tent.'
She was, reported Pelham, 'very pretty' but perhaps her greatest
charm lay in an ability to 'bowl well'. Betty's charm (the same letter
concluded) lay in feeding the chickens and remarking, 'Dada lives
here, oh indeed he does.' As for Agnes, she was left in no doubt that
her husband missed her, if only because 'the bed was devilish
cold'.

The pattern continued up to 1914 with Warner appearing
variously for his own XI, Bearsted, W. T. Fremlin's XI, Milgate Park
(which was Fremlin's own ground) and Leeds Castle. Occasionally
his own side would be styled Caring House. The *Kent Messenger*[13]
gave the games coverage especially when 'personalities' such as
members of the Middlesex and Kent teams were playing. Warner's
best personal performance was 126 out of a Leeds Castle total of
234 against the Kent County Constabulary who were dismissed for
50. Warner kept wicket and stumped two policemen! In the last of
such matches before the war, Warner's XI played the Royal

Marines at Bearsted. R. H. Spooner made 68 for his XI which won easily. The Marines band played throughout the match and among those playing was A. O. Jones, the only other man, besides Warner, to captain the MCC side in Australia before 1914.

Even after the family left Caring House in 1920 and moved to Windsor, Warner kept up his cricketing associations with Bearsted. He persuaded several visiting tourists to have an early April game there before beginning their first-class programme. With the visit of the South Africans in 1929, there ended a personal link going back 22 years. It was something Albert Pellett, whose memory went back over sixty years, told me 'which all the village looked forward to – Mr. Warner's teams coming here. He did a lot for us.'

Life at Caring was not all cricket. There were visits from members of the family such as Pelham's indomitable old mother now in her late eighties and his elder brother Ray, retired and settled in England. Frequent visitors were Sybil and Phyllis, the daughters of Aucher, and occasional ones such as Pelham's elder sister, Dorothy Lubbock and her husband, when on leave from India. There was plenty for visitors to do with tennis in the garden, golf nearby at Bearsted and bridge in the evenings. By now, the links with Trinidad had become tenuous. Only one, Aucher, of the children of Charles Warner's second marriage lived there any longer.

By 1910, the family of four was going for summer holidays to the Norfolk Broads or long outings to the beach at Eastbourne, or Hastings for the day. Warner was a good family man, rejoicing in the company of his children, 'a great joy to us', if striving perhaps a little hard to make a cricketer of Esmond. It was a childhood which Elizabeth Henderson remembered vividly and with warmth. Pelham would 'read to us, teach us tennis, take us for picnics and never lose his temper'. Gradually, a family nickname emerged. They all lived in 'The Rat Hole' (Caring House) and they were Father Rat, Mother Rat and the little rats. The names survived and many years later Father Rat drew up a code of conduct to be followed by the next generation of little rats when they came to stay with 'Grandfather' Rat in his London flat.

These were idyllic years for a family as prosperous as they were. Warner was lucky in a wife who shared his passion for cricket and was ready to spend her money taking the children on tour to South Africa and Australia with him. Their lives after 1914 would never be quite so carefree though they would live at Caring until 1920.

Two things alone marred these years. Warner from time to time was in pain which would eventually lead to a breakdown and a major operation. He was a perceptive man and the gathering clouds of war compelled his attention and sense of duty. It is to his great credit that a man with as frail a constitution as his submitted himself to some pretty rigorous military discipline and training.

The need for larger and more efficient armed forces had become apparent during the Anglo-Boer War, and was in the mind of the Conservative Government which won that war. But only one important pressure group, the National Service League, had urged a period of compulsory military training. The League's main campaigner was Lord Roberts, who had been commander-in-chief in the war and was a friend of the Warners. Roberts wanted a great deal more than any government or, indeed the British people, were prepared to countenance. His fellow-leader in the Anglo-Boer War, Robert Baden-Powell, was more successful in his founding of the Boy Scout Movement with its objectives of patriotism, self-reliance and moral probity.

What the Liberal Government, returned to power in 1906, offered as a formal expression of military preparedness was the Territorial Army, created by the Secretary of State for War, Richard Haldane, in 1907. Territorials were seen as an adjunct to Britain's prime defenders, the Royal Navy. Haldane's scheme provided for local Territorial units based on county organisation. Men recruited would undertake part-time training for four years and remain liable to be called up until they were 30.

Warner, although well over 30, applied for a territorial commission in the 4th Royal West Kent Regiment in 1908 and was gazetted as a subaltern. In the winter of 1910, instead of playing cricket on some tour, he was on a course at Chelsea Barracks involving drill, musketry and infantry training. His principal instructor, Sergeant-Major Levey shared his interest in military history, became a frequent guest of Warner's at Lord's in the following summer but still expected his subalterns (including elderly ones!) to achieve in a month drill standards equivalent to that of regular army privates. A friendship, forged on the 'barrack square' at Chelsea, lasted a lifetime. Levey in later years would be a visitor to Warner in his old age in his London flat.

Warner wrote that he benefited from the military discipline and the military history, both were 'a help towards captaining a cricket team'. He frequently saw cricket in the context of a campaign and much of his writing contained military analogies.

Roberts' plea for compulsory military training was gaining more currency as the international crisis increased and the 'arms race' gathered pace. He recruited Warner to go round campaigning for him in the public schools from whose Officer Training Corps would come the young subalterns of 1914:

I am glad that you are interesting yourself in the work of the National Service League, and will address meetings for us in Norfolk.

I am anxious that the physical side of the question should be brought home to our supporters as well as the purely military exigencies of the situation.

I feel sure that your name – so well-known in the cricket world – will give you an enthusiastic hearing on the general question of the benefits of athletic training which you understand so well.

At Charterhouse, for example, Warner spoke in a debate upon national service and carried the day by a heavy majority. Putting precept into practice, he went in 1910 on army manoeuvres.

A pencilled note to his wife gives us a picture of the 38-year-old Warner taking part in Territorial manoeuvres while still finding a moment to enjoy the civilities of life with an old friend at Oriel:

My darling Fox,[14]
Yesterday we left Uffington at 9 o'clock and got here, Cumnor, about 4–18 miles. We halted for five minutes every hour and I enjoyed it thoroughly. When we started off again presently came the very worst thunderstorm I have ever seen anywhere. The roads were like small rivers and I got soaked through. Only your waistcoat kept me warm. If the thunder and lightning had hit the column it might have been awkward as it would have probably run down the rifles and killed a lot of us. Our camp at Cumnor was a marsh with sheets of water. The CO, who is a ripper, said to me 'You had better walk into Oxford, have a bath and dry your kit.' Excellent dinner with the Dean of Oriel and back into camp by 10 o'clock. I slept splendidly in my flea bag. I am very fit and enjoying it immensely. They seem to think it was a good effort my doing 20 miles my first day. My feet, thanks to your socks, are in good fettle. I am thoroughly enjoying myself.
They are such nice fellows and so cheery and jolly and awfully nice to me and seem to think me a bit of a sportsman to have come at all. All through the villages the people cheer us.

We are reminded that whatever he lacked in physical strength he made up for by sheer determination.

The autumn of 1911 saw another of the 'colonial collisions' between the great powers which brought the prospect of a world war closer. Warner, all set to sail for Australia as captain of MCC, was warned by the adjutant of his regiment that it was doubtful if he would get leave. Not until a fortnight before the party sailed was his leave confirmed. It proved to be the end of his peacetime soldiering, for his illness in Australia led to his being invalided out of the regiment.

He had also experienced something of life in the 'Senior Service' when he accepted an invitation to accompany the Home Fleet on its 1910 spring cruise. He sailed in HMS *Commonwealth* and was at sea for five weeks during which he was invited to play for the Navy in a match at Oporto, making the top score of 41 not out. At Vigo he joined in entertaining officers in the German Navy.

He kept a 'log' of his voyage. Such things are primarily of interest only to the writer and to his immediate family but Warner's 'log' allows us to make some more judgements on the man himself. He was someone who liked people. He delighted in the company of the ship's officers and in the hospitality of his friends the Coverleys who lived in Portugal. Over and over again, 'people were awfully nice to me'. He, for his part, displayed the same qualities which had made him a popular figure in the United States a few years earlier. He was a good dancer and a convivial guest and, as a 'spare man' much in demand by the ladies at the British Club in Oporto where he played cricket – and whose notepaper he used to write most of his log! He concluded his entry, 'danced at the British Club until 2.15 a.m. on Sunday morning. Delightful evening. The girls all danced very well. "Auld Lang Syne" and three cheers for the Fleet. A topping evening. Breakfast at ten then lunch at the Club.'

In 1911 he was again in the Iberian peninsula, this time as the guest of Jellicoe who had become commander-in-chief of the Atlantic Fleet. The Jellicoes had suffered the recent loss of a child and the admiral invited the Warner family to stay at Gibraltar to comfort Gwen Jellicoe. 'It is lovely weather here and it would be splendid for the children. The beach is the finest I have ever seen,' he wrote temptingly to Agnes. So for the two families it was a few days of relaxation and a chance for Agnes to console one of her oldest friends, for it was as Agnes Blyth and Gwen Cayzer that the two women had first known each other, before either was married.

Warner being Warner – and one might almost say, Jellicoe being Jellicoe – there was a cricket match between an XI captained by the admiral and that captained by 'Plum'. Jellicoe, noted Warner, 'fielded very smartly at cover point while I made one, missed a catch, and did not add to my reputation in Spain'.

It was a brief holiday, with memories to be savoured despite the sad circumstances which had suggested it. In a few weeks' time the French occupied Fez in Morocco, Kaiser William II sent a gunboat to Agadir and Jellicoe took his fleet to the southern Irish coast to be ready for any eventuality.[15] By now, in the sense of Sir Edward Grey's famous and sombre words, the lamps were beginning to go out. Soon the ships of the Fleet would have no room for spare-time passengers, however delightful company they proved to be. The men who had marched from Cumnor to Oxford would set their course on Flanders soil. Middlesex played Kent at the Mote Park, Maidstone, just a mile or two from Bearsted, and Colin Blythe took Warner's wicket twice. A record 8000 spectators, as if clinging to a life-line, turned up to see the game. No more would they see Blythe at the Mote Park for he too would join the men in Flanders.

Middlesex struggled on after 4 August 1914 to finish their programme but no man's heart was in it. They played Surrey at Lord's, just as they would in a famous game in 1920. Warner declared with himself not out, just as he would in 1920, and set Surrey a target. But the unreal contest petered out and he left Lord's to report to his Commanding Officer. The sun had cast the last of its golden rays on Caring, on Lord's and on the cricket grounds of England and the Empire. The 'Golden Age' had ended.

5

First Class Finale, 1914–20

The man who had set an example by serving in the Territorials was never fit enough to be a combatant in the First World War but his qualities of leadership were used in the task of selecting others to lead. Warner was commissioned in the Inns of Court OTC and given command of the 'Waiting List'. These were men hoping to serve in one of the four Companies of the OTC.

At first he was told only to accept men under 30 until he persuaded his colonel that many a batsman did not reach his prime until past 30. One of the over-thirties whom he recruited was a man of 48 who wrote to him long after the war recalling the 'kindness and help' which had got him onto the 'Waiting List' and ultimately into the army itself. By December 1914 he was commanding some 1400 men, all potential officers, and carrying responsibility for their training in Regent's Park 'in plain clothes and headgear which varied from Panamas to bowlers'.

At the end of five months 1900 men had passed through his hands and, on being posted to the War Office, he was told he had 'not made a single mistake in the selection of officers'. This was high praise and does him credit, not least because he was not always a shrewd judge of character and could be deceived into thinking that charm and good manners were all. His new War Office appointment in January 1915 called for the same powers of judgement where his job was to select officers for the infantry of the Special Reserve, men who would become the subalterns in Kitchener's Army. At the end of a year he had interviewed 6000 of them – about 35 a day – from all over the Empire. Perhaps a cricketing background helped, as in the case of the young man arriving from Australia with a letter of introduction from the old Test player Clem Hill and the added claim that he had himself bowled Warner out. We cannot know who came before his Board but he must have been painfully conscious of the loss to England and to English cricket through the deaths of so many of those young men. Warner's friend of Caring days, Geoffrey Hopley, was killed in 1915 and the next entry to his obituary in *Wisden* was that of John Howell, killed in Flanders, the best schoolboy bat of 1914, 'potentially an England batsman' and one who had scored 45 for Surrey 2nd XI off Sydney Barnes' bowling while still at school. They were two in a list of nearly three hundred.

Distinct from the death in 1915 of these young cricketers with their careers before them was that of W. G. Grace. The war made it impossible for the cricket world to be as represented as it might have been, but on a bitterly cold October day Warner, with Harris and Hawke, went to the funeral on behalf of MCC. The year 1915 also saw the death of his mother-in-law with whom he had had the pleasantest of relationships.

Meanwhile, his work at the War Office continued – demanding, yet not without its congenial aspect. He would sit at a desk in a large office where five or six other officers were similarly engaged. They included dons from Oxford and Cambridge, some of whom had already seen active service and been severely wounded. There was something of the 'club' atmosphere which all his life appealed to him and he 'would not have missed it for anything'.

But miss it he did in the spring of 1916 when he was in King Edward VII Hospital for Officers for three months and, after a few months back at work, was ill again in December. He was then given six months' leave to be followed by 'light duties'.

Caring House was still their home and from time to time Warner was able to join the family and his convalescence was spent there. His children, Betty and Esmond, were old enough to realise the horrors of the war but the principal effect of it on their lives was the frequent absence of their mother who had joined the Volunteer Aid Detachment of the Red Cross. At Caring, Warner would write letters to those of his friends who mourned the loss of their menfolk in the war and he would also write to those who were wounded. Among the most moving was his letter to William Benton:

> Caring House
> 18 August, 1916
>
> Dear Old Benton,
> I am so grieved to hear that you have lost a leg, and hope you may get alright again. What a *splendidly gallant* fellow you are;

I have heard all about it, and you deserve a V.C. if ever a man did. I am proud to say I know you.

Do let me know if ever I can do *anything for you* and please do not hesitate to say so and anything in my powers I will be only *too proud* to do.

I feel so much for your poor wife. It would be absurd for me to say 'keep your pecker up' – for you have been doing that all the while – but 'just get hold of the bat tightly' you know what I mean. I shall be thinking of you a lot, and hope they will be able to send you home soon. I will come and see you.

God Bless you,

Yours ever,

P. F. Warner

Benton had served in the Anglo-Boer War and subsequently was ordained. He was the curate at Bearsted and had made a few appearances for Middlesex under Warner's captaincy besides playing for the village. When war broke out in 1914 he had volunteered as a combatant officer and he died of his wounds on the day before Warner's letter was written.

Warner's appointment to 'light duties' in September 1917 led to his serving in the Department of Information in the Foreign Office. His immediate 'boss' was John Buchan, who had been a few years his junior at Oxford. Buchan, in 1917, was far from the distinguished public figure he would ultimately become but he had established himself in the publishing firm of Thomas Nelson and he had begun to write. Both men were often plagued by ill-health though Buchan served for a spell in France and experienced the battle of the Somme. A more positive bond was a common interest in the Law. Both enjoyed the company of lawyers and of the Inns of Court while never seriously practising it as a profession. Cricket held no interest for Buchan though his close friend Andrew Lang had written some fine things on the game which Warner loved to quote.

Warner was the first to recognise his own academic limitations and to admire the talents of others. In his brief friendship with Buchan, he realised he was in the presence of a man of commanding intellect and ability not yet fulfilled. They went together to France in 1917, stayed in a chateau and visited the Lines where, Buchan told Warner, the German commander opposite was the Jacobite pretender to the British throne. In after years they occasionally dined together, 'a delightful talker and companion', wrote Warner but there was little ground to sustain a friendship.

Warner's job at the Foreign Office involved him in 'briefing'

American, colonial and neutral press correspondents. His best moment came at Dover early in 1918 when he had to 'host' a dinner and was commended afterwards for his concern in watching over the expenditure of public money: cigars and champagne were not passed round, as had been previously practised! But, alas, ill-health struck again and in March 1918 he resigned his commission and was granted the rank of honorary captain.

It says something for the friendship between the Warners and the Jellicoes that the commander-in-chief of the Grand Fleet (as Jellicoe became in 1914) could find time to write solicitously from HMS *Iron Duke* to Pelham about his health while saying to Agnes, 'I would just love a little of your bottled fruit and it would be all the sweeter for your bottling.' On the eve of Jutland he thanked her for a present of soda mints which he took not for medicinal reasons but because he liked the taste and he expressed the hope to see them both again 'when this business is done. When will that be?'

Warner's absence from work on sick leave during the summer of 1917 had not precluded him from playing cricket at Lord's, where the game was resumed for the first time since the outbreak of war. The immediate reaction of the public in 1914 had been to regard participation in any sport as an unpatriotic activity. Nets put up at The Oval in the spring of 1915, for example, were scarcely used because, in the opinion of William Findlay, then the secretary of Surrey, players 'would be afraid of being jeered at by men on the tram cars'. But gradually boxing and billiards had become acceptable and by 1917, the editor of *Wisden*, Sydney Pardon, felt it high time that cricket was played again.

Warner was responsible for arranging two matches at Lord's for the benefit of war charities. In the first game, he captained an England Army XI, which included Douglas, Hendren, P. G. H. Fender and Blythe, against an Australian Army XI whose principal name was C. A. Macartney. The *Westminster Gazette* report (not written by Warner himself) declared:

Lord's presented a sight by far more reminiscent of the long-ago days of peace than any of us would have believed possible while the war lasted. It must have cheered Captain Warner's heart to hear the acclamations which went with him all round the ground when he fared out to bat. Most knew how ill he had been and rejoiced to see him, with the old Harlequin cap on his head, so much his old self again. It was just like his old self, too, that he batted – a fine, finished exhibition.

He batted for 80 minutes for his 34, much of it with a runner, in a game in which runs were hard to get on a green outfield.

A month later he led a Navy and Army XI against the Australian and South African forces. The 'colonials' won easily and the match proved sadly memorable for Colin Blythe's last wicket in cricket, Macartney giving a low catch to Warner at backward point. Three months later one of the greatest of slow left-arm bowlers was killed in France.

That same summer against Eton and Westminster Warner captained MCC sides which contained Lord Hawke and Lord Harris, at that time respectively president and treasurer of MCC.

In 1918 he was responsible for organising six matches, three of which were between England and the Dominions. The *Spectator* published a lengthy report on the first game, cheering the reader with references to 'an ideal gala day; the sprinkling of muslin frocks and gay parasols' and 'Plum Warner out in the field against his old rival Macartney', then striking a more sombre note in describing those spectators 'in the pathetic blue of the hospitals' and ending:

> We seem to see beyond the smooth turf and the group of white figures to those fields in France and Flanders, in Italy and in Mesopotamia, where the greater and ghastlier game is being played in which many of these men have played and will play again and in which many have played their last ball and closed a noble innings.

Ten thousand people watched the first game, which the Dominions won easily, Warner being left with 35 not out in England's 94. The second game was visited by King George V, on behalf of whose fund for sailors the match was being played, while the third was the first occasion on which cricket had been played at The Oval since 1914.

Warner took sides to play against the Bradford League, against the United Services at Dover and also raised an XI to play F. S. Jackson's XI at Lord's. His own record in these matches was:

Innings	Runs	Times Not Out	Highest Score	Average
8	142	2	45*	23.66

Much more important was the contribution his organisation and enterprise had made both to public morale and to several war charities. Had he but known it, he would be similarly engaged on a much wider scale 20 years later.

Warner's final piece of 'war-service' came in the winter of 1918–19 when he was attached to the Appointments department of the Ministry of Labour to work in the resettlement of ex-servicemen. One of his colleagues was Dr C. R. Williams, later headmaster of Chislehurst and Sidcup Grammar School, who recalled his membership of the panel as 'stimulating company'. 'He invariably sent the applicant away after his interview happy even if no job was in sight.'

Shortly after Warner had taken this work he was invited by Jellicoe to 'get some sea-air' and accompany him in HMS *New Zealand* on the first part of a voyage round the world. Jellicoe had been asked by the Admiralty to advise the countries throughout the Empire on the best form of future naval defence.

Warner's superiors saw this as an opportunity for servicemen in the Near East to be put in touch with resettlement plans, as well as helping the morale of men, bored while awaiting demobilisation, by having a famous cricketer among them.

He embarked at Portsmouth, visited Gibrâltar, sailed through the Mediterranean and landed at Port Said 'basking in the reflected glory of being a guest of the Commander-in-Chief of the Grand Fleet', and enjoying the company of naval officers, 'the best type of Englishmen'. His letters to Agnes provide some comments on his fellow-passengers: of Lady Jellicoe, their friend of so many years, 'I hope Gwen will be tactful in India and Australia; she is not very so'; of Reginald McKenna, a former Chancellor of the Exchequer, 'a good sort and financially sympathetic towards fathers with children like me. Says buy war savings certificates.' Of his host, he wrote, 'Jack and I talk about all sort of things, from Jutland to public schools.'

The 'holiday' part of the programme ended when he left HMS *New Zealand* and began to visit units in the Near East. A pattern established itself; he would stay with some senior officer, give lectures on the bureaucracy and policy of Ministry of Labour schemes, conduct personal interviews in which particular requests would be noted and give a talk on cricket to those who might be interested. As the man who had won the Ashes twice, he was a prestige figure and, with the possible exception of Fry, there was no one else of his generation from the pre-war cricket world who combined this reputation with an ability to speak.

He wrote to Agnes from Cairo, 'I am in the office by 9, then after luncheon tennis or something until 5, and then back to the office until dinner. The work is most interesting and GHQ are screaming for Pero[16] to lecture.' His social life included a dance at Shepheard's Hotel ('You never saw such an ugly lot of women') and the races at Gezira ('won a pound or so'). His absence from home for some weeks meant that we have letters from him which throw light on him as a family man. He would write to Mother Rat and to the little rats, of whom there were now three since John Jellicoe, to whom Jellicoe became godfather, had been born in June 1918. Warner's devotion to his family comes out strongly in the long letters he wrote at four-day intervals. He missed them dreadfully, complained of being 'rat-sick' for home, and was concerned that Agnes should take her 'tonic, eat a lot and be sleek and fat' for his return.

His letters from Acre were descriptive of the Holy Places and Betty was given precise instructions to look up in the Old Testament the stories about where he had been. Esmond, he hoped, would practise in the nets and the garden boy was instructed to 'get the pitch and tennis court in order and roll them twice a week'. Agnes was encouraged to explore the possibility of subletting Caring House ('it would be splendid as it would be quite a nice lot of £sd') which in the end did not take place. Towards the end of his tour, there was some pathos in the comment, 'Pero does not like travelling without his Mother Rat and little rats.'

Despite the bouts of 'rat-sickness', Warner enjoyed himself hugely – the hero-worship which came his way ('Plum Warner seems a magic word'), the cheapness of the trip ('I spend nothing but tips'), the historical appeal of the Holy Land – and recognised the good fortune which had come his way. Yet one cannot escape the thought that some men might have hesitated to leave a wife with two young children and a 9-month-old baby for a trip which was by no means essential and had, in a sense, been 'engineered' by himself and Jellicoe. By Easter he was home again, ready for the first post-war cricket season and shortly to be rewarded for his services in the war with an MBE.

This modest decoration had not been undeserved. Within the limits imposed by his age and health, he had carried out his duties to the satisfaction of his superiors. He had been recommended for a staff posting in France with the observation that 'he would do remarkably well' but he was not fit enough to take it up. Subordinates had found him, as had so many cricketers, a good man to work under. Letters of regret at his departure would follow him after each appointment, one such declaring that 'all fell at once under the charm of the one and only P.F.W.'.

First-class cricket resumed in 1919 with the experimental introduction of two-day county championship matches. It had been a controversial recommendation of the Advisory County

Cricket Committee and those who had opposed it were proved right. Long days on the field were exhausting and, as the editor of *Wisden* put it somewhat inelegantly, 'by 7.30 the craving for food had become stronger than the passion for cricket'. Schoolboys might be enthusiastic but 'not men of thirty and upwards'. Still less men over 45, as Warner found to his cost. He was, he wrote, 'a dead-dog' by the middle of July and he played in little more than half of Middlesex's matches. He scored 170 runs for them all season for an average of 13.07 and at the end he suggested to the secretary, A. J. Webbe, that the time had come to resign. Webbe persuaded him to try another season when three-day cricket would be restored and pointed to his performances in the three-day games in 1919, in which his batting average was 38.87. He had, indeed, been more successful with a century against the strong Australian Imperial Services side and solid contributions of 57 and 34 in the Lord's and Oval Gentlemen v. Players games.

At the end of the schools' season he raised a strong XI to play the Public Schools. His own team included Spooner, who made a century despite having been badly injured in the war, and two former South African Test captains. The boys' side contained Jardine, Chapman, R. C. Robertson-Glasgow and G. T. S. Stevens, who had already (while still at school) played for the Gentlemen v. Players. Thanks to two half-centuries by Jardine, the boys just had the edge in a drawn game.

For him, personally, the 1919 season had been something of a 'hiccup'. Middlesex had done badly and so (in Middlesex terms) had he. The decision to play for one more year had been hesitantly taken. Men born in the early 1870s were by now very rare birds in the first-class game and more likely to make occasional appearances for MCC or the Free Foresters than to sustain a regular place in a county side. But he had allowed himself to be persuaded and, for the last time, the nets at Caring[17] were a bracing introduction to cricket in an English May. And there were many reasons for continuing: the young all-rounder Stevens to be encouraged, the tall Jack Durston to be directed into wicket-taking, the pre-war professionals Hendren and Jack Hearne to be coaxed into prodigious scoring, the post-war amateurs Frank Mann and Nigel Haig to be groomed for captaincy. Who can blame the old trouper wanting one more turn before the footlights when crowds in their thousands flocked to cricket grounds and the game had regained all its old appeal?

First there was a gentle outing to the Parks where Oxford had picked the previous year's schoolboys, Stevens and Jardine. Both made lots of runs and Warner's 36 on the last afternoon was a vain endeavour to save the county from severe defeat. The *Daily Mail*, which had earlier called Middlesex 'dark horses' for the Championship, saw them flounder to the Dark Blues in the preliminary Stakes.

A defeat in the Parks before sizeable but casual crowds scurrying back to some tutorial was placed in its proper perspective by the earnest loyalty of the packed stands at Lord's, who saw Warwickshire walloped and Sussex savaged with only 11 Middlesex wickets falling all-told, and the captain averaging over 200. For the Whit weekend crowd, all 14,129 of them, he made 139 out of an opening stand of 241 in a game in which he, H. W. Lee, J. W. Hearne and Haig, the first four in the Middlesex order, all got hundreds.

By the end of June, Hampshire (twice), Lancashire and Somerset had been laid low and only Nottinghamshire had defeated Warner's men. While the captain himself had made no more large scores, there were plenty of others to do it for him – Hendren, who had missed the fiesta against Sussex, contributed a couple of 183 not outs and Lee's double-century took care of Hampshire. Getting runs had never been a Middlesex problem nor, in 1920, was getting wickets as side after side crumpled to Durston and Hearne. The end of June brought, so to say, a half-term holiday for Middlesex who were not scheduled to play again until mid-July. They lay fifth in the Championship, worth backing either way but only seen as a winner to the punter with pounds to spare.

Warner donned his morning suit and top hat to watch a rain-ruined University match and see Eton decisively beat Harrow. He had his articles to write for *The Times* at three guineas apiece and there were domestic 'chores' such as a problem with the roof at 15 Tedworth Square and another with the garden at Caring, for he was still both landlord and tenant of these respective properties. His playing days were over for the Gentlemen and he went to watch them meet the Players at Lord's.

Just when schoolboys were contemplating their long summer holidays, the Middlesex 'term' resumed. They played Essex twice in succession, drawing and then losing at Leyton by four runs. Nobody made very many for Essex at Leyton on the Saturday and shortly after lunch on Monday Warner, at 22 not out, retired – not hurt but to obey the command of Lord Harris to be at Lord's and 'offer his opinion' on the side to go to Australia in a few weeks' time. He was not a selector but Harris wanted in attendance the wisdom of a former successful captain. To balance things out, Douglas, the Essex captain (and already the nominated England captain), went with him. Next day both men were back and Middlesex struggled in vain for the hundred or so they needed. No one could withstand Douglas's pace and swing that afternoon and it was left to Warner to 'farm' the bowling until, at 46, Douglas beat him. It almost spoils our story to hint that those four runs by which Middlesex lost might have mattered so very much and might have been secured had Warner not obeyed Lord Harris's injunction, though why he had not chosen to open the innings the previous Saturday night must remain conjecture.

Sussex were well beaten at Hove, with the prodigy Stevens taking 13 for 60, 'bowling well enough to get out any side in the world', said Warner, his patron.

By now it was August and Warner would play every day of the month except Sundays. His lot, he must have felt, was cast in an idyllic world: cricket day by day with a team which he had moulded together, who responded to his leadership, called him 'the general' and with whom he enjoyed a relationship that transcended those absurd conventions assigning them to different changing-rooms and decreeing who should be called 'Mr'. From Hove they went to Canterbury, to the tents and pennants, to the bands and parasols, to Frank Woolley and James Seymour. Woolley's claim to fame needs no introduction. Seymour's was about to be established. He had had a benefit earlier in the week and he would successfully challenge the Inland Revenue's right to tax him on it and so take a place in tax history.

Kent were beaten by five runs, the Middlesex captain leaping with joy 'like a young kangaroo'. As events turned out, it was the last game that month he would enjoy so light-heartedly. Victory meant that Middlesex had become serious contenders for the Championship though the complicated percentage system called for the skills of Pythagoras to work out who might eventually be successful. So from Canterbury, pilgrims in reverse, they came to London to do battle with Surrey at The Oval before a crowd of almost thirty thousand where, in beating a side with Jack Hobbs in it by an innings, they reflected the 'well-oiled machine' which Warner declared that his team had become. Jack Hearne, with his 178 and match figures of 9 for 101 had been the architect of Middlesex's victory.

Indeed, match after match had thrown up one or more heroes whose performances – great, not merely good – sealed successive victories. Next time it was Hendren with a double-century against Nottinghamshire who were beaten early on the third day. There was time for Warner to slip home to the flat in Ashley Gardens before catching the evening train to Bradford and talking to reporters at the station. In some ways he was now as much a public figure to the press as he had been when he had brought back the

Ashes in 1904. Not since 1912 had England been involved in a Test match, so that the public and the press were caught up in the excitement of a domestic competition in a way difficult for a later generation to comprehend. It was an excitement to be cherished and relished, not offering instant success but a continuing pleasure as the days went by. You had, of course, to enjoy cricket but that went, in 1920, for a sizeable part of the population.

There were no tents and pennants at Park Avenue: just a dour Yorkshire Saturday crowd which accepted as their due the dismissal of Middlesex for 105 by Rhodes and Rockley Wilson. Warner had won the toss and chosen to bat on a green wicket. Only he himself was undefeated with an eight which must rank among the most defensive rear-guard eights he ever made! By the end of the day Yorkshire had done scarcely as well and Warner could spend his Sunday in Bradford reflecting that all was not yet lost. He also spent the day writing letters and visiting Lord Hawke.

By the Tuesday Yorkshire had a whole day to get 198, and by late afternoon they still needed 57 with the last pair together. 'Now we've got them, sir,' exclaimed Stevens, to be met with an explosion of anger totally out of character in his captain. As so often, Warner knew his opposition, knew what Wilson and Abram Waddington were worth, understood Yorkshire grit. The 19-year-old wrist-spinner at last got his chance to make amends. As he bowled, with five runs needed, a Yorkshire voice cried, 'you're beat Ploom'. Stevens heard it and probably so did Waddington. It impelled the bowler to send down a faster one which ended Waddington's enterprise, gave Middlesex their fifth victory in a row and did nothing for the blood-pressure of 'the general'.

Wilson, who had remained undefeated in the partnership was an Old Rugbeian (almost of Warner's vintage) and a master at Winchester. He (and Waddington) had just been picked to go to Australia with MCC. He and Warner were friends and in their old age would reminisce nostalgically on that game in 1920.

By now, Middlesex had four matches to play. Ten men had played regularly in the immediately previous games and the eleventh place had been variously contended. The Singhalese doctor, Churchill Hector Gunasekara, had played whenever medical work allowed and had made a strong contribution. A. R. Tanner made a solitary appearance (but took two wickets). H. K. Longman appeared the most frequently and it was he who 'clinched' the eleventh place. His selection for what were vital matches is an interesting commentary on the times. Longman had opened the batting for Harrow with a man who later won a VC. He himself was a regular soldier with a DSO and an MC. He was approaching the age of 40 and his contribution to Middlesex's achievements was extremely modest. He was a friend of Warner's but it seems unlikely that Warner selected him for these – of all matches – for that reason. It seems much more likely that it was not quite as easy to get a side together in 1920 as one might suppose. There were five regular professionals – Hearne, Hendren, Lee, Durston and Murrell. Jobs were hard to come by in 1920 and amateur cricketers holding them could not with undue frequency ask for 'three days off'.

The Somerset match at Lord's was won comfortably enough, Warner himself batting low down and getting 28. On Saturday morning, 21 August, the papers recorded Middlesex as top of the Championship by 0.44 per cent (whatever that might mean). Matches still had to be won: draws were not enough, and in a summer of uncertain weather, rain was another enemy. All went well against Warwickshire at Edgbaston thanks, in part, to a vital partnership between Warner and Mann just when things might have gone wrong. Warner's 45, together with the 67 he made against Kent in the next match, gave an extra dimension to the final stages of Middlesex's bid for the Championship. The captain had led with astuteness, observation and knowledge: now he was making runs as well. He was also conserving his energy. A long partnership with Hendren in the Kent match in which, said the critics, he used his feet with rare rapidity against A. P. Freeman, meant that he let everyone else (except Durston) bat in the second innings before declaring. Durston's job was to get Kent out, which he did most convincingly.

Cricket, like history, is so often the story of the victors. On Saturday 28 August, a disconsolate and vanquished Worcestershire, with 15 defeats in 17 games to their name, crumbled against Lancashire at Old Trafford. By evening Lancashire led on the first innings and by Monday night there was scarcely anything left for them to do on the following morning.

A Lancashire victory against Worcestershire would ensure them the Championship unless Middlesex won their final game as well. This Warner knew, and knew full well. He had, in the closing days of his great career, all to play for in a way no fiction writer would have dared create. A part of him must have wished he had batted on at Leyton and given Middlesex just five more runs instead of obeying Lord Harris' behest – especially as Harris had left Canterbury a few days afterwards at the end of Middlesex's match there without a word of congratulation. For all the links which bound them together, the two men were always a little distant, Harris dominating and Warner subservient.

But Harris was there in the Lord's pavilion on the morning of Saturday 28 August to see the nearest thing that English cricket in the 1920s could offer to a cup final. The two London counties, Middlesex and Surrey, from north and south of the Thames would play before over thirty thousand of their supporters for an intangible title that only one of them could win anyway.

Of the occasion, Warner wrote a year later, 'it may be imagined with what tense feelings I look forward to the match'. Ronald Mason in his excellent *Plum Warner's Last Season* enlarges upon Warner's understatement:

> The cumulation on [his] nervous system of all these concen-trated crises – the chance of a ninth win, the chance of the snatched Championship, the allied, but separate tensions, induced by the fact that this would be his very last match, his very last after all those crowded unforgettable years, the delivery of a piece of himself into the shadows – would have inhibited many lesser men into quivering incapability.

There is, in all this, something of the atmosphere – on a lower plane – created by Hugh de Sélincourt in his picture of Paul Gauvinier's last match for the village of Tillingfold. The circum-stances were, of course, entirely different but we can see in de Sélincourt's fictitious character the same awareness of drama and finality, the personal urge to do well, the ambition for the side (much more important), and the crowd desperately wishing for him both individual success and collective triumph. De Sélincourt could end his tale as he wished: Gauvinier would make a few runs and Tillingfold would win. Part of the craft of those writers of cricket fiction such as himself and R. C. Sherriff was to create a happy ending.

Reality might be very different as Plum Warner walked out to bat at Lord's that Saturday morning, with the Middlesex score at 35 for 3, to be cheered by the vast crowd and to be greeted by the Surrey attack of J. W. Hitch and Tom Rushby supported by an outstanding fielding side striving for another breakthrough. 'Runs were terribly hard to get,' remembered Warner and they continued to be as Hobbs controlled the off-side and Miles Howell (whom Warner in light relief nicknamed Spion Kop after the year's Derby winner) frustrated runs in an arc wide of mid-on. The *Daily Sketch* had tipped a horse called Plum for the 1.45 race at Derby that day but he proved to be a non-runner.

Runs remained hard to get all through the day as wickets fell steadily at one end and Warner stayed there, resolute, defensive, even criticised. At half past six Middlesex were 253 for 8 with the captain 70 not out.

On Sunday he was again the family man. Agnes had been as glued to the scene as he to the crease. This day she and the children claimed him, Betty and Esmond with an awareness of how important the next two days were (after all, they had both accompanied him to Australia with the 1911–12 side), John with the boisterous demands of a 2-year-old.

In those days the last Monday in August was not August bank holiday, yet 20,000 Londoners managed to have the funerals of great-aunts to attend or a sudden attack of 'cricketitis'. They saw Middlesex add another 15 (Warner 79). Then Hobbs went cheaply, mistiming a slower ball from Hearne, and Andy Sandham stayed throughout the innings for 167 not out.[18] Fender declared 73 runs ahead leaving Middlesex a nasty 40 minutes in dull grey conditions which C. H. L. Skeet and Lee survived. That evening Lancashire needed only 41 more to beat Worcestershire with all their wickets standing and Warner wrote a letter to *The Times*, dropping it off at Fleet Street on his way home.

Challen Hasler Lufkin Skeet's parents must have had great things in mind for their offspring in bestowing on him such imperishable names. Thus equipped he spent a lifetime as a colonial servant in the Sudan but not before he made two memorable impacts on the Middlesex season of 1920. At Edgbaston he took a catch off a ball hit higher than Warner believed he had ever seen a ball hit. At Lord's on this final day of Warner's career he made the only century of his own tantalisingly brief one. He and Lee (H.W.), the solid, if unspectacular, professional who would serve Middlesex for 24 years took Middlesex to 208 soon after lunch. They had scored at the rate of 86 an hour and their partnership made possible – rather than probable – a Middlesex victory. Warner asked for 'quick runs', got them at the cost of wickets, and came in himself at no. 9 to join Stevens. In eight minutes they added 25, the old man matching the youngster run for run and end for end while doing complicated sums in his head as to when he might declare. At four o'clock Surrey set off with three hours to get 244, a manageable target. It mattered not that Surrey might get the runs; it mattered very much that Middlesex should get them out. By ten past six, nine Surrey wickets had fallen and 50 minutes were left. This time Stevens kept his own counsel (Shades of Bradford!) and simply bowled out Strudwick to win the match, the Championship and Warner's eternal gratitude.

They carried Warner off the ground; they called for him to speak from the pavilion; they pursued the professionals so irrationally banished to their own obscure quarters; they trudged home, those Middlesex and Surrey supporters to Hampstead and Pinner, to Streatham and Brixton. No cup for the winners, just 2.39 per cent.

It was a pity that Warner had written a letter to *The Times*. It had been published that Tuesday morning under the signature of 'Fair Play' and it challenged the prevailing percentage system, arguing that in no sense should Lancashire emerge as champions.

COUNTY CHAMPIONSHIP

POSITION OF LANCASHIRE.

To the Editor of *The Times*

Sir, – There is a probability that Lancashire may, on the present system of scoring, which, by the way, has been universally condemned, finish at the top of the County Championship, but even their staunchest supporters will agree that their form against Middlesex, Surrey, and Yorkshire, the three strongest counties on general form, does not entitle them to this position.

It may be of interest to set out the results of Lancashire's games against these three counties. Middlesex beat them at Lord's by an innings, and played an even draw with them at Old Trafford; Surrey defeated them at the Oval by nine wickets, and at Old Trafford by 200-odd runs; and Yorkshire beat them by 20-odd runs at Bradford, and had the better of a drawn game at Old Trafford. Their record, therefore, against Middlesex, Surrey, and Yorkshire works out as follows:

Matches played.	Won.	Drawn.	Lost.
6	0	2	4

And yet Lancashire may be, on the system of scoring now in vogue, champions! The truth is that their present place in the Championship is very largely due to the fact that they have scored a very large proportion of their points against such weak sides as Worcestershire, Derbyshire, Northamptonshire, and Leicestershire. In common fairness, all lovers of cricket will hope that the Committee of M.C.C., who by the rule governing county cricket, which runs, 'At the close of each season the Committee of M.C.C. *shall* decide the County Championship' will use the power they possess and decide which is the champion county for 1920. Middlesex, Surrey, Yorkshire, or Kent may all be described as champion sides, but Lancashire on this season's form have no right whatever to the title.

I am, Sir, yours faithfully,

FAIR PLAY.

It was an appalling suggestion. While admittedly not claiming the spoils necessarily for Middlesex, it proposed that they should retrospectively be denied to Lancashire because they had failed to beat any of the major counties.

By lunchtime on the Tuesday Lancashire were drinking (prematurely) champagne at Old Trafford, doubting the prospect of a Middlesex victory. Copies of *The Times* in the pavilion would have been far less in evidence than those of the *Manchester Guardian* but anyone who glanced at the correspondence columns would have thought 'Fair Play's' letter displayed anything but a sense of fair play.

Among the letters Warner received was one from the Lancashire secretary: 'It would be idle to deny that we in Lancashire are a trifle disappointed that we have not come out on top but we are sportsmen, and we can give all honour to our opponents in their triumph.' *The Times* correspondence columns, in the circumstances of the Middlesex victory, had no follow-up to Fair Play's letter and carried instead next morning a leading article on P. F. Warner written by R. B. Vincent.

Perhaps Warner regretted that impetuous letter and was glad it had been anonymous. Let it fade from our thoughts in the face of the hundreds of letters of congratulation he received from politicians, cricketers, soldiers and well-wishers.[19] Cartoonists and essayists had a field day. *Mr Punch* added his tributes. All that remained for him was to play for Middlesex v. the Rest of England at The Oval, come off the field with 19 not out, and field out 600 runs. At last, Longman, with 66, justified his captain's confidence in him.

6

Journalist and Selector: I, 1920–32

The end of Warner's first-class career coincided with the decision to leave Caring House and lease the more modest Riverside, in Datchet, near Windsor. It was a solid red-brick Victorian building of uneven proportions and angles. The garden, partly concealed by a high wall, also continued across the Windsor road down to the Thames. There was room enough for a tennis court and a wicket. Although the pre-season traditions of Caring did not continue, there was always a net for anyone who wanted. Among those who remembered pleasant afternoons there during their time at Eton were Lord Home (as Lord Dunglass) Ronald Aird and Sir George Allen. Later the house was made into flats and the present owners discovered in 1985 the remains of cricket balls deep in the shrubbery. Warner would have liked that; the ammunition of the battle-field still to be found in the trenches.

The house itself became the centre of their family activities as Doris Smith remembered. She had joined the Warner household in 1923 and stayed with the family for over thirty years. She was brought up in Windsor and vividly recalled for me the long hours which her father worked as a chef in the royal household. 'During my childhood, when King Edward was on the throne, there were huge meals and he'd be in the kitchens all night. We really saw very little of him for when the Court moved to Balmoral or Sandringham he went too.' A chance conversation of her father's got her into the dressmaking trade, which led, in turn, to her becoming lady's maid to Agnes Warner. Doris moved a mile or two down the road to the Warners' home at Datchet.

I was lonely at first. I didn't eat with the rest of the staff and my room wasn't in the servants' quarters. But there was plenty to keep everyone busy. I made some of Lady (*sic*) Warner's clothes and I had a lot to do when Miss Betty was being presented at Court. There were constant lunch and dinner-parties, bridge, dances, tennis and people for the week-end. The children brought all their friends as well. Ascot was an especially busy time.

There were the years of the 1920s, the gay abandon after the First World War when hedonism prevailed and pre-war standards were desperately pursued. The Warners lived the lives of the comfortably off upper middle class as they had done before 1914. They kept a cook, housemaid, parlour-maid, daily woman and gardener besides Doris. To all of them Warner showed his usual courtesy when he met them.

Despite his longevity and sporting prowess, his life would continue to be punctuated by bouts of ill-health. Twice in the years this chapter considers, he was seriously ill, though an operation in 1923 'made me really free from pain for the first time in 30 years'. In 1930, illness again struck. 'In three weeks I lost two stones and as I am no Falstaff, I could not afford to do so.' He was able to recuperate on a visit to South Africa, accompanied by Betty. One wonders why Agnes could not have gone too. The heart condition, which would later confine her to bed for the last years of her life, had first struck in 1928: a voyage might have done her good.

Among family events was the 'coming out' of Betty in 1925, a compensation in happiness for the very serious car accident which had led her to be one of the earliest patients to make a complete recovery through the techniques of plastic surgery. In 1932, with her father unable to be present as he was on the way to Australia, she was married in St Martin-in-the-Fields to Lieutenant-Commander Harold Henderson, RN. The Hendersons would make a home for Warner in his very last years. Esmond went to Eton and Magdalen College, Oxford and in 1931 was commissioned in the Coldstream Guards, the same year in which John went to Eton. Aucher, Warner's brother, retired from the attorney-generalship of Trinidad in 1922 and he and his wife settled in England.

Among family friends of long standing of whom they now saw more were the Allens. Walter Allen and his wife Pearl were both Australians of several generations who moved to England in 1909, subsequently living in Datchet. Walter, whose brother Reginald played cricket for Australia in 1886–87, was called to the Australian Bar, but later made his career in England in the Metropolitan Special Constabulary, eventually becoming commandant and receiving a knighthood. Pearl Allen, whose life-span was almost identical with that of Warner – both were born in 1873 and she died a few months earlier in 1962 – was a lady, E. W. Swanton has recorded,[20] who 'kept at a discreet distance a string of admirers of whom Plum was not the least'. The two families, Warners and Allens, had first become friendly before the war, a friendship cemented by propinquity, by Walter Allen's keenness for cricket, and by the interest which Warner took in the cricket career of the Allens' younger son, Gubby, one of whose three appearances in the Eton v. Harrow match at Lord's (that of 1920) coincided with the Warners becoming his parents' neighbours in Datchet.

Indeed, Warner, as a carefree young bachelor, may have admired Pearl, a young married woman, when he visited Australia very briefly with Hawke's 1902–3 side on the way home from New Zealand. The team played New South Wales at Sydney in March 1903 and he possibly met the Allen family at their home at Thaxted, overlooking Sydney Harbour. Whether that early meeting between Warner and Pearl ever took place or not, Agnes Warner was a little jealous of Pearl Allen in the earlier years of the family friendship though always very kind to Pearl's children, Patricia, Geoffrey and Gubby. That jealousy was sad, for as Lady (Patricia) Dickson and Elizabeth Henderson both thought, 'she had very little cause'. Warner remained devoted to Pearl Allen all his life. During the Second World War, a daughter-in-law could recall his excitement when she was coming to tea. But by then time had mellowed the relationship between Agnes and Pearl and both were very friendly in their old age.

There is an amusing tale told of the occasion when Warner and Allen, acting as escorts to daughter and sister respectively, took them to Paris to a finishing school. Having shown the two girls around Paris and then, a few days later, deposited them at their place of education, the two men spent an evening at the Casino de Paris. Presently a searchlight played over the audience and stopped at Warner while a young lady descended from the stage to present him with a box of lady's make-up for being 'le plus chauve'. To Allen's comment, 'for Heaven's sake, Plum, put your hat on', Warner replied, 'not at all. I haven't been in Paris for 20 years and here I am getting first prize'. The two girls would remain close friends all their lives.

The Jellicoes continued to be their friends of many years. It was a friendship depending on correspondence in the early 'twenties while Jellicoe and his wife were in New Zealand. One letter describes how Jellicoe, who was the Governor-General, entertained MacLaren's team in New Zealand and how he himself took 4 for 28 'as a bowler in my old age'. When the Jellicoes returned in 1925, he was to become deeply involved in the British Legion as its first naval president and the friendship was resumed on a more personal basis. Busy and distinguished men such as Jellicoe could always find time for Warner because he was a good host and a good guest, a responsive correspondent and a great enthusiast. The two families spent the Christmas of 1927 together at the Jellicoes' home in the Isle of Wight. Plum was agitated that there seemed to be no way of knowing how England was faring in the Test match against South Africa at Johannesburg. Heavy snow prolonged the visit and one day Lady Jellicoe served venison for lunch. Plum disliked it and said so. On the following day, he complimented his hostess on her cottage pie and asked for a second helping only to be told it was the venison rehashed. The friendship could stand these crises!

Warner's career as a first-class cricketer effectively ended in 1920. Four matches in 1926–27 in South America were classified as first class and there was a final game for MCC in 1929. He continued to play some minor cricket in the 1920s, taking sides to the Channel Islands, Scotland and Holland as well as on a more important South American tour.

Cricket in South America had been established through visits by the Royal Navy and the growth of British business communities. Lord Hawke had taken out a side in 1912 and Warner's was the second to visit with matches being played in Argentina, Uruguay, Chile and Peru. The party was received by presidential heads of states, and the British ambassador to Argentina wrote to the secretary of MCC calling the players 'worth all the ambassadors in the world'. One of the party, Lord Home, could use the occasion to widen the experience he would one day draw upon as a British Foreign Secretary and Prime Minister. As for the elderly skipper, he made 81 against Montevideo and 46 against Argentina at Belgrano. The South American sides were, of course, all composed of expatriates, and letters such as this one to Warner provide a vivid commentary on how welcome were teams from England to those who felt isolated by distance and years from the homeland:

You can have no idea what an excellent thing it has been for British prestige to have you and your MCC team in our midst. Do not imagine these are just idle words, for having been resident in Chile for 33 years I can size up the effect on the Chilean community.

C. H. Gibson, the Argentine captain (and hero of MacLaren's match against the Australians in 1921), wrote, 'knowing most of the British community I cannot conceive a more popular figure than you have been on the field of action and off it. Your name will be talked of here with the greatest respect for many moons to come.'

As for Warner himself, the tour had again demonstrated those qualities of leadership which he had displayed as a young England captain. Lord Home wrote to him, 'I shall never cease to be grateful that I was under so sympathetic a captain. It was indeed a lovely day for me when you selected me to come, as had selection depended solely on qualification I am afraid mine would not have stood the strain.'

Sixty years later, Lord Home told me he saw no reason to change his views and he believed that Warner 'was a very good Ambassador for the game, and for Britain abroad'. Another player wrote, 'your kindly advice taught me a tremendous amount about the game. I could never hope to play again under such a personality.'

It had been a tour with its fair share of interest: trains with marble baths; an earth tremor at Valparaiso which shook off the bails; a deputation of West Indian cricketers greeting them at the Panama Canal; and a crossing of the Andes.

At Christmas, Warner had written a long letter to his family from Buenos Aires. It has all the excitement of a small boy writing home from his preparatory school:

> I came straight off the ship and hit three sixes, all drives. It was a small ground but two were big hits. I got a tremendous welcome, all the crowd, including the Montevideo team, cheering me. I had a slog after tea and was only in one hour ten minutes. People apparently think it a tremendous honour that so famous a cricketer as Pero should come to play cricket here. We are staying at the Hurlingham for the 'Test' match with cricket and polo grounds, squash courts, racquet courts, tennis courts and wonderful baths – a paradise. I love playing cricket again and captaining a side. I think of you all so much. By the time you get this, Esmond will be going to Oxford and John to school. How is Betty's ——— [indecipherable]?

The letter had also talked about the roulette they had played, and the systems they had devised which had produced wins of £120 and £50 for two of the party but nothing for him.

Warner's approach to money had not changed. He was always conscious that his wife had a comfortable private income while he depended on what he earned as a journalist (about £10 a week in the cricket season), as an author (with, as Cardus once observed, better sales than any other cricket writer in his time), as editor of *The Cricketer* (£600 a year) and, later, as a broadcaster (about £20 a year). Ready cash was another matter and Warner was often short of it. When he went to Australia in 1932–33, the players regarded it as more economical to give him a thousand cigarettes to start off with (at his usual ten a day, they lasted three months) rather than meet his frequent requests. To be short of 'ready cash' can, of course, be the stylish gesture of a prosperous man. The prosperity of the Warners suffered after the 1929 Depression when Agnes's shares fell considerably. John, as a boy at Eton, could remember his parents anxiously discussing finance. Poverty is only relative and John did not have to leave Eton nor did Warner resign from his clubs – but there was some retrenchment. The Datchet house was given up and the family returned to live in London. Tedworth Square was sold in 1930 and in 1931 they moved to 6 Bourne House, a flat in Sloane Street.

Nevertheless, appearances were kept up. Bradman, who first met Warner in 1930, thought him 'a rich man'. He was never remotely so. Such money as he could call his own came, and continued to come, from his talents as a writer and broadcaster.

To summarise Warner's activities in the decade or so after he gave up playing for Middlesex: he was appointed in 1921 cricket correspondent of the *Morning Post*, continued to be an occasional contributor to *The Times* and edited the 1920 edition in the Badminton Library on cricket. He also founded, though the idea was that of G. N. Foster, *The Cricketer* with which he would be associated for the rest of his life. He was chairman of the English selectors in 1926 and 1931–32 and was a pioneer performer in the new medium of broadcasting.

Warner launched *The Cricketer* on 30 April 1921 as a weekly in summer and a monthly in winter costing sixpence, together with a winter annual for half a crown. In many ways it was a brave decision. In economic terms, the post-war boom was over, the prices of British exports were tumbling, unemployment had doubled in the three months before publication of the new magazine and *The Economist* described 1921 as shaping up to be 'one of the worst years of depression since the industrial revolution'. It was no moment for a new sporting periodical, especially as none on cricket had ever flourished for very long. The magazine was registered as *The Cricketer* Syndicate Limited and its offices, between the wars, were mainly in Wine Office Court, off Fleet Street. They were in a small late eighteenth-century building opposite 'Ye Old Cheshire Cheese' and near to Dr Samuel Johnson's house.

On the face of it, events and history were not on Warner's side but a closer examination suggests that the enterprise might prove viable. Sport had won a large following immediately after the First World War, and cricket had had a fair share of that support. The dramatic interest taken in Middlesex's winning of the Championship at the end of the previous summer of 1920 persuaded Warner of the hold cricket had on the public imagination, only offset to some extent by England's devastating defeat in Australia in the months which followed. He was, by nature, an optimist (as Fry told him at the time) and a romantic. Cricket was one of the better offerings which might help a weary post-war society to recover the good things of life. The opening words of his first signed editorial expressed his convictions:

> The popularity of, and interest in, cricket not only here but in every part of the world where Englishmen are gathered together was never greater than at the present time. Cricket, indeed, as Tom Brown has told us, in the best of all school stories, is an institution and the *habeas corpus* of every boy of British birth, for it is a typically British game. The very essence of cricket is camaraderie and good sportsmanship, and the contributors to *The Cricketer* will strive to write in such a spirit.

The contributors whom Warner recruited and who aspired to these high ideals were distinguished names. G. L. Jessop began a series of 'Reminiscences', Harry Altham his 'History of Cricket';[21] D. J. Knight wrote on 'Batsmanship' and A. C. MacLaren 'For the Schoolboy'. Together they offered a blend of information on the game's past, perhaps more for the older reader, with instruction for the current player including those still at school. MacLaren's essay included the sweeping assumption, 'any fool can play forward to the ball' as a prelude to telling schoolboys how to play off the back foot.

The first issue also carried a full-page review of the editor's latest book, *My Cricketing Life* (on the principle if you don't sell your own wares, no one else will sell them for you),[22] together with articles on the recent series in Australia, the selectors appointed for 1921 (at this stage Warner was not writing yet in judgement upon himself), and a review of counties. The reader was offered, for his sixpence, 26 pages only one of which carried advertisements. There were two cartoons by Charles Graves, one of them depicting the cherubic Plum Warner taking guard, and three action-pictures.

A pattern was quickly established of printing full score details of all first-class games and of many club and school games with rather less attention to the leagues. The first winter annual consisted of 132 pages, well illustrated, and had the usual contributors together with the historian F. S. Ashley-Cooper, the acting celebrity and former England cricketer C. Aubrey Smith, the novelist and cricketer A. Conan Doyle, the essayist E. V. Lucas, the journalist E. H. D. Sewell and Jack Hobbs himself. No one could fault Warner for not going in search of his authors. Furthermore, a feature of the winter monthlies was an article by F. T. Sellicks on Rugby. Other contributors who joined (in the 1920s) were Sir Home Gordon, G. A. Faulkner, who ran a successful coaching school, 'A Country Vicar'[23] (whose recollections rather rambled on and might have benefited from some sharp editorial pruning), G. D. Martineau, mostly with poetry, and R. C. Robertson-Glasgow (of whom more, below). In the early 1930s came Alfred Cochrane, the cricketer antiquary, E. W. Swanton, J. A. Armitage (who often reported the Tests), Frank Mitchell, R. A. Young, Fender, I. A. R. Peebles, and E. L. Roberts (the statistician). Not until 1936 did Fry become a contributor, while in 1929 there appeared, briefly, some fine etchings of cricketers by Juliet Somers.

At the start of the magazine's second year its weekly coverage extended to 36 pages and Warner had secured advertisers for nine of them, a vast improvement on 1921. There was only a net gain to the reader of one page on cricket, but it was becoming a more economical proposition to the publisher. By 1925, though, the publication of the monthly issue in the winter was suspended because it did not pay its way. The Winter Annual was retained and supplemented with a Spring Annual.

By the end of its first five years it had become established. The Winter Annual in 1926 was widely reviewed and, despite the somewhat formidable 24 pages of closely printed statistics on England v. Australia, 1878–1926, by Ashley-Cooper, was well received. It was, said the *Port of Spain Gazette*, 'a journal which gives all news of the grand old game from every playing field in the five continents'. The *Cambridge Daily News* wrote, 'one of the best half-crown's worth we have come across'. To the London *Evening Standard*, it furnished hours of delight and to the *Yorkshire Post* it was attractive and interesting.

By 1931, *The Cricketer* could boast that it went to over two hundred places outside Britain, 'from Batavia to Barbados', as the sales caption ran, 'it has imperial value'. All this encouraged sales and helped advertising. A letter to Warner from the Managing Director of Slazenger's in March 1930 is representative of many satisfied customers, 'we experienced splendid results from our advertising with you this year and a great deal of business has come our way'.

In editorial terms, Warner at first played a large part not only by his written contributions but in dictating the policy of the magazine and securing copy. A. W. T. Langford has left on record that Warner visited the office virtually every day until 1939 and that any thoughts that 'he would be largely a figurehead' were quickly dispersed.

No account of *The Cricketer* can be complete without some discussion on the relationship between Warner and Langford. Arthur Langford was introduced to Warner in 1923 and his suggestion that he might contribute notes on club cricket was accepted. There began an association between the two that would last the 40 years until Warner's death. At the time, Langford was a club cricketer in his late twenties, about to get married, and pursuing a career in journalism. The reporting of club cricket became an important feature of *The Cricketer* and, as such, helped its circulation. After five years as a columnist Langford became a permanent member of staff, the lone survivor of a financial crisis which ended in Warner parting with a rather unsuccessful advertising manager and appointing Langford as an 'unsung' assistant editor, with both editorial and advertising responsibilities. There were Warner himself, Langford, a secretary and an office boy.

The two men made an ideal partnership. Warner was the 'front' man, always keen (as his letters to the BBC would indicate) to have his name identified with *The Cricketer*. Langford put in countless hours composing pieces on the schools, reviewing books or writing his Club Notes. Much of his work was anonymous or pseudonymous. He was the 'backroom' of the enterprise, not projecting his name upon the reader. Warner took advantage of Langford's good nature. Langford was a man without great ambition, happy enough to find his livelihood and his hobby as one. His employer left him alone, free to turn out for the Jesters or Hampton Wick when he liked so long as the weekly paper came out on time. By 1932 he had become indispensable to Warner. The older man (now almost 60) was spared the day-to-day responsibilities, and could concentrate on his numerous other activities, besides continuing to draw his £600 from *The Cricketer*. The younger man, with a wife and small child to support, was hard up yet continued to offer an almost dog-like devotion which led him to write, 'I have had a wonderful time with *The Cricketer*, almost every day I tell myself how fortunate I have been to have such a delightful and happy job of work: it was a great day in my life when you said, "Why don't you call me Plum?"'

From the start, Warner was determined that *The Cricketer* should not just be a source for what was going on in the first-class game. Indeed, today's magazine, with so much first-class cricket to cover, is directed far more at that level than it was in the 1920s. One is struck by what mines of information the 'inter-war years' issues were. Apart from the reporting of the activities of well-known clubs such as the Butterflies, the Free Foresters, the Incogniti, the Mote, North Devon and the newly formed Buccaneers (to name but a very few), where else would one find full match details of such contests as Kobe v. Yokohama, the Irish Guards v. the Club Cricket Conference at Constantinople; Shanghai v. Kowloon; Perak v. Penang; Elmers End v. the South Eastern and Central Railway; Philadelphia v. All Bermuda and Abbottabad v. Subalterns' Course, Kabul? Warner's catholic selection gave much encouragement to cricketers in countries such as Holland and Denmark and throughout the Empire.

Cricket in the Services, universities and public schools, as one would expect, received very extensive coverage. The matches between Oxford and Cambridge and between Eton and Harrow got three pages of reporting in those days. They were, of course, occasions played to a packed Lord's and providing important social events in the English cricket season. Reporting depended to some extent on material being sent in. Indeed, my own first piece as a cricket writer appeared during the Second World War. On finding that the master in charge of school cricket had not submitted a report at all, with the brashness of youth I wrote it myself the following year and it duly appeared: no comment was ever made – perhaps the school authorities never saw *The Cricketer*!

Quite early on, several pages were devoted to letters from correspondents together with a page of answers which occasion-ally gave the impression of being an 'agony' column meeting the desperate hopes of those who sought statistical information, guidance in skills, the whereabouts of cricket books, and the affirmation of *their* choice of teams. In 1925, *The Cricketer* made capital out of the abiding delight found in choosing teams and launched a competition for a World XI of all time to play Mars at Lord's: first prize, five guineas.

The Cricketer (or its editor) was capable of laughing at itself. Amid all the reports of England's great victory at The Oval in 1926, it included the comment of the New York paper, *The World*, which wrote:

We rub our eyes to see whether cobwebs are not growing on the wicket. Nor is this impression of slowness an illusion on the part of those who are strangers to this game. It stands to reason when one of the players is 49 years old. Why, this game would be more closely related to tiddly-winks than baseball. If the English like this sleepy game, well they like it!

Robertson-Glasgow wrote a series of articles entitled 'The Letters of Phalaris' comprising humorous letters to the editor together with answers to correspondents of which the following may serve as an example – though the reader is not given the questions to which they relate: (i) We had to pay threepence on your letter. (ii) The umpires wanted to catch a train. (iii) Eggs and bacon. (iv) Have you confused Fuller Pilch with Quiller Couch? (v) His batting average was 0.5. (vi) You have forgotten the byes and summertime. Robertson-Glasgow was something of an acquired taste. Like his bowling for Somerset, he could sparkle with brilliance on some occasions and be erratic on others. But Warner gave him plenty of opportunities to appear for *The Cricketer* over the years and deserved rather better of Robertson-Glasgow than his comment that 'Warner was as bald as an ostrich and could talk about nothing but cricket'.

Perhaps writers such as Robertson-Glasgow gave some justification to the assertion by *The Cricketer* that 'its circulation is amongst the moneyed class who appreciate and buy high-class articles, not only those of direct application to cricket but also which appeal to a cultured taste'. Warner's critics have identified him with a conservatism in attitude and convention in which cricket had a secure niche within a structured and sheltered social order. Cricket, he believed, was one of the linchpins that strengthened the foundations of that society. It is worthwhile, therefore, to examine how far he used *The Cricketer* as a vehicle for making cricket more widely acceptable and available to the young men of an urban working-class background. In his editorial in 1922, launching the second year, he wrote: 'What chance has the young man in our great industrial towns for a game of cricket, except possibly under the railway arch or in some backyard bisected by a clothes-line? If only recreational grounds could be opened in all these towns.'

He praised the growth of sporting facilities being provided by firms, many of which were being established in London suburbia but he saw this as providing for a social class of greater economic status than those he had in mind. He contrasted the opportunities which the poor might have on the village green with those they were denied in towns and concluded: 'Games have a wonderful influence for good. We may say that the lives of seven-tenths of the nation are drab and colourless, and the more games we can give them, the healthier and happier we shall make them.'

The year before, the Oxford Boys' Cricket Scheme had been established, rather on the lines of the public school missions to youth in the cities which had existed for some fifty or sixty years. It aimed to make college grounds at Oxford available for boys in cities during the vacation. *The Cricketer*, as Warner's editorial suggests, soon lent its backing, giving it publicity, advocating its cause and reiterating its support over the years. A few years later, in 1925, the National Playing Fields Association was formed with similar objectives and a link with politicians and sources of public money. Warner, in 1928, approached various politicians and asked them to identify themselves with the need for more playing-fields and resources. Lloyd George, for example, wrote to him, 'it is philanthropic and commonsense to save our future manhood and womanhood from the massacre and disease of the slum'. *The Cricketer* asked all clubs in towns to make their grounds available to working-class lads.

In 1929, Warner took up the theme again when he wrote:

Want of space crowds out many youngsters who would really prefer to play cricket. The shortage of grounds is a serious matter in every branch of sport. The rich can look after themselves. The large industrial firms, to their credit, are doing all they can for those in their employment. It is for the artisan class that the National Playing Fields Association is doing such good work. The little boy in the street whose bat is a bit of old packing case and whose wicket is an old tin can is the gentleman we want to catch. Let us agitate for more open spaces and a freer use of the public parks. Why not? Mitcham Common produced Tom Richardson, Parker's Piece, Tom Hayward and Hobbs.

He returned to the subject again in 1932: 'We who have been accustomed to take a good cricket pitch for granted will assuredly sympathise with those whose lot in life is cast in less happy circumstances. Here is the opportunity to make happy many a little boy.' He was one of the sponsors, that year, of a ball at the Dorchester in aid of the National Playing Fields Association.

We may credit Warner with a sense of social concern matched possibly by the hope that fresh sources for professional cricketers might be tapped. The cynic might find another motive. Warner, like many another of his class in the 1920s in the wake of

Bolshevism, feared social revolution. Only semi-humorously had he written in 1921, 'can you imagine a cricketer being a Leninist?' and, in 1928, 'cricket is the antidote to all the "...isms" in the world'.

Hand in hand with *The Cricketer* went his work for the *Morning Post* between 1921 and 1932 which involved reporting major matches, writing articles on topical issues and contributing obituaries. As just one example of his reporting, we may notice how he handled the record first-wicket partnership of 555 between H. Sutcliffe and P. Holmes at Leyton in June 1932:

The present Yorkshire first-wicket pair have long been famous. All men praise Herbert Sutcliffe for his great skill, his cool temperament and his magnificent fighting qualities. His record is not surpassed even by 'The Master' and in a tight corner he is the equal of any batsman that ever lived. Always in the pink of condition, he loves a fight. The bigger the occasion, the greater the man. His partner Holmes is a good many years his senior but there are those who argue that in purely technical skill he is the equal of his more famous colleague.

There were some brief references to the milestones of the partnership, and an awareness of the famous 'no ball' which secured the record. The piece was at once factual (though mildly inaccurate) and historical, though the critic might comment with reason that it was much more an essay on two great players than an informed statement of the day's play.

His obituaries of J. W. H. T. Douglas and Lord Harris were revealing pieces. Of Douglas, who was drowned in 1931, 'a little *difficult* and did not always take kindly to the duties which are inseparable from a tour abroad'; of Harris, who died in 1932, 'unquestionably the King of Cricket, the Nestor and Fidelis Achates of that great game in which he had attained every possible distinction. He used his authority wisely and fairly and would be "just".'

In 1926 Warner became chairman of the selectors. He had first been one, as we have seen, in 1905 when still very much a player and the victorious captain in Australia the previous year. It had been an early instance of him filling more than one role in a situation, which would later cause some embarrassment. The position in 1905 had caused no problems. Now, 20 years later, Warner was chairman of the selectors and editor of the influential *Cricketer* (besides writing for the *Morning Post*).

He had, as chairman, two colleagues in P. A. Perrin and (after 1931) T. A. Higson of whom something should be said. Percy

Perrin had had a distinguished career as an Essex batsman, playing for the county from 1896 to 1928, making 66 centuries including, in 1904, an innings of 343 not out against Deryshire. The match had its own interest, apart from Perrin's score, in that Essex lost. Both sides made over 500 in their first innings and Essex were then dismissed for 97 to give Derbyshire a nine-wicket victory. Yet Perrin never appeared either for England or the Gentlemen, primarily because he was so slow in the field.

Higson had had very little experience of the first-class game, making occasional appearances for Lancashire between 1905 and 1923 in which last year he played only once – captaining the side in a five-wicket victory over the West Indies. He was, however, a prominent administrator in Lancashire, served on the committee for 49 years and represented the voice of the North of England in the meetings of selectors, important when there was less travelling to see players. Higson, as early as 1934, had made a plea for brighter cricket and advocated single innings matches.

Warner was thus the only one of the three selectors with Test match experience. Perrin was a very good judge of a player but he was a quiet, retiring man, and he was ready as often as not to fall in with Warner's opinions. Higson, too, was very much Warner's man, though he showed his mettle when Warner failed to consult him in a last-minute substitution of Allen for Harold Larwood in the first Test against New Zealand in 1931. Only when Allen had made a century in the match was Higson appeased.

We may turn now to an examination in more detail of Warner's role as chairman in 1926. With Perrin and A. E. R. Gilligan, who had led the MCC side in Australia in 1924–25, together with the co-option, for the first time, of two professionals, Hobbs and Rhodes, he faced the daunting task of composing a side to regain the Ashes so disastrously lost in 1920–21. They appointed A. W. Carr as captain and, as was customary, co-opted him as well. For the second Test they took the decision, momentous as it was to prove in a few years, to bring the Nottinghamshire fast bowler, Larwood (whose county captain Carr was), into the side.

For the third Test at Leeds there was an overwhelming case for including the Gloucestershire left-arm slow bowler, C. W. L. Parker, in conditions, following rain, which would have been particularly suitable for him. Warner advocated his omission in favour of G. G. Macaulay on his own Yorkshire ground and he carried the day in committee. The England captain put the Australians in, Macartney and W. M. Woodfull made hundreds, and Australia had made 366 for 3 when rain stopped play at twenty minutes past five.

The omission of Parker was unfortunate, to say the least, and was held to be so by all sections of the press. It had an even more unfortunate consequence for Warner three years later when he was the guest of honour at the Gloucestershire Annual Dinner in April 1929 at the Grand Hotel, Bristol. He was, of course, feted as was proper to an invited distinguished speaker. He was in a mellow mood, the talk was pleasant, the wine flowed and people congenial in their conversation surrounded him. In his speech he paid a very warm tribute to W. R. Hammond, just returned from his memorable trip to Australia, and to another West Country player (but not a Gloucestershire one), J. C. White.

Meanwhile, at another table, one might suggest on the lower deck, rancour was fermenting and Charlie Parker was being contained with difficulty by his friends. He had never forgiven Warner for keeping him out in 1926 and now he was not even worth a mention in the speech. 'He blacked my career,' he grumbled to Reg Sinfield. The evening ended and Warner set off for his room. Fate threw them together in the confines of a hotel lift – the patrician and the plebeian of their generation, the one a man of appeasement, the other looking for trouble and nursing a grievance.

Versions of what happened vary but the gist of the matter was that Parker grabbed Warner by the neck, ripped his bow-tie and uttered some unparliamentary remarks. Warner went very white. Sinfield, who himself had received very slight attention from the selectors over the years, prevented Parker from doing Warner serious injury.[24] The incident was kept out of the press and never mentioned by Warner. It does little credit to Parker and reminds us that Warner, popular among so many of the professionals of the pre-1914 era, could be less acceptable between the wars especially among those who identified him strongly with the hierarchy of cricket and, to some extent, of society. By not mentioning Parker's great deeds for Gloucestershire in his speech, the gentleman had forgotten or ignored a great player. The player, however justified his grievance was, had scarcely behaved like a gentleman.

To return to the events of 1926: Warner, in his rather sentimental way, showed his confidence in Carr after the second Test by writing to him:

You are the best captain we have had for ages, and you are worth a hundred runs an innings. Cheer up old fellow. We all have the very greatest confidence in you and I wouldn't be without you for anything. Don't worry for a moment please. Love from yours affectionately, Plum.

He had also, as we shall see below, praised him in a broadcast.

Nevertheless, Carr, by the end of the third Test, sensed that Warner was losing confidence in him. He 'was constantly being advised to do this and that' and he felt the chairman was interfering to an unwarranted degree. Warner, at lunch on the first day of the third Test, had sat 'with a face like nothing on earth' (wrote Carr) contemplating both the catch Carr himself had dropped when Macartney was two and the huge partnership which Macartney and Woodfull were establishing.

The press wanted to know if it was entirely Carr's decision to put Australia in to bat and Sewell asked in the *Daily Express* whether or not Carr was simply carrying out a policy dictated by the selectors. The fourth Test was ruined by rain and, more significantly, Carr was unable to play on the second day owing to tonsillitis. Hobbs thus became the first professional to captain an England side in the twentieth century. There remained the fifth Test and Warner has left on record his impressions of the meeting of the selectors on Sunday 8 August 1926, writing, 'the prestige of English cricket seemed to depend on our decisions. England had won only one Test against Australia out of the last nineteen.' Those decisions included the dropping of Carr, the captain, and his replacement by Chapman.

The official Minutes of the meeting recorded that 'Mr A. W. Carr, who had not been in good health recently, generously offered to resign his place in the England XI and, after due consideration, this unselfish act on the part of Carr was accepted by the selection committee with the greatest possible regret.'

Carr's attack of tonsillitis had been ten days earlier and he had not offered to stand down nor had he expected to be excluded from the side. He felt blamed, by implication, for four drawn matches, none of which was scheduled for more than three days and three of which were affected by rain. The selectors also decided to select one of their own number, Rhodes, who had played in a Test match with W. G. Grace in 1899. Thus both the co-opted selectors, Hobbs and Rhodes, took part.

As every cricket-minded schoolboy (and schoolgirl?) knows, England won the match and regained the Ashes last secured by Warner's own side in 1911–12. 'This was a landmark,' Warner wrote, 'in our cricket history. Had we been beaten, despondency would have crept over the land.' Hobbs and Sutcliffe made centuries, Larwood got six wickets, Rhodes got another six. The chairman of selectors went off to his club, had a whisky and soda, and wrote his piece for the *Morning Post*, for which 'next day I received warm congratulations from the editor'. In an uncomplicated world, or so it seemed, all was sweetness and light. The successful journalist and selector packed his bags a few weeks later to go on his tour of South America.

So many telegrams and letters flooded in upon him that one might be forgiven for thinking that he had won the match off his own bat. Among them were 'simply marvellous' from his daughter Betty, and 'hearty congratulations to your committee' from the Argentine Cricket Association.

E. G. Wynward, the old England and Hampshire player, wrote:

Now that you have achieved great success I am astonished at the meagre recognition that the selection committee have received from the press. A good many of the writers have found it difficult to go back on their continued malignant prophecy of disaster. But cricketers are entirely sensible of the very great debt of gratitude to you.

From M. R. Jardine, father of D. R. Jardine and a contemporary of Warner's at Oxford, came, 'I would like to thank you for what you have done as much as for the way you have done it.'

Perhaps the letter he valued most came from his old friend Altham:

To you our victory must have meant so much for I know how wholeheartedly, wisely and courageously you have worked and schemed for it. Three months ago I felt in my bones that *Auspice Pelhamo* we should win through and so we have and I do feel it is far from the least of the many services you have rendered to English cricket.

One job remained to be done and Warner, always better at doing unpleasant tasks on paper than face-to-face, wrote to Carr:

I cannot say how deeply I feel for you in what I know is a great disappointment for you. I believe I feel it almost as much as you do; in fact, I can think of nothing else. It was a horrid and beastly job that faced us and we only tried to do the right thing. Take it in the grand manner and don't be angry and hurt with me. You giving up your place will give you an even greater hold, if such is possible, on the affections of the cricket world.

The game was always greater than the man and Warner could feel vindicated in his rejection of Carr and choice of Chapman.

Carr would reappear twice more as an England captain though not when Warner was a selector.

How did Warner handle these events as a journalist? What he wrote in *The Cricketer* was substantially the same as that which he wrote in the *Morning Post*. In his reporting on the second Test he said, in *The Cricketer*, that A. W. Carr was 'a really good captain who placed his field excellently and works his bowling well. He is absorbed in his job and is the best captain England has had for many a long day.' A few days later, after the third Test, he confined his criticism on Carr's decision to field to saying, 'it was a mistake to put Australia in but it was Macartney who upset all calculations'. His reporting of the fifth Test was an essay in success. Only the final paragraph gives any indication that the man who commented on Chapman's captaincy has also chosen him:

> One more point and I make it with bated breath. Those who were responsible for the selection of the England teams had only one goal in view: what was best for England. And if, as a result of these deliberations, we caused disappointment to any individual, it is certain that none felt that disappointment more keenly or had greater sympathy and understanding than his colleagues who for many weeks had striven, in conjunction with him, with the one object in view, the defeat of our 'gallant friends the enemy'.

There had also been some consolation for Parker. Warner wrote, 'he should be a proud and happy man in the knowledge that he has obtained 200 wickets for the fourth time. All followers in the game will unite in congratulating him on his unique distinction.' But, as we have seen, it was not consolation enough and Parker nursed his grievance over the years.

A few months later appeared Warner's *Fight for the Ashes*, published by Harrap. It was the first of a long sequence of books by various authors to bear this title.[25] Warner's account of the matches was largely based on his own (or others') press reports but in his closing pages he touched on the issues in dispute during the series. Of Parker's omission, he wrote, 'Carr had exactly the side he wanted.' Of Carr's decision to put Australia in, he wrote, 'Mr Carr consulted whoever he thought fit.' And of Carr's subsequent omission in the last Test, 'it was essential, in the interests of England, that the best possible side on the form of the moment should take the field'.

On the second and third points, Warner need not be criticised, but on the first he distanced himself quite distinctly from the decision to omit Parker and laid the blame fairly and squarely on Carr. It is an instance of the 'half-truths' of which even Sir George Allen believed Warner could be guilty.

Warner was not unaware of the conflict of interest created by his being both a selector and a writer. He himself has indicated that his appointment to the chairmanship in 1926 was in jeopardy because of his journalistic activities. That he was not reappointed in 1927, despite having won the Ashes and a sheaf of congratulatory letters, we may surmise was partly because of his dual role. He received almost as many letters of commiseration as he had done a year earlier in congratulation but to them he replied that he had 'no hurt feelings', that Leveson Gower, his successor, was 'an experienced selector' and that the Board of Control had frequently varied the composition of its selection committees.

In 1928 the Board passed a rule that selectors might not contribute to the press. Three years later Warner was reappointed as chairman of the selectors and the editor of the *Morning Post* released him from writing on the Test and Test trials. This, in a sense, reduced possible tension though, as later events were to show, Warner's reporting of a Yorkshire v. Surrey match at The Oval in 1932 rebounded on him in 1932–33.

Nevertheless, by the late 1920s Warner had been writing much less himself in the way of new material in *The Cricketer*, though using it as a vehicle for his own existing writings. Between 1926 and 1933, for example, his *My Cricketing Life* was serialised, a set of articles he had written for *The Times* in 1919 on 'Other Days' was reprinted and a broadcast talk he gave in 1928, when WG would have been 80, was reproduced. In this he paints an amusing picture of WG and himself going out to bat, Warner admitting to be less than half the weight and half the girth of the Grand Old Man. From 1929 onwards, the leading article on page one of *The Cricketer* was written by 'Second Slip' and later, entitled 'In the Pavilion', by Sir Home Gordon. Here might be made the comments which Warner himself could not make.

Something on which he could report with no serious conflict of interest was his last appearance in first-class cricket. The occasion was at Chatham in July 1929 and brought together two of his great interests, cricket and the navy. MCC scored 333 against the Royal Navy and the Royal Marines, Warner – in the euphemistic phrase – failing to bother the scorers. The Services side, 220 behind, were asked to follow on whereupon they scored 382. The innings included a ninth-wicket partnership of 120 and 11 overs by Warner, the highest number he had ever bowled in a first-class match. They may be said to have 'contained' the opposition in that he conceded only 28 runs but he failed to add to his career-aggregate of 15 wickets. Set, rather surprisingly, a target of 163, MCC failed by 23 runs to achieve it. Warner was dismissed for eight by Sub-Lieutenant Arnold Pomfret. The young man went on to become an admiral and Warner would have appreciated that: bowled by an aspiring admiral in his last first-class innings. He enjoyed his three days as the guest of the navy at Chatham dockyard in what had been, in earlier days, 'Caring House country' to him. There had, indeed, been one last appearance for Bearsted (after an interval of nine years) in the previous summer of 1928 when he captained the village against H. L. Tennyson's XI, though the village cricketers were largely displaced to make room for four men other than Warner himself who were past or future England captains in Jardine, Chapman and A. E. R. Gilligan and A. H. H. Gilligan.

Warner returned as chairman of the selectors in 1931 and his colleagues had to choose a side to play one Test against New Zealand but their main concern was to pick the MCC party to go to Australia in 1932. Jardine was appointed captain against New Zealand whose performances earned them two extra Tests. In the following summer of 1932 he captained England when the Indians made their Test debut, declaring when close to his own century to ensure an England victory. His subsequent appointment as captain of the MCC side to go to Australia proved the grindstone of Warner's troubles on that tour. The journalist confined himself to saying in *The Cricketer*, 'may we conclude by congratulating D. R. Jardine very heartily on his selection'.

In 1925 Warner began an association with the BBC which was to last for over thirty years though not without its ups and downs. The original British Broadcasting Company invited him to give a fifteen-minute talk on 'Prospects for the Season' at 'our ordinary fee of five guineas'. Unlike the story of the don in the 1950s who accepted an invitation to appear on television with the comment 'how much do *I* have to pay?' Warner asked for a larger fee. It is a comment on the postal services of those days (and the non-use of the telephone) that an exchange of six letters took place between 20 and 25 March (inside a week) in which both parties haggled.

Warner replied to John Stobart that as he and Warner were 'both at an extraordinary school, I think with respect you ought to offer me more than an ordinary fee'. Stobart, the old Rugbeian, replied, 'In view of the circumstances you mention, we would spring another two guineas.' Warner asked for ten and finally settled for eight, Stobart writing, 'if you won't tell anyone but it won't do to make it a precedent'. Warner had also used the argument that he was an 'expert', to be told tartly that 'we get the most tremendous experts for five guineas!'

After all this fuss, his opening words of his first broadcast were: 'Some years ago when I was playing cricket in Australia one of the newspapers remarked that so polished a brain as mine had seldom been seen beneath the Southern Cross.' He added that there was not a 'great deal of grey matter inside' and asked for sympathy in this, 'my first Test of an unusual kind'. He also took the opportunity to correct the interpretation which had been put on Lord Hawke's speech of a few months earlier, saying that what Hawke had meant to say was that 'it would be a bad day for English cricket when no amateur could be found good enough to play for or captain England'.

In 1926, when newly appointed as chairman of the selectors, Warner gave a talk on the evening of the first day of the second Test praising the qualities of the team he had chosen and Carr, the captain – words which would later rebound on him. By then the BBC was looking into the possibility of having brief commentaries during county matches. Warner was asked to a lunch to discuss it and he gave the first broadcast of a match when Essex played New Zealand at Leyton on 14 May 1927. He had asked to be introduced as editor of *The Cricketer* but the BBC had demurred, replying that it was like introducing 'Mr Churchill, author of a history of the recent war'. Warner won his point only to upset the editor of the *Morning Post* who insisted that Warner must be designated *their* special correspondent or not broadcast at all. Jealousy and suspicion of the potential rivalry of the new medium was evident.

Others beside Warner were being experimented on as sports commentators and Warner had the first hint that he was not entirely acceptable to the Corporation (as it had become) with a letter from Hugh Brennan – not an old Rugbeian – in August 1927 saying, 'Captain Wakelam put up quite a good show last Saturday. He has not got your knowledge of the game but he is an expert in the art of narrative and he is being given a trial.' Warner replied by sending Brennan a letter from a 'fan', a Buckinghamshire parson, who wrote of the 'delightful and human way in which you commented'. But the Buckinghamshire parson could not save Warner and he was never to be in demand as a commentator. For the moment he was given no reason. The correspondence between Warner and Brennan reveals the one trying to establish a warmer relationship ('you and your wife must come to dinner with us one night when John has got over his tonsillitis') and the other keeping the relationship formal. There came a request to do the piece on W. G. Grace and Warner accepted without even discussing a fee. Brennan found the text dull, lacking in any sense of personal reminiscence, and thought Warner's presentation at rehearsal 'melancholy'. The broadcast duly took place in 1928 and became another historic 'first'; the first time a cricket broadcast from England was heard in Australia. Warner received a letter from Grace's widow, Agnes: 'I write to tell you that it was greatly appreciated by me and my youngest son who, with his wife and child, lives with me.' There was another attempt to have the Brennans to dinner although no date was given, and the somewhat uneasy relationship terminated when Brennan replied towards the end of 1928, 'it would be best to fix up your arrangements without thinking of us' and wrote on Warner's file, 'melancholy delivery'.

That, for the moment, was that. Warner, never slow in later years to write and suggest himself as a broadcaster, did not reply and he waited until he learnt of an internal change in BBC staffing. This had come by 1932 when he approached Seymour de Lotbinière who had the courage to tell him what was on the file. Warner replied, 'if I am a good enough cricket authority to speak on cricket, all this fuss about my dossier of four years ago seems out of place'. Lotbinière agreed to 'abandon researches into the past' and asked Warner, chairman of the selectors again, to speak about the side he proposed to send to Australia in 1932–33. As early as June (interesting in the light of later events and decisions) Warner said on the radio that 'our fast bowlers are likely to be Larwood, Voce, Allen and Bowes'. Lotbinière gave him a 'good report', paid him ten guineas and Warner replied, 'I am glad my Melancholy has gone for ever. Everyone was very nice to me [a typical Warner response] and I hope I will be asked again.' He was! The invitation came to say a few words preceding the Empire News Bulletin the night before sailing to Australia. His first seven years as a broadcaster had indicated that he was of less value to the BBC in the new developing art of commentating than as a spokesman on general cricket themes. But even in that direction judgement was qualified.

Meanwhile, for the journalist, selector and broadcaster, other duties called for he had been appointed manager of the tour to Australia. The greatest trial of his career awaited him.

7

The Burden of Management, 1932–33

Warner's association with the events known to cricket as the bodyline bowling controversy introduced the unhappiest period of his life. It began, as we have seen, with his appointment in April 1931 as chairman of the selectors with the ultimate object of choosing the side for the 1932–33 MCC visit to Australia. It ended when MCC had said its last word on the subject two years later.

The task of finding a side to beat the Australians had begun, in a sense, immediately after the 1930 series in which Bradman dominated the Tests with even more authority than had Hammond in the 1928–29 Australian tour. Bradman, it seemed, had added a new dimension to the game and bowlers needed to be found to get him out. Warner was quite aware of this. He wrote the comment in the *Morning Post* after Bradman's 334 at Leeds that 'England must evolve a new type of bowler and develop fresh ideas, strategy and tactics to curb his almost uncanny skill'. And again, after the fifth Test, 'one trembles to think what lies in store for bowlers during the next 15 to 20 years.'

Neville Cardus had written in similar vein about Hammond a few years earlier, 'the possibilities are beyond the scope of estimation: I tremble with delight at the very thought of the grandeur he will spread over our cricket fields.' No doubt these remarks were conventional journalism to whet the public appetite. When Warner was presented with the prospect of seeing bowling which might contain Bradman, he was less than happy with what he saw. The scene was Yorkshire v. Surrey at The Oval in August 1932 and W. E. Bowes was bowling to Hobbs. Hobbs protested at the nature of the deliveries he received and Warner wrote in the *Morning Post* next morning:

I am a great admirer of Yorkshire Cricket. I love their keenness and the zest with which they play, but they will find themselves a very unpopular side if there is a repetition of Saturday's play. Moreover, these things lead to reprisals, and when they begin goodness knows where they will end.

Once again I appeal to all who control Yorkshire cricket, the president of the club, the committee, the captain, to men like Sutcliffe, to see that things are altered. I have written, I hope, honestly and fairly, and I am certain I echo the opinion of all who care for cricket and who wish to see its high traditions and prestige maintained.

These were brave words directed at – no less – his old friend, Hawke, president of Yorkshire and chairman of the MCC Cricket Committee. A few days later, Warner repeated them in *The Cricketer*:

Bowes should alter his tactics. He bowled with five men on the on-side and sent down several very short-pitched balls which frequently bounced head high and more. That is not bowling. Indeed it is not cricket, and if all fast bowlers were to adopt his methods there would be trouble and plenty of it. He would be a far better bowler if he concentrated on length and cut out all this short stuff. He is not doing justice to himself, his ability or to the game by such methods.

What Warner wrote would be remembered by Australian journalists in later months especially as Bowes was a last-minute selection approved by Warner for the MCC party and Jardine had faced him in that match at The Oval. For Jardine had been appointed captain of the side to go to Australia. It is not difficult to understand why Warner and his colleagues chose him. He was the reigning England captain (*already* appointed by Warner in 1931 against New Zealand) and a man of authority with a good cricket brain. Moral judgements apart (and this is to anticipate events), the technical skill of his captaincy went unquestioned, then and later. Warner wrote some years afterwards:

When in 1931 I came into closer contact with Jardine I realised – it was easy to do – that there was a man who was a thorough student of the game of cricket, keen and competent, one who had thought much and pondered deeply over the tactics and strategy of the game and, incidentally, a stern critic of his own cricketing abilities.

The coming tour appeared to him in the light of a crusade, and it was certain that he would put his whole soul and endeavour into the work in front of him. Backed by my colleagues, I recommended him to the MCC committee.

E. W. Swanton has written that the choice of Jardine 'was widely approved'. And, in the opinion of the survivors of the tour, there was at the time no other significant candidate. 'The ideal man when selected,' thought R. E. S. Wyatt – a generous comment from a man who had been captain at The Oval in 1930 and whom Warner had displaced. Warner would have brought down coals of fire on his head if Jardine had not been selected.

If added evidence of his abilities to play against the Australians were needed, two instances might be cited. He had made 96 not out as an Oxford undergraduate against the 1921 Australians and he had toured Australia in 1928–29.

Yet there were almost as many arguments why he should not have been chosen. Even the 'Australian' evidence was counter-productive to his cause. He had nursed a grievance against the 1921 Australians because they had insisted on playing a two-day game at Oxford to give themselves a rest day. Had they agreed to an extra over he would have got his century – though *Wisden* caustically reported that he might also have done so had he displayed 'a little more energy'. On the 1928–29 tour he had found it difficult to come to terms with the Australians as a people. Instances abounded of his aloofness and his inability to tolerate barracking. He had formed a dislike for Australians which would grow out of all proportion. He was, indeed, the current England captain – but only since 1931. Neither his university nor his country (until 1931) had invited him to lead a side. A few tongues wagged despondently at the appointment. His old schoolmaster at Winchester, Rockley Wilson, who had himself gone to Australia with the 1920–21 side, remarked that 'we would win the Ashes but we might lose a Dominion'. But, for good or ill, the deed was done.

At this stage in the argument, Warner might be blamed for choosing a man whom he must have known to be unacceptable to the Australians. How far ambassadorial qualities (or lack of them) mattered, is open to debate. P. G. H. Fender felt 'not very far' and he welcomed the choice of the man who had superseded him as captain of Surrey. Years later, Sir Donald Bradman told me, when discussing Hammond, that he regarded the captaincy of a touring team as needing 'the leadership and tact required of an overseas diplomat', qualities which Warner himself had had.

There is another aspect to Jardine's appointment which we cannot ignore – that he would be a 'hard' man against the Australians. He had been so against the Indians in the single Test in 1932. Warner and his fellow-selectors would have been severely criticised if they had passed him over for his qualities of 'hardness'. Memories of the Australians between 1921 and 1930 were too recent to allow that sort of emotional attitude to prevail. There is a certain irony, in the light of later events, in Warner's own approach to the matter of winning, for he – just as much as Jardine – sought success. His sense of history led him to hope that a side he had selected to go to Australia would be as successful as the two he had led there. So, with victory in mind, Warner gave Jardine the bowlers he wanted – Larwood, W. Voce, Allen and, at the last minute, Bowes. What a fast bowler with a packed leg-side field could achieve, he well knew. He had seen it, for instance, when W. B. Burns of Worcestershire had bowled against Middlesex in 1910 – though it did not do Burns much good! He got 0 for 28 in Middlesex's 361. Warner, after facing him for a few overs, was out to one of G. H. Simpson-Hayward's lobs. Foster had employed a similar attack in the 1911–12 tour of Australia in which Warner was captain. This much is not in dispute. What we must presently consider is how far Warner was aware of Jardine's thinking between his appointment and his arrival in Australia.

A month before the Surrey–Yorkshire match on which Warner had aired his views in the press, he had been appointed manager of the MCC tour. As early as February Lord Hawke had sounded him out about the possibility and Warner had spent 'several sleepless nights' before allowing his name to go forward, although it had not been on the original short-list. The MCC Committee met on 4 July and 'after careful consideration' Hawke's nomination of Warner was accepted as joint-manager with R. C. N. Palairet. Palairet was to look after the financial side, an area in which Warner's competence was doubted.

The appointment was greeted with some surprise not only because it was (then) unusual to nominate a former captain as manager, but also because Warner was both chairman of selectors and a journalist. Among those who toured with him, opinion was divided whether he was the right man to be chosen. Bowes believed that his journalism should have excluded him.

Later in the month, the MCC Committee considered a request from Warner that he be allowed to broadcast on the tour. He was told, however, he might broadcast on three occasions only and for no fee – at the start in Perth, in Sydney and at the end in New Zealand. A later Committee meeting in October turned down his written request to be allowed to broadcast in Adelaide during the third Test. Finally, Warner's financial terms were agreed upon: he would get £500 plus expenses, an arrangement he regarded as satisfactory.

On 17 September MCC sailed from Tilbury on the *Orantes*, cheered on their way from St Pancras and at the local stations en route. It was still true, in the 1930s, that no sporting occasion in the Empire matched the Anglo-Australian Test series.

To return to the question of Warner's awareness of his captain's plans: according to Jardine's daughter, as quoted in Laurence Le Quesne's *The Bodyline Controversy*, Warner and his fellow-selectors were certainly aware that he intended to use leg-theory during the tour, although Warner was not present at the dinner in a London hotel when Jardine discussed how to beat the Australians with Carr, the Nottinghamshire captain, and the county's fast bowlers, Larwood and Voce.

Once on board ship, there were inevitable discussions among players as to how they might win. Allen believed that none of these discussions raised the tactic which eventually became known as bodyline. He and Wyatt regarded it as something which evolved rather than was preconceived. As for Jardine, he kept himself very much apart from the team, mixing little and creating an aura of aloof authority. Both then and up until November 1932, in the collective opinion of the survivors, neither Warner nor anyone else really knew what Jardine proposed to do. Bowes commented, 'I doubt if Warner knew anything' and L. E. G. Ames remarked, 'in my view, he knew nothing'.

Although it might be fair to say that a man so close for so long to the corridors of cricket power and to the press box might have grasped that 'something was in the wind', the balance is very much in his favour that he was ignorant of Jardine's tactical planning. When the storm broke, his letters to his wife, hitherto unpublished – to which frequent reference will be made in this chapter – indicate a surprise which was not feigned.

Although it bore no relation to cricket policy, a letter from Allen to Agnes Warner written on 15 October when the party had been a month at sea is revealing in the light of later events:

There have been no rows and everyone seems very happy but I am terrified of Douglas [Jardine]. For a well-read and well-educated man he is easily the stupidest I know and conceited as well. I am not saying I don't like him, as I do, but one can't help noticing his shortcomings.

About the same time, Arthur Mailey noted the manager's role on board ship: 'He was the best chairman of a ship's sports committee I have ever met but what a dictator! and what an autocrat! He did things off his own bat without calling a committee meeting, consequently everything ran as smoothly as possible.' Mailey also noted the boyish enthusiasm with which Warner looked forward to seeing Australia again after 20 years.

It is difficult, in these days of instant travel and an abundance of sporting occasions of international calibre played out all over the world, to comprehend the immense excitement that the arrival of an English team 50 years ago caused in Australia. The Australian, while fiercely patriotic, felt cut off from 'home' by thousands of miles and months of travel – a 'home' to which he had never been and might never go. So the visitors were a link and they were at one with their hosts in the imperial connection. The Empire mattered and cricket was the Empire's game. Who better then to utter that philosophy to the waiting crowds at Fremantle in October 1932 than Pelham Warner – born in one far-flung outpost of Empire and twice a visiting captain in this other far-flung one? So he sounded the right imperial noises and no one blushed with embarrassment when he declared that cricket was the game that 'stood for all that is true and honest'.

To say 'that is not cricket' implies something underhand, something not in keeping with the best ideals. There is no game which calls forth so many fine attributes, which makes so many demands on its votaries, and, that being so, all who love it as players, as officials or spectators must be careful lest anything they do should do it harm.

An incautious attitude or gesture in the field, a lack of consideration in the committee-room and a failure to see the other side's point of view, a hasty judgement by an onlooker and a misconstruction of an incident may cause trouble and misunderstanding which could and should be avoided. This is the aim of the Marylebone Cricket Club, of which I am a humble if devoted servant, in sending teams to all parts of the world to spread the gospel of British fair play as developed in its national sport.

Someone in the crowd cried 'Bowes!' and asked, was Bowes the answer to Bradman and did not Bowes bowl bumpers? Warner replied, 'Bowes is a splendid bowler and have not fast bowlers bumped the ball before?' And in his 'permitted' broadcast from

Perth he hoped Bradman would play: the game will be the loser if he 'should not'.

J. H. Fingleton, both Test cricketer and journalist, believed that even in those expansive days of cricket and the Empire Warner overstated the case for British fair play as if he anticipated trouble and set out to place himself 'above the dust of the discord'. A tiny shadow, no bigger than a man's hand, had crept over the clear southern skies. The storm-clouds would gather.

On the same day as the team arrived in Fremantle, the Melbourne *Age* devoted a long article to the leadership qualities of both captain and manager. Jardine, for instance, was 'a man in whose hands the game would lose no credit'. The Australian cricket-loving public would find him 'a strong, purposeful leader, thorough to a degree, a sportsman who would scorn to take advantage of an opponent'. Warner brought 'the heart of a boy, the experience of a veteran and a vast accumulation of knowledge of inestimable value to the team he directs'. How far Warner would be allowed to offer such knowledge depended on his captain's view of the managerial role. Jardine quickly indicated that he regarded the manager as of no consequence in policy on the field and, in fairness to him, it was an accepted contemporary opinion. Only Ames, of the survivors, believed that Warner took too literally the view that he should not interfere with the tactics of the captain. The Sydney *Herald* also chose to feature the two men, calling Jardine 'astute, observant and possessing a brand of humour which people mistake for cynicism' and Warner 'a born diplomat whose personal charm, like wine, improves with age'.

After two matches at Perth, the party moved to Adelaide and Warner spoke at the dinner of the Oxford and Cambridge Association of South Australia. It was an atmosphere in which he was completely at ease. Ninety men of the two universities gathered in Adelaide when MCC played there and their guests were the Oxford and Cambridge men in the MCC side. Warner's speech consisted of witticisms about each of them, or of reminiscences of their fathers' times as undergraduates. What the austere Jardine made of a limerick about himself which began 'There was a young fellow of New' must be imagined. In retrospect the evening was one of the last occasions of the tour when Warner must have felt so contented and relaxed.

A few days later MCC met an Australian XI in Melbourne. Woodfull, the Australian captain, got hit over the head by a ball from Larwood. Its echo reverberated through the cricket world and, like the shots at Lexington in 1775, prefaced a colonial war. The picture told its own tale and the reporters told theirs.

Londoners read in the *Evening Standard* of 'supercharged fast bowling' and in the *Star* of 'very dangerous stuff'; the one remark, written by Bruce Harris who (then) did not know a great deal about cricket, the other by Hobbs who had faced Bowes just a few months earlier. If Jardine were setting out to soften up the Australians, he was succeeding. Before rain stopped play, Larwood had dismissed Woodfull and Bradman for a baker's dozen between them.

In the view of Fingleton (who carried his bat for 119 not out) the next game at Sydney brought 'bodyline in deadly earnest'. The press were beginning to coin the phrase (with a hyphen at that stage). To Fingleton, the hyphen seemed immaterial when you rubbed your bruises. He believed that from then onwards bad feeling existed between England and Australian players. His own mother was so shocked at the treatment her son received that she refused to go and see him play in the Test matches.

Meanwhile, in Sydney, Warner went to another Oxford and Cambridge dinner and (reasonably enough) told the same jokes. He met old friends of his previous visits to Australia at Lady Fairfax's cocktail party and chatted to the doctor who had attended him in 1911–12. But, as he wrote to his wife on 29 November before he left Sydney, he was now deeply in conflict with Jardine – not on policy at this stage but on attitudes:

D. R. Jardine is a very difficult fellow – such a queer nature – rather 'cruel' in some ways, and generally got his knife into some one for no reason at all. He is not easy or pleasant, really on the contrary but is *very* keen. Hates Australians and his special hate is now Bradman! Not an easy task to keep things nice and even, but so far, alright, but he is not the right fellow to be captain. Long ago, but for me, there would have been a row with the Press. He was entirely in the wrong as he was *very rude* to the Press for no reason at all. One *simply cannot* like him and I have tried very hard. He says cruel things of people and his language is poor at times. Not often but he uses awful words on occasions in talking, eg. of Bradman. He is very conceited, only He knows, and arrogant.[26]

He was also shocked at a remark Jardine made when some of the tourists went to look at the newly opened Sydney Bridge. Some aircraft of the Royal Australian Air Force flew over and Jardine turned to him and said, 'I wish they were Japs and I wish they'd bomb that bridge into their harbour.' The manager was appalled: this young captain, too young to have known war and drawing, perhaps, on what he had read about the Japanese bombing in Manchuria, so hated all things Australian.

So, within a few months of choosing Jardine as captain, Warner was regretting his decision but for him bodyline bowling was not yet the issue even if it were for the Australian players. He had added in his letter, 'our fast bowlers are very good: some of the Australians have got out to horrid strokes, thinking the ball is going to bounce and it goes on and hits the wicket'. This, of course, as Jardine demonstrated throughout the tour, was part of his overall strategy. A man experiencing short-pitched bowling might well fall to the one particular ball which was a full-length one.

Now for the first time, another word appeared which would re-echo in the months to come and which even had antecedents long before the tour. Warwick Armstrong, the old Australian captain, introduced it in his cable to the London *Evening News*, on the eve of the first Test: 'As to England's attack, I say frankly there will be trouble if the fast bowlers go for the body instead of the wicket. In Australia, bowling at the batsman is regarded as *unsportsmanlike.*'[27]

The first Test immediately after the New South Wales game was something of an anti-climax. Bradman was allegedly unfit to play,[28] no one was hurt by an English bowler, S. J. McCabe scored 187 not out off an English attack which had its share of high-rising balls and the Australian public, despite seeing a ten-wicket defeat, were confident that Bradman's return would be the assurance of success.

The match had ended after only a few minutes' play on the last day, England needing to take one wicket and then make one run. At the end of the previous evening, Warner made a telephone call to John at Eton who recalled the excitement of the occasion:

> I was told the evening before to expect the call at 10 past 8 in the morning. I went to my housemaster's study and heard the link-up, Paris? Colombo? Sydney? and then my father's voice, 'the Australians are coming off the field at 164 for 9 which makes their score, after two innings, level with our 524. They're coming in the pavilion as I talk to you. . .' Then we couldn't think of what to say to each other. He said it was 'hot', I said it was 'cold' and that was that!

So John went into his house for breakfast announcing he was the first person in England to know the Test match score. It had been an imaginative gesture on his father's part to accept the offer of a free telephone call to England from the Australian broadcasting authorities and make it to a schoolboy. He had given his 'statutory' middle of the tour broadcast, as allowed by MCC, but his contract forbade him to take payment for it. It was something pleasant to remember in the dark days immediately ahead.

For within a few days of the Test, as MCC were making their way from Wagga Wagga to Launceston in Tasmania, the Sydney *Referee* of 14 December launched a full-blooded attack on Warner. It called him a 'double personality' finding what was 'abhorrent to him in English county cricket, the very essence of true sports-manship in Australia'. His words from the *Morning Post* of the previous August had been thrown back at him and he had replied, first of all, 'misreported' then, 'I'm not allowed to give interviews', pressing the paper to make no reference to having even been questioned. W. M. Ruttledge, the reporter, with almost the entire front page of the paper at his disposal, ended with the statement that while Warner in England 'had no authority to check Bowes', he had 'in Australia very wide and definite powers as manager'.

> Without challenge he can exert disciplinary action upon any member of the team. And he can, if he chooses, stop this short-pitched body theory that he so strongly abhorred before he left England. He is, by his official indifference, helping to breed a feeling of bitterness, not only between the opposing teams, but between the peoples of the two countries of the Empire.

So the storm had broken and Warner wrote, rather lamely, to Findlay, the MCC secretary, 'it would be silly to disregard the hostile feeling which has been created by this type of bowling. One of these days there will be a terrible accident.' But he added that Larwood 'kept more or less a length'. The letter reached Lord's during the second Test – which Australia won by 111 runs. By the same post, Findlay got a letter from Jardine:

> So far our bowling has in general been a shock and an unpleasant surprise to the old hands in Australia. The papers have put up a squeal rising to a whine about bowling at the man. Nothing of the sort but we have by dint of hard and, I hope, clear thinking got a field suitable for attacking the leg stump.

The fact that the Australians won that second Test at Melbourne over the New Year period led Findlay, back at Lord's, to assume that no great crisis existed. He replied to Warner that it was 'difficult to discover here to what extent this leg-theory' was being used. To those back in England, such as Findlay, the state of play between England and Australia might be seen as a 'draw' in two senses; both sides had won a game and, in the second Test, Bradman had scored a duck and a not-out century. Although the England attack was directed primarily at his dismissal, honours were even. There were, of course, things that hardly anyone knew such as Allen's refusal to bowl to a packed leg-side field.[29] Allen, as an amateur, could afford to take an independent line and, to his great credit, he did so. He indicated his intentions to Warner, who was upset at this sign of dissension in the camp and remarked that one of the reasons Allen had been picked was for his ability to 'get on so well with Douglas'.

The criticism of the Sydney *Referee* in December was followed by that of the Melbourne *Truth* in January, on the eve of the third Test: 'Australia is fed up to the neck with the hypocritical humbug of Captain Jardine and sees little to enthuse over in the seemingly guileless evasions of manager "Plum" Warner.' The manager, remaining outwardly uncommunicative, wrote to his wife that he felt good 'off-the-field work' by himself could compensate for Jardine's attitude to the press and to the public. It was an optimistic assessment of events as they stood. It was not proving a happy tour.

The Adelaide Oval, its pastoral mood enhanced by the backcloth of the Lofty Mountains, provides a gentle and beautiful setting across the river Torrens from the city of spacious streets and unhurried pace. On the surface, it was the least likely of places in which the sparks of a smouldering dispute would leap into flame with all the urgency and terror of a forest fire in the nearby mountains themselves.

Yet embers there were all too ready to be ignited when circumstances arose. The Adelaide Test became the occasion, and the mood of the State of South Australia the contributory cause. Sir Alexander Hore-Ruthven, the Governor, believed there was a sensitivity among the people which bode ill for progress and which contributed to a gathering economic crisis. In his confidential report to the Dominions Secretary in London he wrote, of the population of South Australia as a whole:

It is a difficult matter to open their eyes to the fact that they have much to learn from the outside world. The slightest hint from an outsider that all is not perfection, causes offence at once. The narrow and confined outlook of the people is in inverse proportion to the breadth and expanse of the country, and accounts a good deal for the lack of progress.

If this were true – and the whole career of Hore-Ruthven in Australia over 17 years suggests that he understood the country very well – then offence might well be taken in more than just a cricketing sense to the events which took place at Adelaide Oval in January 1933. On the political and economic state of the Commonwealth of Australia as a whole there will be occasion to comment later in this chapter.

All roads, on Saturday 14 January 1933, led to the Adelaide Oval where 50,000 people (one in ten of the total population) packed themselves into the ground. England resumed at 236 for 7. Hopes among the crowd that they might see Australia bat before lunch were dashed and it was three o'clock before Woodfull and Fingleton opened the Australian innings. Fingleton went at once to the popular English (but Australian-born) Allen. Larwood bowled the second over to Woodfull to an orthodox field and Woodfull staggered away from the wicket, hit on the heart, as he had been at Melbourne. One over later, with a packed leg-side field, Larwood knocked Woodfull's bat out of his hand. Before the close of play, Bradman and McCabe had both been dismissed by Larwood, Woodfull had gone to Allen and the Australians had scored 109 for 4.

Such is the tale in barest detail. It says nothing of the antagonism of the crowd or of their booing and shouting. It does not convey the picture of the magisterial Jardine in his Harlequin cap and silk scarf coolly and determinedly placing his ring of leg-side fielders for Voce and Larwood. It ignores the genuine concern of English fielders, whom only a fence preserved from invading hordes. It stands aside from umpires and fielders contemplating who could grab a defending stump quickest. It forgets the wretched Warner watching helplessly from the pavilion.

The dénouement of the day's events has often been told. Warner walked the few steps from the English dressing room to the Australian one. Little has changed in the 50 years since: the masseur's bed stands in one corner of a room cluttered with the impedimenta of the cricketer's trade. Warner hesitated, knocked at the door and heard someone shout, 'come in'. The place was full of young men, angry and upset at the chain of events. The frail figure in his panama hat and light suit cast a nervous glance around until he saw Woodfull. Various versions of the conversation exist. In essence, Woodfull said, 'I don't want to speak to you, Mr Warner. There are two teams out there; one is playing cricket the other is not. It is too great a game to spoil. The matter is in your hands.' Warner left to return to the English dressing room, shaken, in tears and terribly upset. It was an image remembered by all who saw it.

Warner – the epitome of all the game stood for; the quintessence of sportsmanship and high ideals; the chevalier of cricket – had been identified with a rejection of the very standards he had devoted his life to upholding. 'The matter is in your hands,' Woodfull had said. If there be a day in Warner's life after which the world was never quite the same again, it was Saturday 14 January 1933.

The incident was manna to the press. Warner always believed that Fingleton made it public and he was so upset that a dressing room conversation should become world news overnight that he offered a guinea to anyone who could dismiss Fingleton (which Larwood duly did) in the remainder of the Test. Fingleton denied the fact and resented Warner reiterating his opinion in his *Cricket Between Two Wars* in 1942. Warner's conclusions were based on no sort of evidence and their repetition did him no credit, the more so as he and Fingleton exchanged friendly letters in the intervening years, and Fingleton's family entertained Esmond at their home in Canberra in 1937. In his final book, *Batting from Memory* published in 1981, Fingleton wrote, 'Warner was being more than naïve, in the tumult and tenseness of those times, if he thought a story like that wouldn't surface from the Australian dressing-room.'

A second consequence arose out of Warner's own statement to the Australian press that Woodfull had apologised. Woodfull denied it and stood by his original remark. This, too, filled the Australian Monday evening papers, at the same time as Warner met representatives of the ABC who asked him to ensure that bodyline bowling was given up. Warner replied he had no responsibility for tactics on the field. In the opinion of all the survivors of the tour, Warner's reply was a reasonable one though Ames believed that 'had Warner been a stronger personality, he might have persuaded Jardine to alter the tactics'. But, he added, 'had Warner insisted there would have been a first-class rumpus, the consequences of which could have been disastrous'. All felt that Warner's loyalty to MCC and to its captain were paramount factors and governed his attitude. Understandably, the Australians at the time took a different view and were not impressed. Warner's silence henceforth was seen as a subject for criticism and his previously quoted opinions a theme for rebuke.

Between the Monday and Thursday, the match took its course, including the injury to W. A. Oldfield whose personal exoneration of Larwood from blame did nothing to placate public opinion. England won by 338 runs, but what happened on the field was, in a sense, subservient to events off it. The ABC sent off their first cable to MCC containing the emotive word 'unsportsmanlike' in its description of the policy being pursued by the English team. Warner's proffered advice on how the cable might be drafted was ignored, understandably since he had indicated he could not interfere in tactics.

There was another way in which Warner could have interfered. He could have telephoned MCC at Lord's. With the benefit of hindsight two of the survivors of the tour thought he should have done, and had he done so he would have been given 'plenipotentiary powers' to act as he thought fit. Those who felt he should not have done so argued that the poor telephonic reception of the days would have led to 'vital words and passages being lost' and to misunderstanding. There was also, in Warner's mind, as a letter to Agnes indicated, the very real hope that events might still be contained.

By the evening of Wednesday 18 January all England could read the contents of the cable in the London and provincial evening papers, while the Thursday morning papers, published a few hours after the Test itself ended, carried comments such as the *Daily Herald*'s belief that there should be 'no sentimental climbdown', and accused the Australians of 'undignified snivelling'.

The Times stated:

It is inconceivable that a cricketer of Jardine's standing chosen by the MCC to captain an England side would ever dream of allowing or ordering bowlers under his command to practise any system of attack that is not cricket. In all probability the present delicate and difficult position would never have arisen but for the irresponsible chatter of elderly critics in the pavilion and in the press and the craving in some quarters for sensational news-stories which has magnified words or incidents natural enough in the heat of a hard-fought battle.

Sewell wrote in the *Daily Sketch*, 'what kind of effeminacy has entered Australian cricket that relations are supposed to be jeopardised for such trivialities?'

Among those who challenged the prevailing opinion was Neville Cardus, in the *Manchester Guardian*. After the second day's play he had written that 'the morality of such bowling' was open to question. On 17 January he spoke of 'violence and intimidation'. The leading article, probably also written by him, declared:

If this is how Tests are played, we would be better off without them. This happy game has been translated during the Tests to the very stratosphere of gloom, as though the acrimonious explosions could only fitly be dealt with by the League Council, Assembly, and Committee of Nineteen. Therefore, we might cancel the remaining two Tests and agree to play no more for ten years, by which time we might have made the great decision to play them in a friendly way without humbug, or never again.

Cardus was in Manchester and his writing was influenced by the reports of the Australian papers.

The Daily Telegraph reported the views of cricketers of an older generation (Warner's generation, indeed), in Ranjitsinhji and Jackson. Both men were critical, Jackson in particular, drawing the distinction between 'leg-theory' and short-pitched bowling. Among other cricketers who expressed concern in varying degrees were Foster, who had been Warner's fast left-arm bowler in 1911–12 and A. E. R. Gilligan, the captain of the 1924–25 MCC side. Foster, especially, voiced disapproval, the more so as Jardine had picked his brains before departing for Australia. But in Australia, the Board's cable was not without its critics within the Australian press. The Melbourne *Herald* felt it was 'holding a pistol at the head of the English authorities', and the *Age* said that nothing could 'justify the terms of the cable'.

After the Test had ended, *The Times* still refused to take events in Australia seriously. Its fourth leader, traditionally an occasion for humour or satire, on the following day was entitled 'The Bowler Hat'. It suggested that bowler hats might be worn by batsmen against certain bowlers – 'would they arouse as much barracking as a Harlequin cap?' In the next column, in letters to the editor, A. A. Milne asked if the time had come to admit that cricket was a game for batsmen only.

While the English nation was making up its mind where it stood, MCC was thinking out its own position. Findlay, the MCC secretary, on Wednesday morning 18 January, had on his desk the Australian cable together with ones from Jardine and from Warner, whose texts have not survived. A letter written that morning by Findlay to Lacey contains a draft reply cable and it throws some light on what Jardine and Warner between them may have said.

Much regret contents of your cable. Marylebone assured that no English bowler bowls at the man but at leg stump which is said to be the weakness of certain batsmen. Cricketers of today have not had great experience of fast bowling and the open stance of batsmen necessarily increases risk. Of all considerations friendly relations and the game itself paramount. If remaining Tests cannot be played in this spirit and appreciated by players and spectators alike would it not be well to consider substitution of state games.[30]

Two days later, on the suggestion of the president of MCC, Lord Lewisham, another cable was drafted whose last sentence read differently from the earlier one: 'If Australian Board consider that Larwood is too fast a bowler to be safe on present Australian wickets Marylebone feel sure that Jardine would give the utmost consideration to their view.' Privately, Findlay noted that the ABC were rather tiresome gentlemen and that the fuss was rather unfortunate. He completed a busy few days by cabling to Jardine, 'best congratulations. Thank you all very much.'

The English players joined in the applause from London by taking the unusual step of issuing a press statement declaring they were 'and always have been, utterly loyal to their captain under whose leadership they hope to achieve an honourable victory'. They did this partly because of wild rumour in the Australian papers of internal dissension and even beer-throwing.

How much this public display of loyalty to the captain owed to Warner may be conjectured. Ames believed that some credit was due to him for encouraging a gesture which might 'save the tour from complete disaster'. Wyatt believed Warner was in close contact with some of the players, such as Hammond, but doubted whether he would have raised the issue of loyalty. F. R. Brown, the youngest in the party and on the periphery of events, had no doubts at all about the sense of collective loyalty which the team felt. Larwood considered that Warner's concern to demonstrate collective loyalty arose from a desire to win which was almost as strong as Jardine's, and that under that 'dignified and affable exterior there was a shrewd brain and dominating personality that would not hesitate to drive home any advantage'. It is a view which, as so often, does not accord with the private despair Warner felt.

Yet the issuing of such a statement at all was a little tongue-in-cheek. Loyalty to Jardine was expressed but nothing said about bowling on which it is known differing views were held. From later evidence, Wyatt, Allen and Hammond were all known to disapprove of the captain's policy.

Jardine had had a vote of confidence from both the players and the majority of the English press and it would have been difficult, at this stage, for Warner to distance himself from him in public. To Agnes he wrote from Sydney on 27 January:

I wish Martin Hawke would not make speeches. He always says something stupid. I think the Board will withdraw the word 'unsportsmanlike' – they certainly ought to, and then things may be happier. I am hoping that this wretched row will die down. The Board's telegram was silly, tactless and rude.

To have been so critical of his good friend of so many years – 'my best pal,' as he had told Agnes in 1904 – suggests how tense the whole affair had made him. Hawke's major 'crime', as reported in the Australian press, had been to say 'remember the 1921 Tests'. And the Warner who had vilified Jardine so much in an earlier letter described to his wife how he and the captain had made up a four with two ladies and gone to a supper party and dance. Warner's evening was 'made' when his partner told him 'she wished some of the young men danced as well' as he did. Another dinner party, a piano recital and some tennis provided a weekend far more enjoyable than that at Adelaide the week before.

But while the word 'unsportsmanlike' was the spectre at the feast there could be no real cause for joy. By the end of January, the English press were looking for some firm answers. Cardus returned to the attack. He wrote in the *Observer* on 29 January, in lines clearly directed at Warner:

> The Australians object to a deliberately planned attack made up largely of half-pitched, high-kicking balls which look to be dangerous to limb, if not to life, and which compel a batsman to think first of all of his personal safety. If the bowling of Larwood and Voce in Australia has not in any way justified this impression of it, why have we not received an emphatic denial of these accusations by somebody in responsibility on the spot?

Cardus was still running against the tide of opinion in England and the second Australian cable published the next day, though moderate in its language, echoed the same sentiments about 'dangerous' bowling which he himself had done. The English press, as a whole, were not prepared to be told that England's bowling was contrary to the 'spirit of cricket'.

Meanwhile, world events of more significance than cricket were taking place. On 1 February the press was full of Hitler's assumption of the chancellorship of the Reich, 'the summit of his ambitions'. Jardine's ambitions, said *The Times*, taking up the word, must be to win the Ashes and 'with the full support of MCC, to employ such methods, allowed by the laws of cricket, as he considers most likely to win the game'. It was not bodyline bowling which would bring England and Australia to loggerheads, but barracking.

Most of the Australian press had criticised Warner immediately after the third Test, the Sydney *Referee* repeating his words in the *Morning Post* of the previous August and adding: 'P. F. Warner's opinion was written by him just before the Englishmen left the Homeland on their present tour; and he has since maintained an indefensible silence, while he sees our batsmen's bodies being battered and bruised, and the game of cricket heading to its doom.'

Then the Australian press discovered and reported the most damning piece of evidence yet to show where they thought Warner ought to have stood. He had written in his article on 'Captaincy' in the 1920 edition of the Badminton Library volume on cricket:

> It is, of course, nearly always possible in a one, two or three days' match to prevent your opponents winning, in the event of their getting level or ahead of the clock, by instructing your bowlers to bowl a good length outside the leg stump, with six or seven fieldsmen on the leg-side, but for ourselves, and we believe the vast majority of cricketers, *we regard such tactics as unsportsmanlike, and quite contrary to the spirit and traditions of the game; and we would scorn such a manoeuvre, and would rather suffer a hundred defeats than put it into practice.*[31]

Here was the very word 'unsportsmanlike' being used a dozen years earlier by the England manager of tactics on which he now uttered no comment. It gave pertinence to what the old Australian Clem Hill had said to him at Adelaide one evening, 'come off the fence, Plum'.

It was at this point that the politicians began to take an interest. Stanley Baldwin, a former and future British Prime Minister and a future president of MCC, wrote to Findlay approving of the MCC cable. Findlay replied that he was glad Baldwin approved and added that he had heard 'our fellows have had a pretty bad time'.

More significant than Baldwin's interest was the concern of the Dominions Secretary, J. H. Thomas, who arranged a meeting on 1 February at his office. He was joined by the Attorney-General, Sir Thomas Inskip (also a member of MCC), and a delegation from MCC led by the president, Lord Lewisham. That the entire MCC group were all noblemen or knights and that the youngest was Sir Stanley Jackson (a mere 62!) is an indication of the sort of men serving on the MCC committee. They were men of wisdom (if age begets wisdom) with the experience and ability to make tempered judgements. Their careers had been in politics, law and diplomacy and they understood the importance of preserving relationships within the Empire. But with the distinct exception of Jackson (a former England captain), they were less able to contemplate the nature of what exactly had happened in Australia. They were joined by Hore-Ruthven and it was he, in the context of that meeting and of later events, who really mattered.

Hore-Ruthven was a man of outstanding qualities. As a young officer serving in Egypt at the end of the nineteenth century he had won the Victoria Cross. He had first come to Australia in 1908 as military secretary to the Governor-General. He was several times decorated in the First World War and retired from the army as a Brigadier in 1928. He was appointed Governor of South Australia and his tenure of office coincided with a difficult phase in internal politics, involving a split in the Labour Party, and bringing the Governor dangerously close to political involvement. The tact and diplomacy with which he handled matters won him popularity and respect in almost all quarters so that in 1934, when his governorship expired, he assumed a similar post in New South Wales where, again, political problems dominated the scene. Hore-Ruthven's continuing success led to his appointment as Governor-General, at the urgent suggestion of the Australian Prime Minister, in 1936. Lord Gowrie, as he became, continued in office until 1945. Throughout his time in Australia, he made it his business to understand the mood and the temper of Australian people in all walks of life. The hallmarks of his career were a sense of goodwill and imperturbable commonsense. These qualities were brought to bear on the cricketing crisis which had arisen. He continued to offer his advice and judgement in the following years, and his letters to Warner, as we shall see in the next chapter, throw an important light on his assessment of Australian attitudes. He also used Warner as a vehicle for conveying his opinions to MCC. Eventually Gowrie himself became president of MCC in 1948, appropriately enough a year in which the Australians were the tourists.

All this is to anticipate. Hore-Ruthven was on leave in England at the time of the Adelaide Test and it was a telegram from his private secretary, Legg Winser, which urged him to ask for the Dominions Office meeting. Winser, who was well known in political and cricket circles in South Australia (where he had been secretary to successive Governors since 1915), had been approached by influential businessmen in the city to get the Governor to act quickly. Hore-Ruthven did so.

All were agreed that moderation must prevail. After the meeting

Lord Ullswater told Findlay that a cable should go to Australia making the assumption that 'the good sportsmanship of our team is not in question' and these were the words employed, cast into a rhetorical question (in a cable!) in the message sent the next day, 3 February, to the ABC. A spokesman for Thomas told the press that the Dominions Office had not been in touch with British representation in Australia, adding that for the Dominions Secretary 'to intervene in an official capacity' would be absurd. Maybe, but Thomas was to leave on record that no political issue in the British Empire had caused him so much trouble during his tenure of office.

Up to 1 February Thomas had not contacted Britain's accredited representative in Australia but Warner had. Immediately after his relaxed weekend in Sydney, MCC had gone north to Toowoomba in Queensland and on the very day (1 February) on which the Dominions Office meeting was taking place in London, he sent a telegram to the head of the British Mission in Canberra, E. T. Crutchley, who had travelled back from leave in England on the same ship as the MCC party: 'Have under consideration cancellation of remaining matches of tour including Test owing to failure of Board to withdraw stigma of word unsportsmanlike in their first cable. Beg you use your influence to get word withdrawn. Matter very urgent.'

It was the first positive step Warner had taken to bring the matter to a head. Crutchley approached Joseph Lyons, the Australian Prime Minister, to see if any bargaining were possible: in effect, the English were 'sportsmen' if they modified their bowling. Crutchley wrote in his diary:

I phoned the PM at Melbourne. He said to start with, 'It looks as though we were leading two armies'. I told him exactly what had happened and he agreed that the cancellation of the tour would be a very grave thing, for Australia especially, just when feeling was so good. He promised to get hold of Dr Robertson, chairman of the Board of Control, and see what could be done.

On that same day, the Prime Minister saw A. W. D. Robertson and sought the withdrawal of the offending word. In a telegram which Robertson sent to W. H. Jeanes, the secretary of ABC, he wrote, 'if we do withdraw, no doubt attack [i.e.: bowling] will be modified. Government afraid success of Conversions endangered.' To the significance of this last point we will return later.

Because a postal official revealed Warner's telegram to Crutchley to the press, his initiative in negotiating with the Australian

Government was known all over Australia and in London (just) before the MCC cable of 3 February was dispatched. Palairet, the other manager, made one of his rare interventions on the whole issue when he told a reporter at Toowoomba that it was no use denying that an approach had been made to Crutchley and he hoped it would prove fruitful.

Warner himself was in Brisbane and he entered into discussions with the ABC representatives there on the weekend of 4–5 February. The Brisbane *Telegraph*, welcoming the talks, wrote, 'it is time that oil was poured on troubled waters. The matter has been drifting so far from the realms of cricket proper that a commonsense attitude by all parties is long overdue. The situation that has developed is likely to make the game a laughing stock.' The paper also reported that Warner had let slip to journalists on the train to Brisbane that he thought bodyline would ruin the game. In the jargon of the 1980s one might call it a deliberate 'leak'. Combined with the result of the discussions, suddenly it seemed relations between England and Australia were becoming as warm as the Brisbane climate when the ABC agreed to withdraw the word 'unsportsmanlike' unequivocally. Warner wrote to Agnes that he had had to stick to his guns on that point.

To the question, how far Warner deserved credit for his part in this, Ames replied, 'unreservedly yes'. No one else was quite so emphatic but Wyatt believed he had done his very best 'to ensure better relations'. Clearly his role in the direct cricketing negotiations is important but it cannot be detached from the political factors – and it was he who had approached Crutchley. We must pursue that cryptic comment 'success of Conversions endangered', and to do so we must plough, however lightly, the furrows of contemporary Australian politics.

The Commonwealth of Australia is a federation, inaugurated in 1901. As such there are certain powers acquired by the Federal Government, and a residual legislative power left in the hands of each State. Both Federal and State politics had significance for Anglo-Australian relationships in the 1930s. Australia had shared in the economic consequence of the Depression and, like Britain, had experienced political instability in the process. The Federal Government in 1932–33 (to use the years of the MCC tour) was led by Lyons, a Labour politician who headed a United Australia party. The parallel with Britain's National Government under Ramsay MacDonald is close. The State Government of South Australia, whose capital was Adelaide, scene of the third Test, was led by L. L. Hill, a Labour politician kept in office by Conservative support. The State Government of New South Wales, in whose capital of

Sydney a final farewell dinner to MCC would take place, was led by B. S. B. Stevens, who also headed a United Australia party.

Thus, at Federal level and at two relevant State levels, government depended on some form of coalition or other. In each case, the coalition was sympathetic to the British link at a time when there were some Labour politicians in Opposition who advocated a more Nationalist approach. This factor, albeit entirely accidental, did much to reduce the tension when the bodyline crisis was at its peak. Warner, in approaching Lyons through an intermediary (Crutchley), was approaching an experienced politician, tried in the fire of Australia's great political crisis of 1929–31 and ready to do all he could to prevent the cricket crisis of 1933 getting out of hand.

The political situation was closely linked to the economic one. The coalitions at both Federal and State level had come about partly because of differing views on how to restore financial stability after the collapse of the economy in 1929. Overseas confidence in Australia had been lost, wheat and wool prices had fallen, and exports had declined. British investors, in particular, had suffered by the suspension of payments on government bonds in New South Wales. Lyons had come to power, at Federal level, pledged to create economic recovery. In 1933 he proposed to float a £17 million conversion loan on the London Stock Exchange. British holders of existing Australian State Loans were to be asked to convert them into a new 4 per cent Commonwealth Loan and British Treasury approval would be needed for the new Overseas Issue.

Hence, the stark cry in Lyons' telegram to the ABC, 'Government afraid success of Conversions endangered.' If Anglo-Australian relationships really were seriously damaged, the British Government would not feel it the right moment to approve a new issue of Stock affecting Australia nor would the British investor be enthusiastic about investment there. To a country seeking much needed capital, the consequences were alarming. One doubts if Warner understood much about this though the subject of money was a constant personal worry! But the matter serves to show into what deep waters the manager had now been plunged.

Hard political and economic facts had therefore played as much a part as had dialogue between cricket administrators in easing the immediate crisis. And on 8 February Warner could take stock on the eve of the fourth Test and write a long letter to Agnes:

> Queensland Club
> Brisbane.

Nothing can compensate me for the moral and intellectual

damage which I have suffered on this tour. D.R.J. is very trying and is now a bundle of nerves. Job, Balaam's Ass and PFW are the three most patient men that ever lived! D.R.J. is half-mad but the men are splendid and stick to me when I tell them that only the end matters. Bear with him until we win (or lose) and then say what you like to him. Hammond says I 'have a wonderful nature and character'. He is a great fellow both on and off the field. Obby [Allen] is a great help and such a good cricketer. But they are all good fellows and very loyal and patient but D.R.J. must not captain again. He is most ungracious, rude and suspects all. He really is a very curious character and varies like a barometer. He is very efficient but inconsistent in his character and no leader. I ought to get a prize for Patience or Tact and good temper if not a Knighthood!! 75% of the trouble is due to D.R.J.'s personality. We all think that. D.R.J. has almost made me hate cricket. He makes it war. I do hope the Test will go happily. I rather dread it.

It was the fullest picture which Warner has provided of his opinion of Jardine. None of the survivors of the tour felt that his public relations with Jardine were good despite an outward display of loyalty. One player believed that any rapport between the two men ceased after Jardine's rudeness to Warner on board the *Orantes*. Another remarked that a relationship was 'non-existent'.

The letter also throws light on Warner's association with the players as a whole. His comment that they were 'all good fellows' was a judgement which they broadly reciprocated. Towards them he was 'friendly and warm' and those who turned to him with any problem received a lot of sympathy and found him a good listener. It was a tour in which the amateur–professional barriers fell considerably and he made a strong contribution to that change. To Ames, 'he had the interests of every individual very much at heart'. Only one of the survivors thought otherwise. One also suspects that the links between Warner and Hammond were firmly forged on this tour. He, Wyatt and Allen would all be appointed England captains in their turn by Warner.[32]

One person to whom Warner could turn was his brother-in-law Ormond Blyth, who had retired from business and come out to Australia to see the cricket. With him he could relax and talk about family affairs such as the arrival of Betty's wedding photograph, followed by the news of her tonsillitis; how much money Warner was *not* spending on the tour and the state of Agnes's shares; and

1   (top left) Charles Warner,
PFW's father.

2   (above) Ellen Rosa Cadiz,
PFW's mother.

3   (left) In Port of Spain, Trinidad,
aged 6, 1880.

4 Lord's as PFW would have seen it in the 1880s. *(BBC Hulton Picture Library)*

5 Ninety-nine not out at lunch. Rugby v. the Free Foresters, 1890.

6   The Ran Dan Wine Club at Oriel, 1894. R. C. N. Palairet (centre), the president, was succeeded by PFW. They would be joint-managers of MCC in 1932–33.

7   Oxford University XI, 1895. Back row: R. P. Lewis, H. A. Arkwright, G. B. Raikes, G. O. Smith. Middle row: F. A. Phillips, H. D. G. Leveson Gower, G. J. Mordaunt, C. B. Fry, H. K. Foster. Front row: P. F. Warner, F. H. E. Cunliffe.

8 Batting for Lord Hawke's XI v. St Vincent, 1898. His 156 was 'the most magnificent score in the annals of the island'. *(MCC)*

9 MCC in Australia, 1903–4. Back row: A. A. Lilley, A. E. Knight, A. Fielder, E. Arnold, A. E. Relf, L. C. Braund. Middle row: J. T. Tyldesley, R. E. Foster, P. F. Warner, G. H. Hirst, B. J. T. Bosanquet, T. Hayward. Front row: H. Strudwick, W. Rhodes.

10   Setting off in Sydney for the first Test, 1903–4. *(MCC)*

11   (left) A cartoonist's view of England's victory in the first Test at Sydney, 1903–4. *(The Bystander)*

12   (below) PFW at the time of his marriage, 1904.

13 Agnes Blyth at the time of her marriage, 1904.

14 PFW's XI v. Bearsted, 1907.

15   Caring House in Kent, the Warners' country home from 1906 to 1920.

16   Agnes, Esmond and Betty on the beach at Cromer, 1910.
PFW, the photographer.

17   MCC in Australia, 1911–12. Back row: H. Strudwick, S. P. Kinneir, E. J. Smith, F. E. Woolley, J. Iremonger, C. P. Mead, J. W. Hearne, W. Hitch, J. Vine. Front row: S. F. Barnes, W. Rhodes, J. W. H. T. Douglas, P. F. Warner, F. R. Foster, J. B. Hobbs, G. Gunn.

18   C. A. Macartney c. PFW b. Blythe at Lord's, August 1917. This was Blythe's last wicket before his death in France three months later.

the first hint that he might not be working for the *Morning Post* on his return to England.

If the fourth Test, which began on 10 February, had been an occasion similar to the third, there would have been grounds for Warner to dread it. Luckily for him (and we may feel he needed a bit of luck by this time), it was a reasonably even contest until the closing stages. Voce was unfit, the wicket was even-paced, the weather was too hot even for Larwood and no one was hurt. Six days later England had won the Ashes. The only 'brush' between manager and captain had been over Jardine's insistence that E. Paynter return from his hospital bed to bat. Jardine's answer to Warner's remonstration was one calculated to appeal to Warner's use of military analogies – 'what about those fellows who marched to Kandahar with fever on them?'

The telegrams poured in: 'Splendid, well played all. My heartiest congratulations' from the MCC president. 'Well Bowled. Congratulations. Marylebone.' from the Club. 'Heartiest congratulations to you and your team' from Ramsay MacDonald, the British Prime Minister. Even J. H. Thomas, no doubt mightily relieved, joined in: 'Bravo, the Ashes are won. But they are secondary to the great fighting spirit and good sportsmanship shown by both sides.' Finally came the royal accolade: 'As patron of the MCC I wish to convey to the team in Australia my warmest congratulations on their victory. I have followed with closest interest the ups and downs of the match. George R.' George V, as King of Australia, presumably had to be neutral in his allegiance. As patron of MCC he was perhaps allowed some royal bias.

Woodfull went to the English dressing room with his congratulations. That evening there was a reception at Government House, Brisbane. Warner spoke of the loyalty Jardine, as captain, had inspired. The press of both nations was almost unanimous in its praise of Jardine's leadership. The Brisbane *Mail* probably came nearest to a sound appraisal when it said 'whether the body theory is right or wrong one must admire Jardine as a skilled tactician and an exceptionally clear thinker about the game. He can have very few equals among England's captains.' *The Times* wrote, 'the biggest factor in England's success has been the captaincy of Jardine. He has beaten the Australians at their own game.' The sourest note again came from Cardus in the *Manchester Guardian*. Quoting Dr Johnson, he wrote of Jardine's philosophy of cricket, 'knock the man down first and be compassionate afterwards'.

On the day England regained the Ashes, Archie Jackson died at the age of 23. He had been the youngest Australian to make a Test century on debut in 1928–29 and he had come to England with the

1930 side. Ill-health dogged him thereafter but as late as the time of the Adelaide Test he was able to make 77 in a Grade match at Brisbane. He had watched something of the series and wrote for the Sydney *Mail*, 'may it be left to the cricketers themselves to furnish the only possible answer to the legitimate tactics employed by the Englishmen'. It was a generous view of events by a great Australian player whom Warner visited in Ingarfield Hospital, Brisbane, during the Test on the day before he died. Later, Warner was asked to preach at a memorial service in Balmain Central Methodist mission in Sydney, 'a compliment and a gesture', he wrote to Agnes, 'which showed clearly that amidst all the trouble there was still some good feeling remaining'.

A few days later, at the age of 59, he made an appearance on the field of play himself for MCC against Northern Districts at Newcastle, scoring a single and being in the field while A. G. Chipperfield, a future Test player, made 152. It was nearly thirty years since he had first played on Australian soil as captain of Hawke's team against Victoria.

By now the tour was in its closing stages. He made an attempt to get Jardine to agree to abandon bodyline for the final Test but without success. After the calmness of the fourth Test the players were inclined to think it was no longer an issue and all the survivors saw it very much as a personal gesture on Warner's part. Indeed, the Test was broadly free from incident although Bradman was hit for the first time by Larwood, and Jardine himself was hit by H. H. Alexander. The crowd cheered at this, 'a disgraceful exhibition', wrote *Wisden*. But they also cheered, crowning irony, when Larwood (sent in as night-watchman) made 98. Their applause, and their genuine regret at his not getting a century, emphasised the Australian attitude throughout the summer; Jardine, as the instigator of a particular policy, was the target for attack, Larwood was only the paid professional instrument of that policy, a man to be welcomed in Australia when, 16 years later, he made his home there.

During the match there was a dinner given by the New South Wales Government. Everyone who was anyone in State and in cricket circles was invited. The speeches set out to leave a pleasant taste at the end of what had been a bitter tour. The speech of the premier of New South Wales must have caused many an Australian player to have gulped down his drink and leap for another one quickly:

[W]hen they say a thing is 'not cricket', they express an attitude of mind common to Australia and England. Our visitors have played cricket in the best traditions of the British people. Our function tonight has been primarily to show our appreciation of the sportsmanlike manner in which they have played the game throughout the Tests.

To such remarks Jardine had no need to plead *mea culpa* nor, of course, in any circumstances would he have done so. Warner's speech was slightly sentimental, a little sad and a far cry from what he privately thought. He hoped, the press reported, that the 'little ruffles on the surface would be forgotten and everything unpleasant relegated to the dustheap of oblivion'. He congratulated Jardine on the fighting spirit he had shown and he believed the spirit of cricket and sportsmanship had not been forgotten. The jinx word 'sportsmanlike' or its kindred noun was pushed to the front by both Warner and the New South Wales premier, almost implying that the more you said it, the more it was wholly believable by everyone and its validity should never have been put in doubt. At the end, he reminded his audience that he was an old man who greatly loved the game of cricket. Tears came easily to him and he stood before that large crowd of guests emotionally overcome and with the memories of earlier and happier tours crowding in. He would live another 30 years but he would never return to Australia.

It was a speech of diplomacy, deliberately putting the events of the past months in a low key. The survivors of the tour felt it struck the correct note. Warner had, said Allen, done his best to get Jardine to modify his policies. He had sought, thought Brown, peace at all costs. On an occasion such as a State dinner he had said, all agreed, the right things.

He had told his listeners that he 'loved the game'. But to his wife, he wrote, two or three days later, 'D. R. Jardine is a trial. I never wish to see him again. His outlook and mentality are all wrong. Wyatt and Gubby say "he is the man who made the game impossible". I think I hate cricket now. It has been such a worry.'

Before he left Australia, Warner was asked to Canberra where he met the Governor-General, Sir Isaac Isaacs, and the British representative, Crutchley, with whom he had made contact earlier. Social occasions are not the subject of Minutes and we can scarcely more than guess at what was said. But writing to Agnes before he sailed for New Zealand he indicated that he had been asked by the Governor-General (the first Australian to hold the office) to seek a restoration of good Anglo-Australian relationships when he got home.

MCC broke new ground by going on to New Zealand. Larwood,

because of a foot injury, went straight back to England. The cricket was different, the opposition (in those days) a lot weaker,[33] Hammond averaged 563.00 in the two Tests (227 and 336 not out), Jardine in his speeches got in some jokes against the Australians but the best joker of all, his bodyline bowling attack, was kept firmly in the pack.

Warner, with the Tests behind him, indulged in a flurry of letter writing to Agnes. From Melbourne he wrote on 5 March that, 'thank heaven, the most unpleasant tour ever' was nearing its end. He described Woodfull as making 'a complete fool of himself' at Adelaide and 'fanning the flames'. He declared once more that he never wished to see Jardine again. For no particular reason, Hammond was again singled out as 'a good fellow' whom Warner liked immensely and he scribbled on the margin, 'am not going to serve on any more selection committees'.

On the voyage to New Zealand he wrote her a long letter mostly about money. He was anxious to go on writing for the *Morning Post* but not on a daily basis though 'of course, we must consider the £ s d'. He hoped MCC might give him a bonus (they did not). Finally – and Agnes must have alternated between worry and boredom by this time – he had another 'dig' at Jardine, 'very difficult man and heavens how he loathes Australians'. His son John believed that Agnes was more bored than worried by the repetition. The criticism of Jardine was not entirely valid for the captain was a welcome guest in many an Australian home, as was Warner, during the tour. 'How he loathes Australians who barrack,' might have been fairer.

Another letter was written to her as he crossed the Pacific homeward-bound via the United States. He told her he wanted to take the chance to see New York ('I shall never have another one') and he proposed to 'find a cheap hotel to stay at'. No doubt this was genuine enough but there was an underlying reason. Warner was acutely aware of the sensation which would arise when MCC met the English press. Some of them, he had heard, proposed to join the ship for the crossing of the Atlantic. So he had successfully cabled to MCC to be allowed to leave the party at Toronto, thus avoiding (as he told Agnes) 'possible interviewers and Fender who will want "news"'. He also touched on his relations with Palairet, the other manager. The two men had known each other since their Oxford days and Warner, as an undergraduate, had stayed at the Palairets' family home. But they had not got on well on the tour despite a clear definition of their respective duties. Warner believed (correctly) Palairet had Jardine's ear rather than himself and he considered Palairet was cast too much in the Jardine mould

– 'very cross at times and able to be rude, very rude to servants, not a pleasant travelling companion'. It was a comment several of the survivors accepted and they were not unaware, at the time, of a certain antipathy between the two men. Significantly, and scarcely surprisingly, it was Palairet, the junior manager, and not Warner, who wrote a foreword to Jardine's book on the tour – Warner gets four inconsequential 'mentions' – and it was Palairet, and not Warner, who was asked to Jardine's wedding a year later.

Finally, he wrote a scribbled letter in pencil on pages torn out of an exercise book as he crossed the Rockies on the Canadian Pacific train. By now everything had been said and there was much repetition – D.R.J., Allen's character, Palairet's rudeness, his own job with the *Morning Post*. Presents had been bought for the family (some Greenstone 'to make you a piece of Jewellry') and John's housemaster at Eton had been asked to let him home for the night when his father returned. The snow and ice from the train windows were as remote as could be from the climate of the southern hemisphere. 'Longing to see you all. No more tours for me.' He had made the same remark to William Ferguson the scorer, adding, 'not if I were paid £10,000'.

It says a great deal for the ethics and conventions of the day that a party containing two managers at mild variance, an autocratic captain, and players who had private differing views on policy could represent such an image of collective loyalty to the outside world over eight months. In our own times, and over a much shorter period of time, dissent would certainly 'out'. It also says something for Warner. The word 'loyalty' was never once used in his letters to Agnes. In a sense it was in the letters alone that he could be 'disloyal'. They provided a safety-valve and the outlet for his emotions. Outwardly, he stood for loyalty to MCC whose servant he was. Inwardly, he could release his pent-up anger and tension in his letters, and to some extent, to Allen ('I do not know what I would have done without him.').

He had been depressed by the miserable send-off MCC had received as they left Australian shores. By comparison with 1903–4 (even 1902–3) and 1911–12, it did not bear thinking about. He believed that his own reputation in the country was damaged beyond repair. But his son John came to think that the memory of his father as a great England captain in Australia far eclipsed that of him as the hypocritical manager in 1932–33. He attached import-ance to the invitation Pelham received to preach at Jackson's memorial service in Sydney and he told a tale when he himself was in an Australian train in the 1950s. Denied a bottle of wine by the oddity of Australian licensing laws, John Warner asked the waiter if he remembered 'Plum'. The man knew the legend of earlier days rather than the drama of later ones and instantly produced a bottle. 'It was one of the rare occasions in my life when I chose to use my father's name,' remarked his son. Meanwhile, for his father, there would be the respite of New York, a quiet Atlantic crossing, a report to prepare, and the inevitable post-mortem.

8

The Legacy of Discord, 1932–33

Today a touring team completing its programme in New Zealand would be back in England 36 hours later and, in a sense, its arrival home would not be 'news' since everything about the tour would have long since been seen on television, and reported in commentaries. The press, meanwhile, would have provided the public with the opinion of numerous reporters – not so 50 years ago. It is essential to an understanding of the MCC tour of 1932–33 to realise that meaningful reporting was comparatively slight. Jack Hobbs' views in the *Star*, as 'ghosted' by Jack Ingham, were reported simplistically and few papers had any representation at all. Reuter's Agency gave a very muted picture of events.[34] A 'hungry' public had to wait until the team returned for a fuller picture of what had happened. Jardine's men came home via Fiji, Honolulu, America and Canada so that a month elapsed between the last ball bowled and their return to Glasgow, where a pipe band greeted them and 10,000 Scotsmen cheered them with the fervour that might have been reserved for an English defeat at Hampden Park.

Warner himself arrived in England on 13 May at Plymouth, having, he said, 'not seen an English paper for weeks', and he declined to make a statement to the press. Within a few days, his report on the tour was in the hands of MCC but before we turn to the implications of that, we should notice what developments had taken place in those six weeks he had been out of contact with the world of cricket.

Broadly, three things had happened. The ABC had submitted a proposal for change in the Laws of cricket governing the fairness of the bowler's delivery. This was covered by the (then) Law 48 and the Australian suggestion may, for convenience, be thought of as the provision of a Law '48(b)'. By it, a bowler who, in the opinion of the umpire, sought 'to intimidate or injure' the batsman would be banned for the rest of the innings. A cable to this effect reached MCC at the end of April.

Secondly, MCC had been approached by the BBC in April asking if Warner might give a broadcast on his return to put the nation in the picture. MCC were unresponsive and the BBC wrote again, with an apology for being so persistent. Ronald Aird, then the assistant secretary, replied that he felt the Committee would not 'be happy' and, a few days later, he confirmed that it was thought 'inappropriate' for Warner to speak. Warner's only involvement with the BBC was a cheque for £1 5s for negotiating on their behalf the commentaries by the Australian Alan Kippax relayed through Paris.[35] To refuse to allow Warner to broadcast was a reasonable decision especially before his report on the tour had been received. The same policy of 'silence' was extended to the proposals of the ABC which were to be regarded as *sub judice* until both Warner's and Jardine's reports were in the hands of MCC. At the Annual General Meeting of MCC two days before the team returned home, members were told that no immediate comment could be made on the events of the tour.

Thirdly, as we have noted, came the arrival of the team and renewed public debate in the press. Larwood (who had come home earlier direct from Australia), despite MCC attempts by cable to 'muzzle' him over the previous month, wrote in the *Sunday Express*. The papers, as a whole, might be described as 'partisan': England had won the Ashes, Bradman had been controlled and the Australians were 'squealers'.

In this atmosphere the England season of 1933 began. On the one hand, there was a public ready to applaud victory against the Australians and not in the least abashed at the tales emerging of how it had been achieved; on the other, there was MCC equally ready to applaud victory but still persuading itself that the tactics employed were not an issue of great concern. Such was the state of feeling when Warner presented his report to the MCC secretary just after the middle of May. No record of this report exists in the archives at Lord's but from Warner's letters to his wife it is possible to suggest the gist of it. Broadly, he must have criticised very severely Jardine's attitude as captain and the tactics he employed. He was summoned by a special subcommittee (under the chairmanship of Lord Hailsham) to give evidence. He left convinced that he was thought to be exaggerating and 'that my opinions were embarrassing'. The subcommittee could hardly avoid seeing Warner but others, such as Wyatt, the vice-captain, Allen and

Hammond, were not seen at all probably because they were suspected of holding the same views as Warner.

To the outward world he maintained the same stoic silence which he had pursued in Australia. He was too much an MCC Committee man to be seen to join issue with his colleagues in public. He had his own vehicle of communication with the world at large in *The Cricketer*. But, as editor, he at first kept a similar low profile to that which he was adopting as the returning manager, as the chairman of selectors or as a member of the MCC Committee. *The Cricketer* expressed its opinion through 'Second Slip', the old Cambridge captain Frank Mitchell. Before long Warner's policy of keeping silence was being criticised in his own 'Letters to the Editor' column.

As a member of the MCC (full) Committee, he automatically attended a meeting on 12 June which dispatched a reply to the Australians' proposals for a 'Law 48(b)'. That reply still ignored the basic realities of the conflict – using the word both in the sense of the cricket which had been played and as a description of relations between MCC and ABC. But his influence can be seen in MCC's concession that the Committee would 'watch carefully (during 1933) for anything which might be regarded as unfair or prejudicial to the best interests of the game'. And in their protests against barracking in Australia he and his fellow committee members were on common ground. Warner had always felt that barracking had fanned the flames in Australia. Jardine, in particular, had been a victim of it, both in 1928–29 and in 1932–33.

Some vindication of Warner's views on bodyline bowling came in two matches in July as a consequence of which his MCC colleagues were the more ready to realise the implications of bodyline bowling, and to relate that realisation to the possibility that the Australians might not come to England in 1934. The first game was the University match. In those days Oxford v. Cambridge was still one of the great fixtures in the Lord's calendar and the sight of Kenneth Farnes, the Cambridge fast bowler, bowling with four short legs to the tail-end Oxford batsmen to the tune of a match analysis of 7 for 71, demonstrated what no newsreels from Australia could have done. Three weeks later, the West Indies bowled with similar effect in the second Test at Old Trafford. E. A. Martindale and L. N. Constantine provided an even better imitation than had Farnes, Jardine to his great credit making an unflinching century off them – though on a more docile pitch than the Australian ones.

Warner at last broke silence and wrote to *The Daily Telegraph* in July 1933 as one who thought of himself as a West Indian:

I was 'sorry the West Indies had recourse to leg theory', or 'Bodyline' (Australian), because I had hoped that my country-men would avoid a type of bowling which I believe to be against the best interests of cricket.

But I agree that its exploitation at Old Trafford will serve a useful purpose in giving Englishmen some idea of what this bowling is like, though it is well known that Constantine is at least two yards slower than Larwood, and also lacks his control of the ball. What is objected to by a great many cricketers is fast leg theory on hard, fast wickets. A bowler must be fast to carry out this plan of attack, but it requires not only speed, but accuracy of direction and control of length. No batsman objects to fast half volleys on his legs, however many fieldsmen may be placed on the leg side. What is objected to is when the ball is pitched short. It is the length of the ball, not so much the pace of it, to which exception has been taken.

Short-pitched very fast deliveries on hard wickets on the line of the batsman's body look – even if the bowler is acquitted of all intention to hurt the batsman – as if the bowler was 'bowling at the batsman', in the sense in which that expression has hitherto been understood by cricketers.

It is akin to intimidation. At the end of the last century, and at the beginning of this, English cricket boasted many fast bowlers – every county had at least one; Surrey two, the renowned Richardson and Lockwood. Some hard blows were received at times.

Sir Stanley Jackson, for example, had a rib broken by E. Jones, the Australian, but these bowlers did not give the impression of bowling at the batsman, and the short very fast 'bouncer', on the line of the batsman and which caused the batsman to duck, was certainly not defended, or encouraged.

At all events, fast bowling was very much in vogue at that time, and no cry was raised against it, whereas today we have practically every Australian cricketer of every generation definitely opposed to what they call Bodyline bowling.

This vast mass of opinion deserves the deepest thought and consideration. To suggest that the Australians are 'squealers' is unfair to men with their record on the battlefield and on the cricket field. Rightly or wrongly they believe that such bowling is contrary to the spirit of the game.

Mr Agate hopes that 'the Australians are now raking the bush for some Hercules who can bowl faster than Kortright, in order that, without regard to length and aiming solely at the batsman's head and heart, he shall, next season, try on the English goose the sauce that has been deemed proper for the Australian gander'.

I should be sorry indeed to see 'a Red Terror' from the 'Never-Never', some Saltbush Bill of Richardsonian proportions, exploiting this bowling against England in a Test Match at Lord's, or anywhere else.

The courtesy of combat would go out of that game in ten minutes: and one of the strongest arguments against this bowling is that it has bred, and will continue to breed, anger, hatred, and malice, with their consequent reprisals.

Admitting it is within the law – there are many things in cricket which by the laws of the game are right, but which are 'not done' – is it worth while if, as a result of Bodyline, England and her greatest cricketing Dominion are to 'fight' each other?

It was not thus that cricket gained its great name, a name synonymous with all that is fair, and kindly, noble, and upright.

Some would urge that the laws should be altered. I do not agree. This is a case where one should rely on the spirit, kindliness, and good will which should be inherent in cricket. But if a change in the law there must be, why not draw a line across the pitch and no-ball any delivery pitched the bowler's side of the line? The cricket pitch might look somewhat like a tennis court, but would that matter greatly if we got back to the old happy state of affairs? For the cricket world today is most decidedly not happy.

Always have I been opposed to this bowling which has aroused so much controversy, and, right or wrong, I am only pleading for what I honestly believe is best for the great, glorious, and incomparable game of cricket. I am not the least of the lovers of cricket.

In the absence of his report to Lord's, it remains the only public evidence of his views on bodyline bowling. In Australia he had felt inhibited by his position from speaking. Now, freed from the ties of being a selector or a manager, he was more able to speak his mind. Much of the detail had already been outlined in his letters to Agnes to whom he always paid the compliment (rightly) of understanding the 'small print' of the game.

Both his letter and those practical demonstrations in July 1933 gave a public airing to bodyline bowling. Behind the scenes two interrelated matters were being discussed, the one the 'Law 48(b)' proposals and the other the England captaincy for 1934. Within the context of the 'Law 48(b)' proposals was the assurance to the Australians that bodyline bowling would not be employed when they came in 1934. In England, Dr Robert MacDonald, the resident representative of the ABC in London, was able to achieve an assurance from the MCC special subcommittee sufficient to satisfy the ABC. The evidence for the 'concordat' which MacDonald reached lies in files in Melbourne, not at Lord's. In effect, the ABC would ask for a formal guarantee that the type of bowling to which exception was taken in 1932–33 would not be used in 1934. MCC would give that guarantee. Pride was saved by the word 'bodyline' being omitted. The exchange of cables between September and December 1933 was the public expression of these private negotiations. So far as can be ascertained, Warner played no part in them.

As for the 'Law 48(b)' proposals themselves, a solution was found at a meeting of the Imperial Cricket Conference (which Warner attended as a delegate for South Africa)[36] at the end of July 1933 at which a resolution was passed affirming 'the principles already laid down by MCC that any form of bowling obviously a direct attack by the bowler upon the batsman, would be an offence against the spirit of the game'. The conference hoped that 'controlling bodies should not permit or countenance that kind of bowling'. Thus 'Law 48(b)', as such, did not come into force. Instead, there was attached to Law 43, the law governing the powers of umpires, an additional instruction on the definition of fair and unfair play.

The other 'behind the scenes' issue was not resolved so easily. This was the question of who would captain England against the Australians in 1934. Warner was much more closely involved in this although in an entirely unofficial capacity. While in New Zealand, MCC had cabled asking him to be a selector again in 1933 but he had declined. We know, from his letters, that he had had enough of it. It was therefore other selectors who chose Jardine as captain against the West Indies in 1933. In essence, they had no alternative. He had won the Ashes, he had retracted nothing, he had the confidence of the MCC Committee and he had come back a popular hero. The outwardly cool and austere figure who was Jardine submitted to the cheers of the crowd when he led an MCC side out against the West Indians at Lord's, in May, with the same look of aristocratic disdain with which he had met Australian barracking. If it proved difficult to 'needle' Jardine, it was equally difficult to worship him. But hero-worshipped he was especially when he had combatted the bowling of Constantine and Martindale with his century.

While the dialogue with the ABC on bodyline bowling was, as we have seen, reaching some degree of mutual acceptance, the captaincy of the England side for 1934, against the Australians, remained the contentious issue. MacDonald wrote to his colleagues back in Australia, in January 1934, saying that he himself had informed MCC that 'there would be a veiled vendetta' if Jardine were appointed captain. Indeed, he went so far as to say that 'victory at any cost [was] common to both Attila and Mr Jardine. If I do Attila an injustice by this simile, I tender an apology to his memory.' A rather more balanced, but still firm, approach came from Hore-Ruthven – and it was in this that Warner was concerned.

During the English winter of 1933–34 he was engaged in correspondence with Hore-Ruthven. Our main concern is with his letters to Warner but we should also note one he had written in June 1933 to Thomas, the Dominions Secretary. By then, of course, he was back in South Australia and he had had time to assess the feeling after the dust of the tour had settled. In a long letter he remarked:

Since I have been back here, I cannot help being rather perturbed over the result of these unfortunate cricket incidents and I am afraid that they have had a serious effect on the good feeling between the two countries. We both had the opportunity of observing the very strong anti-Australian feeling which had been aroused in England by these events, and on my return I find a deep sense of injustice and a genuine feeling that the true facts of the case have not been fairly represented at home. This atmosphere, I feel, we must, at all costs, endeavour to remove. I am forced to the conclusion that the Australian case had far more justification than one would have been led to suppose at the other side of the world.

He was critical of the MCC attitude in their cable of 12 June and of Warner in particular:

To announce, first of all, that they consider the leg theory perfectly correct and later on to say they will express an opinion at the end of the season seems to be hardly consistent. The MCC say they have reached this conclusion after hearing the views of Jardine, Warner and Palairet. Jardine's views are, of course, obvious but what views Warner expressed we do not know – if he supported the leg theory he must have altered his view considerably since he wrote his article in Badminton, and which has been freely quoted in Australia.

He concluded by saying that the Australian press continued to be reasonable and hoped that the English press might be persuaded, through Thomas's influence, to be equally fair-minded.

Nevertheless, Hore-Ruthven, whatever his private opinion of Warner's attitude to bodyline bowling, came to regard him, by the autumn of 1933, as his best way of influencing MCC opinion for the future and he wrote on several occasions to Warner, with letters marked 'private and personal' and with particular instructions to ensure the press got no wind of what was being said. In November 1933 he wrote to him saying that if Jardine were *not* appointed captain he believed all would be well, and went on: 'most members of the ABC, and the general public, were all for finally closing the incident and for nothing being said that might possibly cause further friction'.

He said that the attitude of the Australian press was also one of goodwill with the intent 'to avoid all comment and let the question simmer down'. But the proviso remained – Jardine must not be captain – and he hoped Warner would use his influence to ensure this negative aim was achieved.

Warner replied to Hore-Ruthven in January 1934 in a letter whose 'Dear Sandy' (in days of a much more formal surname relationship) indicates the two men had come to know each other quite well, even if only as correspondents:

Dear Sandy,
Thank you very much for your nice and very interesting letter, and your good wishes for 1934 which I heartily reciprocate. Well, I am delighted 'the row' is over ... The Press and Public will give the team a good reception ... The trouble is Jardine. Is he to be Capt? At present I say 'No' unless he makes a most generous public gesture of friendliness and then I am not sure I would trust him. He is a queer fellow. When he sees a cricket ground with an Australian on it he goes mad! He rose to his present position on my shoulders, and of his attitude to me I do not care to speak. It is hoped he may retire at the end of the Indian Tour, but in many quarters here – where they do not know the truth – he is a bit of a hero. If he is captain in the First Test and not friendly he will not capt. in the 2nd but I would not have him at all.
    We start a New Year here on a wave of optimism – things look good and they say Income Tax will come down. I trust so.

Back came Hore-Ruthven's letter on 5 February, within weeks of the Australian side sailing for England. It was an unequivocally firm and strong letter – whereas Warner's had had a vacillating note about it:

GOVERNMENT HOUSE,
ADELAIDE

Private & Personal   5th February, 1934.

My Dear Plum,
The Jardine question is very important and from what I can see of the signs out here the only thing that could disturb the harmony which players and public are all anxious to maintain, would be to put Jardine in charge again. The whole atmosphere will be altered at once if he is made Captain. The players will go on the field with the feeling of irritation and suspicion, and it will play into the hands of the extreme element here who wanted to demand guarantees that Jardine would not be Captain and that body-line bowling would not be allowed, and they will at once say that 'Gentlemen's Agreements' are no good to them, and in future we must have the written guarantees. And, moreover, the sensational section of the Australian Press will make the most of it and start the controversy all over again.

I know the difficulties of not appearing to let him [Jardine] down, but the question is so vital, not only from the point of view of cricket, but of the friendly feeling between the two countries, that some excuse must be found for leaving him out. As, once the sore is opened again it is going to be very difficult to heal, and all the soothing syrup we have administered of late will be wasted.

We can't get away from the fact that the root of the trouble was the selection of a man of Jardine's temperament as Captain, so why go on pouring sand into the machine until in the end you smash it up?

You may think that I am exaggerating the feeling which Jardine's captaincy would give rise to, but it has been my business to make a careful study of Australian mentality for the last six years and I have no doubt as to the repercussions this would cause on men's minds out here, and these are not only my personal opinions, but are shared by many who are far better judges than I. So I think it is best to speak one's mind openly, and I hope you will forgive me for being so frank.

Before the second letter from Hore-Ruthven had reached him, Warner wrote, on the basis of the first one, to Findlay on 22 February:

Of course if Jardine were captain it might be awkward, but your conversation the other day led me to understand that Jardine would be required by MCC to give certain guarantees which would appreciably ease the situation. I believe that you realise that I was his best friend and supporter. I have no axe to grind and my objections to his methods and manners was because I considered them contrary to the ideals and interests of cricket and the prestige of MCC.

I believe that history will find me guiltless of a wrong appreciation of the situation. I do not consider that Jardine – on his Australian form – can produce the friendly relations and happy spirit which MCC so urgently desire in the coming test matches and which are so very vital for the good of the game.

The note would not have satisfied Hore-Ruthven, though in Warner's defence it may be added that he was more aware than was Hore-Ruthven out in Australia how much the English public wanted Jardine.

What might have been decided by the England selectors – of whom Warner was *not* one – can never be known. Jardine sent from India, where he was captaining the MCC 1933–34 side, a note to the London *Evening Standard* at the end of March saying that he had 'neither the intention nor the desire to play cricket against Australia'. MCC had not, in the end, had to make the decision themselves. How far Jardine might have been asked, as the United States courts would say, 'to plea bargain' over bodyline bowling can only be guessed at. There can be no prizes for guessing that he would have refused such a deal. Warner, in some senses the unfortunate cause of it all – as the chairman who had originally chosen Jardine – could begin to relax and once again learn to love the game he 'had grown to hate'. He made one more rather belated intervention when he wrote to Findlay on 1 May, venturing to ask whether the MCC Committee should 'take any notice of Mr Jardine's cable to the *Evening Standard*':

I desire to speak with restraint in this matter, but it seems to me that Jardine's cable, which he knew was for public consumption, is in direct contradiction of MCC's so-called promises to Australia. The words 'no desire to play against Australia this summer' are really most discourteous and deliberately flout MCC's expressed wishes and desires; and Mr. Jardine is a member of the cricket and selection committees of MCC. I beg to urge that the committee consider this cable of Mr. Jardine and whether any steps are necessary in connection with it.

Nothing came of it, for this time it was in no one's interest to pursue either Jardine (somewhere in India) or his motives. The Australians had already arrived and on the day after Warner's letter to Findlay, Bradman made his customary double-century at Worcester.

Warner's references to Jardine in his two letters to Findlay cannot pass without comment. His claim to have been 'his best friend and supporter' is entirely without validity in terms of Warner's private opinion, as his numerous letters home showed. It is only defensible in public on the grounds that Warner had been careful never to make any statements in Australia against the man or his policies. All along he had felt, in private, that Jardine should never captain England again. By 1934 he was saying, not in public but in his letters to MCC, not only that Jardine should go but that he should be disciplined for his attitude towards MCC.

We are brought back to the essential word 'loyalty'. Warner had been loyal to MCC through and through; to an institution which, like Elizabeth I's devotion to the State, he 'put above all earthly things'. Therein lay what logic there was in his silence in Australia, his private correspondence with his wife and his contribution to Jardine's 'downfall' in 1934. If there were 'a wrong appreciation of the situation' for which history would not find him 'guiltless', it lay in his failure to tackle Jardine head-on at the time of the first Test. To have done that would have needed the rhetoric of Cicero and the courage of Scipio. Nor could he have been assured, in December 1932, that the senators from Lord's would have backed him up. And there remains the thought that he really did want England to win. In the closing stages of the fourth Test, he left the dressing room and listened on a radio, so great was his excitement as the Ashes came England's way. It was another expression of his loyalty. His personal dilemma was in finding it difficult to equate loyalty to the captain and loyalty to the cause.

In the context of a biography of Warner, there is not a great deal more to be said on the bodyline issue. The season of 1934 ran its course not without some embarrassment to MCC. Neither Larwood nor Voce was picked against the Australians, who made an official protest against Voce's bowling when they met Nottinghamshire.

At the end of the summer, at a special meeting of the MCC Committee, Warner pressed for a more forceful application of Law 43 on 'fair or unfair play' and this found expression in the report of a subcommittee, to which he was appointed. It recommended the issuing of instructions to umpires which would advise them what constituted 'a direct attack'. These instructions, which strengthened their authority in interpreting Law 43 together with the introduction of the new lbw(N) law, may be said to have ended, in technical terms, the saga of the bodyline bowling crisis. In Warner's own words, 'it no longer disrupted the cricket world'. Yet, in some ways, it heralded the dawn of a new world in which politics and sport would become inextricably associated, in which the imperial bonds unifying cricket would become weaker, in which – after Warner's time – the role of MCC would be diminished. Lord's, no more than Westminster, could not forever arbitrate upon an Empire which had ended.

What were the consequences for Warner himself? He had been given the task of finding a captain to beat the Australians and he had found one in Jardine, 'a man cast in the toughest Australian mould, à la Armstrong if you like', as Fender had written. Contemporary opinion was agreed he had little choice other than Jardine and he himself had understood Jardine's view of leading a 'crusade'. But crusades are holy wars, campaigns against evil. His chosen captain had cast the Australians as evil and Bradman as the arch-devil. Out of this had sprung the bitter differences between manager and captain. .

He had been forced into taking up a position he found personally unacceptable because he believed that the public role of loyalty to the institution he served was his prior claim. Had he betrayed his loyalty to MCC or distanced himself from the captain, he would have displayed that same lack of courtesy (his word) which he had attached in 1920 to bowlers who used a strong on-side field. It may be that in the pursuit of courtesy – high in his list of virtues – he stumbled. For courtesy's sake he had kept his own counsel. In the end his silence mutilated the virtue and it was only rendered strong again by his letter to the press in July 1933.

That he was aged and shaken by his experience, the survivors of the tour – and his family – agreed. That he lost credibility, opinion differed. Wyatt and Allen, the amateurs, believed 'not'; Ames felt 'in Australian eyes only'; Bowes considered he did so 'in the eyes of mainly professional cricketers but was vindicated by his contribution to the lbw(N) law'; Voce and Larwood appreciated the way he had not 'let down' Jardine at the time.

That he was personally scarred, again opinions varied from the suggestion that he 'never got over it' to the comment that 'all was forgotten'. Perhaps, to this question, he may be allowed his own answer at the time, 'I almost hate cricket.' The relationship between man and game, lovingly built up over 50 years had to be laboriously and diligently reconstructed. Warner was too gentle a person to hate men or institutions for long. Like Lord North, on whose shoulders was thrust the responsibility of handling the colonial conflict with America, he was an ordinary man thrust into an extraordinary situation. If Warner felt he had failed, who would have succeeded? And what would have been the price of success?

9

Journalist and Selector: II, 1933–39

Plum Warner returned to England in 1933 chastened by criticism, saddened by experience and disillusioned by events. He had gone to Australia in his late middle age: he returned, in his own words, 'an old man'. Gradually he picked up the threads of his life as head of a family, as a writer and as a selector. The circumstances and mode of living would change, he would write for a different paper and he would become far busier as chairman of selectors.

In 1936 the flat in Sloane Street was given up for the lease of 3 Malvern Court, at the corner of Old Brompton Road opposite South Kensington underground station. Their new home was a first-floor flat where Pelham and Agnes would remain for the rest of their married life. The pattern of that life changed for a variety of reasons. Betty, now married, and Esmond had left home. John, a boy at Eton until 1937, as often as not spent his summer holidays in Westmorland rather than in a London flat. There was a last 'family' holiday when John and his father joined Agnes at Gibraltar in 1934. She had gone out some weeks earlier. The visit of father and son (during John's Christmas holidays from Eton) was sadly curtailed because their ship spent some days marooned in fog, not arriving until after Boxing Day. The Warners no longer entertained in the way they had done and their standard of living was more modest. By now, Agnes's health had begun its long decline and the days of generous hospitality were over. This was linked to a decline in their finances, or more particularly in Agnes's, brought about by the worldwide Depression and its aftermath. Warner continued to worry about money yet remained curiously naïve about it. John recalled a conversation piece between his parents.

Pelham Agnes, I'm going to Lord's and then to my club. Can you let me have some money?

Agnes Well, yes: I think I have two or three pounds.

Pelham What have you done with all that money you had a few days ago?

Agnes I paid a grocery bill of three pounds and you had the rest.

Armed with what Agnes gave him, he would sally forth to *The Cricketer* office, his club or to Lord's. He might go by tube but would usually share a taxi home.

This is to look at events on the surface. Agnes's distrust of Pelham's finances may be linked to another factor. There had come into her husband's life a lady who was a dancer. Pelham had met Miss E.H. in Australia during the 1932–33 tour and in the distress of that experience she had been some consolation to him. Sometime in the 1930s she had come to England and her continuing attraction for Warner became a financial obligation he had to meet. Agnes, who was nobody's fool, and a woman of much greater perception than her husband, could ask outwardly what he did with the money. Privately she recognised that he was finding affection elsewhere. The liaison kept its secret and Miss E.H. was only a tiny part of the canvas which was Warner's busy life, though there will be occasion to return to her later.

He became more than ever the 'club' man and one finds constant references in his papers to occasions when he dined at the Garrick, the Carlton, the Conservative or the East India. He was frequently someone's guest in either House of Parliament and enjoyed listening to the debates. He still moved in naval circles and from time to time he would take a side down to Portsmouth and dine in the barracks. Army hospitality claimed him when he captained teams against Sandhurst. He continued to relish the company of lawyers in particular and regarded himself as one of their number. He was a frequent guest in the various Inns of Court while crime itself in its various aspects interested him. He would go from time to time to listen to cases in the courts and he liked to read biographies of great jurists. He belonged to the Crimes Club (more dinners!) and as a young man he had rather shamefacedly joined the crowds at Paddington station straining for a sight of Dr Crippen, the first man to be arrested at sea by wireless message. As an old man, he gave talks on cricket in prisons, borstals and in Broadmoor.

There is the temptation to assume that Warner was forever dining out. Such occasions stood out in his memory and he enjoyed them. He was in demand as a speaker and found the exercise effortless, but a part of his life, especially in the winter months when there was no cricket to watch at Lord's, was the normal domestic one of being at home. There he would be constantly writing, dashing off letters to numerous correspondents or scribbling pieces for the press in any corner or chair to hand. He neither used a typewriter, acquired a secretary nor sat down at a desk. He was 60 in October 1933, and he might well have felt entitled to retire from the cricket scene, except as a spectator, especially after the strain of events in Australia. Instead, he resumed his activities both as a journalist and as a selector together with an occasional role as a broadcaster. Indeed, it could be argued that many of the most productive years lay ahead.

He no longer worked for the *Morning Post*. He had cabled H. A. Gwynne, the editor, while in Australia that he wished to write less on the day-to-day account of matches and instead give general impressions of some dozen matches a season. The editor was not keen and, as the season approached, felt he would be left without a regular correspondent. 'It looks as if the MP have given me the sack,' he had written laconically to Agnes on the ship to New Zealand. There were faults of interpretation on both sides and Warner blamed communicating by cable for the 'confusion' which led the editor to part with him. 'Although there was no ill-will,' he wrote later to Agnes, 'I believe I was worth £2000 a year to them in revenue and they were foolish to let me go.' Robertson-Glasgow took over from him and Warner, in 1933 and 1934, had a short spell with *The Daily Telegraph*. It was, again, day-to-day reporting for which he no longer had the energy or the time. Effectively his career as a journalist working for the daily press was over. He had written with authority, confidence and conviction but without sensation. The request for '500 words on Bradman and the girls' from one of his editors simply got stuffed in his pocket, although the mobbing of the young Australian hero by fans was obviously good 'copy'. Because he chose to work in pavilions rather than in press boxes, he was somewhat detached from the 'hurly-burly' of reporting and, in the opinion of Swanton, 'never really learnt the ropes'. Bowes believed that it was the influence of the Surrey members in the pavilion at The Oval, in 1932, which had led him to overreact to Bowes' own bowling to Hobbs compared with other press reports. If so, he was demonstrably hoist with his own petard. In essence, as a journalist, he remained – and perhaps chose to – the talented amateur. It was his editorship of *The Cricketer* which continued to involve him in daily visits to the office up to the outbreak of war in 1939.

For the moment, 'he felt he had had enough of controversy' and he declined invitations to be chairman of the selectors in 1933 and 1934, returning to the post at the very end of 1934. By May 1933 he was back in *The Cricketer*'s office, and making his first public comments on the tour he had managed and whose captain he had chosen. They appeared in an article, spread over three issues in May and June. He began:

It would be improper, both on public and private grounds, to discuss at the present moment, the controversies which arose in Australia, for these matters are still under discussion but there can be no harm in offering a criticism of the play of the members of the MCC team.

The rest of the article was a series of pen portraits of the players on both sides. On Jardine, he wrote, 'one of the best captains in the field England has had for a long day. This is neither the time nor the place to discuss the problems which his adoption of leg-theory raised, but he was an astute observer and thinker.' Warner paid tribute to him as a leader 'unswerving in his attitude' who 'bore barracking and criticism with calmness and dignity'. He also visualised Allen 'as a future captain of England'.

In July *The Cricketer* reproduced an article from the *Morning Post* by his successor, Robertson-Glasgow:

The winning of the game is valued more highly than its playing. It is the time and place for us to think more of what cricket is about. It is all so childish, so petty, the hurt so self-imposed, for the winning or losing of a Test match is nothing to cricket.

The article continued in this vein, and Warner prefaced it with the statement that:

We are in complete agreement with Mr Robertson-Glasgow and we earnestly pray that the 'hate' which has crept into the game in the last few weeks may be deleted with all possible speed. In our opinion it is one of the greatest essays ever written on the game of cricket.

Warner had overreacted in his enthusiasm for a very ordinary, not to say naïve piece by Robertson-Glasgow. Victories *did* matter, as Warner himself had appreciated in 1903–4, 1911–12 and 1926 and had never been tired of reiterating. Test matches would soon have lost their appeal if they had become gutless displays in which genuine partisanship gave way to dilettante appreciation.

Then came, in August, 'the Editor's view on the Bowling Controversy'. It was an article reproducing almost exactly the letter he had written in *The Daily Telegraph* the previous month (see pages 137–9). By now, of course, the correspondence columns of *The Cricketer* were flooded with letters as the English public became more aware of the events in Australia and of bodyline bowling, as presented in milder form, by the West Indian bowlers in the 1933 series. Only one letter, a fierce defence of Jardine and Larwood, carried an editorial footnote, 'we publish this letter as we wish our readers to make full use of our correspondence columns but it must be clearly understood that the Editor must not be associated with the views of the writer'.

By 1935 Warner was again chairman of the selectors. It had been his own choice not to serve in 1933 and 1934. He had not, as some observers have suggested, been temporarily 'dropped'. In an early issue that summer he wrote in an editorial, 'for an obvious reason it would ill become us to make any comment on the selection committee but if we may offer a suggestion, it is that they pay special attention to fielding and give youth a chance'. So, the editor of *The Cricketer* was addressing the chairman of the selectors and no doubt Warner took good note of Warner's advice! Sir Home Gordon, indeed, later in 1935 wrote on how hard the selectors had worked, how much they had travelled and suggested that their 'most exaggerating sin was that they never replied to press criticism'.

Warner, as editor of *The Cricketer* and as chairman of the selectors, avoided serious pitfalls by not writing editorials which compromised his position in any way and not reporting on Test matches which, in any case, Board of Control policy forbade. It was much more as the manager in 1932–33 that he had found himself in an invidious position as a writer in 1933. *The Cricketer*, in the late 1930s, became not so much a paper to which he contributed opinion as one in which he was the senior executive figure. By and large the compromise worked but from time to time the paper was used by Warner as a vehicle for urging reforms. He had long had views on the need to reform the lbw law and *The Cricketer*'s backing was given to the movement which brought, in 1935, the experimental lbw(N). It became ratified as a law in 1936 and forms part of Law 36 in the 1980 Code of Laws.

In 1937 the Advisory County Cricket Committee invited MCC to appoint a Commission to investigate 'the problems confronting the first-class counties'. The Commission, under the chairmanship of William Findlay, produced a very lengthy report highlighting, among recent problems, the wet summers of 1935 and 1936, entertainment tax, defensive cricket and drawn matches and the disparity of strength between the competing sides. (Would a Northants side of 1937, without a win to its name and collecting wooden spoons in triplicate have ever dreamt of the triumphs of a one-day final at Lords?) Among its recommendations were a reduction in the number of first-class counties and a new scheme of scoring points. *The Cricketer* published and supported the report in full, though Warner felt a chance had not been taken to advocate the eight-ball over as a time-saver. His argument won some attention and, in 1939, it was introduced in England as an experiment but it did not reappear in 1946.

In lighter vein, Warner wrote an open letter in 1937 to one of his regular contributors, A Country Vicar, who had opposed the proposal that the University match should begin on a Saturday. Midweek suited the clergy much better. 'Fie upon you! for differing with your Editor! In these democratic days, I want to see the interest in the match much greater.' It had ceased to be the social occasion it had been a decade earlier for 'the men have ceased to wear top hats, except for your Editor and the women now think their second-best frocks will do'. The first time the match was on a Saturday was in 1938 and, as *Wisden* remarked, 'the experiment did not meet with the increased public support hoped for', only 6000 paying for admission. Immediate post-war figures were to be much greater until the sad decline of the 1970s when (in a midweek fixture again) families and girlfriends were the main supporters.

In the 1930s Warner found it less easy to secure contributors to *The Cricketer* who would write articles because 'you love the game, dear boy'. He was able to get Sir Home Gordon for nothing, that diminutive baronet who liked to be 'in the know', said nice things about Warner which Warner published, knew less about cricket than he might have done for a man who watched it so much, presented 'copy' which was a subeditor's (i.e: Langford's) nightmare and had a style so execrable that even Esmond, in his letters to his father, pleaded for him to be pensioned off. Home Gordon and the Country Vicar were the 'amateurs'. The young 'professionals' included Swanton and Gerald Pawle. Swanton would later become editorial director and have a link with the paper for over half a century. Pawle made his first contribution a year earlier than Swanton, in 1931. His career was as a journalist with the *Yorkshire Post* and Warner found him valuable as a source of northern gossip. Gerald Pawle was kind enough to delve through his scrapbooks and diaries for me:

My total emoluments for 1934 season amounted to £7 15s 0d! In 1935 I spread myself in a special feature about the Yorkshire Gents for which Plum paid me £1. In 1936 I was contributing regularly on anything which interested me. I earned £10, about 5/- a paragraph. In 1937 my pay was boosted to £12 and by 1938 I was covering assignments for *The Cricketer* on the Tests v. Australia, Yorkshire and the Northern Schools.

Pawle remarked that Warner took the trouble to write friendly letters to his contributors, 'may I say how much I appreciate anything you write', adding, 'it's a bit of a job carrying on in these days'.

Round about this time Sydney Levey made a double-century on an Optimists tour of Devon. The editor of *The Cricketer* wrote a warm letter of congratulation to the son of his old friend from pre-war Inns of Court days. Levey, as a schoolboy in 1922, had submitted some lines ('real doggerel verse, A is for Armstrong, the big man of cricket') to *The Cricketer* for which Warner had paid him five shillings ('my first literary earnings') and given him the claim, in 1986, to be the oldest living contributor. Then there was the contributor awaiting to be elected to MCC who approached Warner about how long he would still have to wait. 'I consider a cricketer of your ability should be a member of the Club,' replied Warner, 'I will do all I can' and no one was more astonished than the newly elected playing member who was thus compensated in great measure for the meagreness of the cheques.

Meanwhile, Langford soldiered on, no doubt his own compensation including 5 for 11 (with a hat-trick) against St John's, Leatherhead in 1936 and 96 not out against Cranleigh in 1938. With the outbreak of war the services of this man, now aged 43, simply saved *The Cricketer* from extinction. The editor himself, on the declaration of war, announced munificently that 10,000 copies would be distributed free to the armed forces in 1940. It was a flamboyant gesture akin much more to the behaviour of the real newspaper giants of those years rather than to the modest endeavours of a sports magazine. How *The Cricketer* fared in wartime we shall see in Chapter 10.

Warner believed reasonably enough that his own name helped the paper's fortunes and this was one of his reasons (besides a financial one) for wanting to broadcast. He approached the BBC in the summer of 1933, suggesting he might give a talk on the West Indians and this was taken up with rather dire results. The manuscript, in the view of Lotbinière, needed drastic rewriting and, he minuted, 'had too little picturesque and too much historical stuff'. An edited version was delivered and Warner wrote, as a postscript in acknowledging his cheque for ten guineas, 'when are you going to ask me again?' Lotbinière's reply was more frank than had been Brennan's five years earlier:

I would rather leave your postscript unanswered. The fact is that we do not feel that you do yourself justice in your cricket talks. I am afraid we were rather disappointed with the West Indian talk. We feel it was an opportunity missed. A broadcast talk needs a special technique and differs considerably from the literary article. I am sure you realise I very much dislike having to say all that I have said.

Lotbinière was still under 30. It must have taken some courage to write to an older man of such distinction in these terms but Warner respected his openness and frankness and, broadly, took it on the chin. He replied pleasantly enough but he could not resist a final paragraph, 'if you get a so-called cricket authority to broadcast why not let him do it his own way? It is rather like coaching Hammond when he is batting.'[37]

The two remained on friendly terms and would occasionally see each other at Lord's so that Lotbinière could, without embarrassment on either side, ask Warner to be 'twelfth man' at very short notice when someone (already billed in the *Radio Times*) dropped out. The subject was 'At the Nets'. Warner worked hard and used the occasion to plead, as he did from time to time in *The Cricketer*, for more to be done for boys outside the privileged background of the public and preparatory schools. 'More concrete wickets are needed in public parks', he said in commending the London Country Council for its scheme in hiring out such wickets for eightpence an hour. He also used the occasion for a homily against smoking by youth. 'Many of the greatest players, Grace, Trumper, Ranji and Bradman did not or do not smoke' – though neither Warner, nor for that matter, Hammond, set the example at the time. He was again 'twelfth man' when Lotbinière was let down for a talk on the eve of the fourth Test against the Australians in 1934. Earlier that summer he had been asked to comment on the Australians when they arrived. In saying of Woodfull (whose confrontation with him was of such recent memory) that 'there has never been a better liked or more respected captain', he was being personally generous to a fault and, at least, fulfilling the BBC request 'not to drop a brick after all the row'. The year 1934 ended with Warner writing to Lotbinière, 'I am glad to be received into the fold again.'

Yet he remained only marginally acceptable. The BBC found it difficult to ignore such a prominent figure especially when he so persistently suggested himself. They avoided asking him again until the late summer of 1936 when they wanted his comments on the side going to Australia. For a fee of six guineas he gave a four-minute talk in which he said that the captain, Allen, 'promised ideas and decision'. His request to give a second talk on the same theme was refused!

In 1937 he raised with the BBC the possibility of giving a talk on the one hundred and fiftieth anniversary of MCC and got a guarded reply indicating that soundings had suggested MCC were not interested. Warner took it to the MCC Committee who showed interest but left it to the BBC to suggest a broadcaster. Nothing happened, possibly because of the pressing demands of broadcasting the Coronation, possibly because an internal memorandum had just been written on Warner, 'the comments on his broadcasting since 1932 have been uniformly adverse. Used for name, not for manner or material.' It was a harsh and not altogether deserved judgement. Warner, had he been told it, could have countered with plenty of letters of appreciation, as for example, one from the Hawke family when he broadcast a warm tribute on the death in 1938 of his old friend.

Despite Lotbinière's earlier view that there was too much 'historical stuff', it was probably what Warner did best. He had a long memory and was accurate. By contrast, Learie Constantine, who would become a 'producer's dream' (BBC Memorandum) in a few years' time, could never be trusted to get his historical facts right. The two together (and they did broadcast thus once or twice during the war) would have made a perfect pair.

Meanwhile, the new medium of television was making timid and flickering inroads into the parlours of those within 50 miles of Alexandra Palace and Warner earned 13 guineas in two pre-war appearances.

Yet little broadcasting came his way up to the oubreak of war despite a letter to the BBC: 'I hope you will not forget me.' He did a talk on the 1938 Tests, after haggling for seven guineas instead of the proffered five and, a year later, one on the West Indian cricketers. He had been the subject of two internal memos: the one on whether he, Howard Marshall or Wakelam should be asked to give a talk on the 1938 season and he had got the verdict; the other on his payment. This led to a spirited row between accounts and contracts with notes passing backwards and forwards asking on whose authority Warner was being 'paid over the odds'. Certainly he was offered under the odds (so Warner thought) to go to Belfast and take part in the programme 'Ulster Inn' for eight guineas, sleeping berth, first-class rail and 15 shillings expenses. He (although about to depart on a tour as manager of a cricket tour in Denmark) declined on grounds of age! But this period of his life ended with a rare compliment from the BBC. His last broadcast before the war, the one on the West Indians, was reported to be 'quite excellent' and he was told so. In a sense, he was on home ground.

Warner's first task as chairman of the selectors, to which office he returned in 1935, was to appoint a captain against the South Africans. The current captain was Wyatt who believed that Warner was reluctant to have him partly because he had been so seriously injured in the last Test against the West Indies. Warner had been saying openly that he should not be captain for fear of further injury to his damaged jaw. It was a reasonable view but, in the opinion of both Wyatt and his predecessor Jardine, it was not the only reason. Wyatt had received a letter from Jardine on 12 April 1935 with the revealing comment:

I hope you will be quite fit early in the season. You want to start building up a side for Australia this year. Poor Bob! Warner's efforts on behalf of Gubby and Leveson Gowers' on behalf of Errol Holmes bid fair to make the season interesting! Let me know if there is anything I can do at any time, for you know how essential I feel it to be that the skipper should be worth a place in the side himself as a cricketer.

There was press speculation that Allen might be considered. Warner obviously had Allen in mind and to give him some experience in captaincy had arranged for him to lead an amateur side in Gibraltar in the spring. However, an injury sustained when the ship rolled in the Bay of Biscay on the way home ruled Allen out and he played very little in 1935.

Jardine had thought that Allen rather than Wyatt would be asked to captain MCC v. the South Africans in the early season game at Lord's, but the invitation went to Wyatt and, in due course, it was followed by a letter from Warner asking him to captain England against South Africa.

Wyatt had had a fine start to the season, despite the jaw, and Jardine wrote to offer his congratulations and added, 'at the Selection Committee and on the field assert yourself. Peter Perrin is always staunch and sound: 'ware Warner and Higson!'

Captain and chairman clashed over the selection of the team for the second Test at Lord's. Wyatt urged the inclusion of T. B. Mitchell, on the positive ground that he was the bowler to make most capital out of a wicket reduced to a desert by a plague of leather-jacket insects and on the negative ground that R. W. V. Robins should be excluded because he had not pulled his weight in the first Test. Mitchell was selected and had a bad match. Warner recorded in his autobiography that the selectors, 'an experienced body of men, if I may say so', were unanimously in favour of Robins but gave way, 'physically and mentally exhausted', to Wyatt after eight hours of discussion. Warner added that Wyatt, in his endeavour to prove he was right, then 'overbowled Mitchell in the match . . . It was a sad affair.'

Wyatt has challenged both the unanimity of the opposition to him and the length of the meeting – 'I had particularly outspoken support from Perrin.' He believed that, the match having been subsequently lost, Warner was all too ready to lay the blame entirely on his captain rather than accept a corporate error in selection. As in 1926 at Leeds, it was an instance of Warner's reluctance to accept personal responsibility when things went wrong.

In a desperate effort to win the fifth Test, and so draw the series and save the rubber, Wyatt put South Africa in to bat on a good wicket. *Wisden* got rather carried away in describing his decision as 'probably the most daring ever adopted in Test cricket' and the venture proved unsuccessful, both sides accumulating massive first-innings totals. Fry, writing in the *Evening Standard* on Wyatt's captaincy as a whole, was full of praise, speaking of a side which 'had the appearance of being unanimously at his call and gladly so' and which achieved 'as high a standard of corporate efficiency as has ever been seen in a Test match of my time'. Warner also praised Wyatt's captaincy, in particular his field placing and handling of the attack, but he blamed him for the decision to field.

During the summer Warner asked if Wyatt would be prepared to take the side to New Zealand in the coming winter of 1935–36, adding that it might be wiser if he rested with a full tour to Australia in mind a year later. Wyatt took the winter off and Holmes led MCC. The team played briefly in Australia and their presence (with no one from the 1932–33 side) did much to restore Anglo-Australian goodwill.

The first indication which Wyatt had that he might not, after all, lead England in Australia in 1936–37 came when he was invited to play under Allen's captaincy in the match between MCC and the Indians at Lord's early in 1936. A month later, both men played as the respective captains of North and South in the Test trial at

Lord's. Both had 'good' matches and both were picked for the first Test against India but the captaincy went to Allen.

Warner was never reluctant to write consoling letters and always found it easier to 'sugar the pill' in correspondence rather than conversation. He wrote to Wyatt:

My dear Bob,
You know, I hope, how at times in this life one has to do things which one does not like doing. Making Gubby captain in the Test at Lord's will not, I sincerely hope, cause any sort of resentment on your part. There must be disappointment, I know, but you are such a fine fellow that you will bear it with the courage and good temper you have always shown. I shall never forget your loyalty and even temper, and your charming disposition in Australia during some rather grim periods. You were wonderful, and you were wonderful, too, in 1935 when a lot of dogs were barking at you.

> You will know, I believe, how I feel.
> With every possible good wish
> Yours ever,
> 'Plum'

Warner's decision won general support from the press, only *The Times* arguing the case against Allen on the grounds that being 'a fast bowler at once disqualified him'. But even that critic believed that Allen had many of the qualities needed, 'keenness, energy and spirit'. Statistically, Wyatt's period as captain had produced only two wins in 13 matches between June 1934 and August 1935.

In cricketing terms, the selectors were presented with two excellent men both of whom had considerable claims. On Wyatt's side, it could be argued that he had had more experience as captain at both international and county level, that he had played with more regularity, that he had been both a vice-captain and a captain on overseas tours. On Allen's side it might be said that the MCC tour of 1936–37 was intended to bury the bodyline hatchet once and for all. Wyatt had been (indeed still was) close to Jardine and had been his vice-captain though he had scarcely been consulted in 1932–33. Allen had not only demonstrably shown to Australians his lack of sympathy for Jardine's policies in 1932–33 but he had, with his Australian family connections, been the one member of the MCC party who had remained popular with them.

Finally, it was openly accepted that Warner was very fond of Allen, regarded him almost as a member of the family and had encouraged him throughout the 1920s and 1930s. Neither of

Warner's sons were identified with cricket at top level. Allen, by 'adoption', might continue the lineage and heritage of which Warner, in his grander moments, saw himself a part – Harris, Hawke, Warner, Allen: all great men who would give their lives to Lord's and to MCC. In a sense, history proved Warner right.

So one England captain had given way to another and Allen would eventually take the side to Australia in 1936–37. The two men have been friends over a lifetime and, as I chatted to Wyatt in his Cornish home in 1985, a copy of Swanton's newly published biography of Allen lay on the table, given by the subject 'to Bob' with a warm inscription. And, at the luncheon to launch Gerald Pawle's biography of Wyatt a few weeks earlier, the two had sat close by. Nevertheless, Wyatt still believed that Warner, having 'inherited' him as England captain, had at once begun to lay plans to depose him. Wyatt had some grounds for this view. An article in the 1934 Winter Annual of *The Cricketer* by Fender had discussed the England captaincy for the next tour of Australia and not mentioned Allen. Warner, who had just been appointed a selector for 1935 had added an editorial footnote, 'in view of his considerable experience against Australia, G. O. Allen must be considered'. In a letter to Agnes during the 1932–33 tour, Warner had written: 'Gubby should be the next captain of England.' Wyatt believed that Warner's natural inclinations were to prefer those from the Oxbridge, south of England 'stable' and that, more particularly, he saw Allen as the favourite horse. To continue the analogy, we may recall Bismarck's dictum about the relationship between horses and riders. Warner, the chairman of selectors, believed he could have a firmer hold on the reins with Allen in the shafts than with Wyatt. It was, all the same, a disappointing time for Wyatt whose captaincy of Warwickshire was being taken from him in a sequence of events which were far more conspiratorial than the matter of Warner's preferences for the England captaincy. One has only to compare the openness of Warner's letter compared with the barely concealed hostility of those from the Warwickshire chairman.[38]

Ironically, Warner was to find Allen, as captain, as much his own man as Wyatt had been. Indeed, the irony went further for one of the issues at stake around the selection meeting for the tour of 1936–37 (once Allen had been duly appointed captain and co-opted to the committee) was whether Wyatt should go as a player. Allen argued the case for Wyatt while Warner wanted Paynter. Allen got his way but on the tour itself Wyatt was injured early, only coming into the side for the fourth and fifth Tests, although he came third in the tour averages. A more important issue arose over the suggestion of Voce. Allen attended one of the meetings at Lord's in August and found general agreement to pick him. Voce had not played against the 1934 Australians and Allen believed his presence in the tour party would damage the restored goodwill. Warner himself argued the case for Voce despite his own bitter opposition to the type of bowling which Voce had been under orders to deliver five years earlier. Allen threatened to resign as captain but himself suggested the compromise solution which 'worked'. Voce, under Allen's tutelage, made 'a statement' and the author, when interviewing Voce shortly before he died, was left in no doubt of Voce's admiration for Allen and his willingness to serve under him. In the series itself Voce was by far the best England bowler. Warner, in his autobiography, fired a broadside at both 'his' captains over this period: 'It seems to me that Wyatt in 1935 and Allen in 1936 were rather like the Soviet (!): they kept on stressing their own views, and did not give sufficient weight to the arguments of the other side. They appeared to set little store by facts.'

The remark has an ungracious touch to it not least because of the immense success of Allen as a captain, despite losing the Ashes after being two up in the series. At the time, Warner had allowed himself a brief 'editorial' comment in *The Cricketer*. Before the team set off he wrote, 'the lean years are past, done and finished with. We have a bright future.'

So the captain had been chosen. But Warner had also been approached about another matter relating to the forthcoming tour of Australia which harked back to the previous one. As early as March 1936, six months before the party would leave England, he received a letter from Hore-Ruthven, now Lord Gowrie the Governor-General of Australia, asking him to discuss with the Australian High Commissioner in London, S. M. Bruce, how a particular 'gentleman' might be stopped from coming out as a correspondent to report the MCC tour of 1936–37. Gowrie wrote:

My dear Plum,
I cannot conceive anything more calculated to revive the friction and ill-feeling that existed here three years ago than the presence of the gentleman that you mention and the style of articles which he would presumably contribute.

But how to tackle the matter is rather a difficult problem. You know even better than I what these newspaper men are and any action we might take may make things worse rather than better. I am wondering whether a protest from Mr. Bruce, the High Commissioner in London, would have more effect as coming from the Australian point of view, than anything which I can do, or any British official. At any rate I do not think it would do any harm for you to go and see Bruce and explain the situation to him and ask his opinion as to the best course to pursue.

After the splendid atmosphere that Holmes[39] and his lads produced here it would be a tragedy if the whole thing was upset again by the presence of this individual.

We are looking forward very much indeed to the visit of the next team, but if sand is going to be thrown into the machine by the presence of this gentleman it would be better if the team stayed at Home altogether. I will think over very seriously as to whether there is anything that I personally can do but as you will realise one has to be very careful not to play into the hands of the press and make things worse. Let me know if you think there is anything I can do and I need not tell you I will spare no effort to prevent this catastrophe coming about.

We cannot automatically assume that Gowrie was referring to Jardine (now writing for the London *Evening Standard*) as he was careful never to mention a name in the letter, although it is a more than reasonable supposition. These were strong words from a man thoroughly versed in Australian thinking. For whatever reason, Jardine did not go to Australia then and only once again visited the country, on business in the 1950s.

The tour itself was a success despite the loss of the Ashes. 'no one could have led the side better on the field or more happily and with greater tact and discretion off it,' wrote Warner of Allen in *The Cricketer*. Objective support came from Hammond, one who found it difficult to bestow praise, 'Gubby Allen was worth a nip of champagne all round to any team, a popular leader whom nothing could shake.' In 1937, because of work commitments, Allen was not available to captain England v. New Zealand and Warner and his fellow-selectors chose Robins, another Middlesex man and the current county captain. It was a holding operation for two reasons: Warner hoped Allen would make himself free to captain England v. Australia in 1938 while, in the autumn of 1937, came the news, after weeks of rumour, that Hammond would henceforth play as an amateur.

Sir Home Gordon called Robins 'a vivid personality' but if we set him aside, there were now two principal candidates for the England captaincy. Robins himself contributed to the debate by saying in public that 'no cricketer would object to being led by such a great player as Wally Hammond' and the press in general urged his selection as captain of England. There were, of course, powerful arguments against. Hammond had a difficult personality and there was no twentieth-century precedent for an ex-professional captaining England. The *Daily Mail* believed 'the strangling effect of the old school tie' would prevail.

Warner had been an admirer of Hammond ever since, as the *Morning Post* critic, he had written in 1923 of a 24 made for Gloucestershire against Sussex: 'I watched Hammond with special interest. He is very young and he has a good style. I liked his cricket immensely.' Warner had then urged his selection for the Players against the Gentlemen at The Oval and he had made 46. In 1926, when chairman of selectors, he visited the young man, on the verge of death, in a Bristol hospital and told him that the England side of that year 'would have been a great one' if Hammond had been in it. Hammond later wrote that Warner 'gave me the strength to turn the dark corner from hopelessness back to life'. Their friendship was to last over the years and Warner felt that he 'was one of the few to break down the barriers of reserve and shyness' in Hammond. Warner was thus presented with two candidates both of whom he personally liked and this mattered very much to someone of his sensitive personality. But it remained necessary for Allen to make some appearances! Business, as ever, made its claims. While · Warner wanted him to play for MCC v. the Australians early in May, Allen was reluctant to do so as he would have had so little cricket. Warner, according to Allen, was upset by his declining to play and with Allen's comment to him, 'but Plum, I don't think you really understand fast bowlers' problems'. Swanton has commented that it 'must have been a wounding thrust from one in whose career [Warner] had taken an affectionate interest for so long'.[40] In the event, Allen had two good county matches, withdrew from Middlesex v. Australians because of back trouble and was named as captain of the Rest in the England trial, with Hammond as the 'England' captain. Allen declined the invitation on the grounds he was still unfit and he felt that Warner might have indicated in advance that it was 'the Rest' captaincy which he was being offered. The selectors had little choice but to appoint Hammond.

For a spell relations between Warner and Allen were cool and it may be suggested that the favoured son had shown rather too much of a rebellious spirit over the last few years. There had proved to be an independency of mind and attitude in Allen which Warner resented. In Hammond he would have a captain more docile and subservient. At least Warner may be given the credit for choosing an England captain from stables with which he was less familiar. Warner, so often labelled the arch-conservative, had given the England captaincy to a grammar school boy who had been a professional until a few months earlier. He had chosen a player whom he admired, a man whom he liked and a captain of whom he would say in a broadcast at the end of the 1938 summer, 'he was an able, inspiring and sympathetic leader'. It was a view Warner reiterated when Hammond returned after the 1938–39 tour of South Africa, declaring 'that he was immensely appreciated by his side and he was understanding and sympathetic to those who failed'. The comment tells us more about Warner than about Hammond. Hammond was often far from understanding and sympathetic to those who failed, though his biographer felt that there was a shy man inwardly possessing such qualities but desperately unable to express himself.[41]

Certainly, no criticism attached to Hammond's captaincy while Warner was chairman of the selectors. At the end of the 1938 season, *Wisden* called his leadership 'sagacious and inspiring', and Lord Hawke congratulated him. In the last weeks of Hawke's life, it was a gesture which did something to diminish the longstanding criticism attached to Hawke for his badly chosen words on professional captains.

Shortly before he ceased to be chairman of the selectors, Warner wrote an article in *The Cricketer* in 1937 which gave an insight into his own view of the work involved. In discussing the selection of a team to tour Australia he posed the sort of question which had to be considered. Will the captain be a good leader of a side on tour? Will such and such a player make a good travelling companion? Will he put the side first? Will he keep himself fit? Will he suit the climate he is going to? Will he make runs on Australian wickets? A selector, he wrote, had to be 'absolutely unprejudiced and impartial, "know his stuff", be cool, calm and judgmatic, learn from the past, and know the principles of cricket, which – like the principles of warfare – do not change'. He should study how a bowler obtained his wickets and how a batsman made his runs. He should be able to accept with equanimity the criticism of the press which, except for a spell in 1935 and 1936, he felt 'was considerate'. Finally, he wrote, 'I am interested in every detail and phase of cricket. I venture to think that there are few men of my age so much in touch with the present generation of cricketers.'

It was the generation of the rising Hutton, D.C.S. Compton and W. J. Edrich (so far as batsmen were concerned) and Warner, in his last period of office as a selector, recognised their talent. Compton's cricket career was, in his own words, 'made possible by Sir Pelham Warner'.

By others who remembered Warner in committee he was seen

as 'conscientious and informed'. Wyatt conceded that 'he would give way if opposed by sound reasoning'. Outside the committee room, he was known to listen, observe and travel. Sir Home Gordon, in an article in *The Cricketer* (which he forbade the editor to censor), wrote:

I am able to realise the heavy responsibility on his shoulders. It would be impossible to exaggerate how conscientiously, how laboriously, yet how devotedly he fulfilled the trust imposed on him. People would be surprised how wide was the range of his investigations. Players of quite moderate ability were kept under review in case their skills should suddenly develop. Nobody was neglected. Unbiased and unruffled he and his fellow selectors listened to everybody. Sometimes, when Warner paid apparently deep attention to nonsense talked to him, I thought how aptly he fulfilled the behest to 'suffer fools gladly'.

His thoroughness may again be gauged by an exchange of correspondence with Hedley Verity, the Yorkshire professional, in January 1938. Warner wanted a detailed comment on how certain players whom he had in mind for the series against Australia had performed on the 1936–37 tour. Verity's reply is a long one and against it are written Warner's own reactions, for example:

Yorkshire do not play the Australians until the end of July. I have in mind that England's chance would be enhanced if it was possible for Hutton to have a look at O'Reilly before the first 'Test' Match. O'Reilly is the type of bowler who may get anyone out cheaply the first time they are opposed to him, owing to his action and flight. An innings would obviate that danger in the first Test. I know the difficulties, and can only offer the suggestion hoping that some way can be found.

Beside this Warner pencilled, 'not possible I fear.' Hutton duly made a century in the first Test off W. J. O'Reilly and others, as did C. J. Barnett on whom Verity had commented:

'Jaw' about Barnett is due to two things; his English form and game differing from his Australian performances and his habit of talking about himself which makes him unpopular. In Australia, in a cricket sense, he 'did his stuff' as opening batsman. As his pal I know it helped his morale to talk; I encourage it for that reason and incidentally tried to instil the idea that to be No.

1 he must get on top of all the bowlers, get them down, rather than adopt his carefree County methods. Considering the way he did the job he must be considered; he only failed when lame and tired in the last match. He could, however, be talked into doing well lower down the list if more suitable openers could be found. Had we possessed another reasonably successful opening batsman in Australia our success would have been assured.

Warner had also sounded out the possibility of selecting Sutcliffe. Verity replied that he was 'still a great batsman and might prove useful'. Verity supported Warner's suggestion that pace had to be the spearhead of the attack, advocating the selection of Allen, Voce, Bowes and Farnes, of whom only the last two played. It was a letter of such quality and detail as to suggest (had he survived the war) that one day Verity himself would have made an excellent selector.

The story is told that at the end of the 1938 series Warner felt he was being pursued unnecessarily by the press before The Oval Test. He went out for the day and told no one of his movements. Alas! Ames broke his finger and England were without a wicket-keeper. Warner was untraceable and the decision to summon Arthur Wood for his first Test match at the age of 40 (and take a taxi from Nottingham to London to arrive on time) was taken by the other selectors. Warner had spent the day reading in his club with instructions not to be disturbed!

This mild dereliction of duty is far outbalanced by the warm tributes paid to Warner when he ceased to be chairman. Among many letters he received was the following from a member of the Kent County Committee:

> My dear Plum,
> You may be interested to know that I was at a party the other day at which a number of prominent cricketers were present – I remarked that in my view it was a great disaster that you had resigned from the Selection Committee – One and all *most cordially* agreed with me – It was felt that, quite apart from your unique knowledge of cricket and cricketers, you were a tremendous *steadying* influence on the Committee. We shan't see your like on the Selection Committee again but I imagine that you felt it a great tie to have to be touring the country all through the cricket season in search of talent.

More officially, but with equal enthusiasm, the editor of *Wisden* wrote:

It will be no easy matter to find a competent successor to Sir Pelham Warner whose decision not to seek re-election has been received with widespread regret. The game owes much to his devoted work, his encouragement of young cricketers and to his ever-optimistic spirit. It is a tribute in itself that when Sir Pelham has assisted in choosing a team to oppose Australia in this country, England has never lost a rubber.

Yet this was not the end of his career as a selector. Fifteen years later, in 1953, he was appointed chairman of the MCC sub-committee to choose the side to go to the West Indies. Hutton, the captain, was conscious of the presence of a man who had first picked England sides 48 years earlier. 'I didn't want to press my arguments too far,' he recalled and he felt a reluctance to disagree with Warner's views. Hutton also believed that the selection was rushed to fit in with Warner's attendance at the Oval Test. The captain had to combine trying to win the Ashes with selecting the tour party. Warner had let it be known after the war that his experience could again be drawn upon as a selector but, apart from this one instance, other views prevailed and he was not invited.

During these years, Warner's natural instinct to be friendly and to be such a good and regular correspondent meant that contacts with old friends were maintained and new links established. His association with Don Bradman, 35 years his junior, may be cited as an example of this. He first met Bradman in 1930 and, in his courteous way, wrote a letter of congratulation to him upon his performances that summer. Bradman, later in the year, successfully asked Warner to write the Foreword to his first book. Bradman had considerable sympathy for Warner in the position in which he found himself in 1932–33 and, as a witness to the events, described vividly to me, 50 years later, *in situ* at Adelaide Oval, how ashen and shaken Warner was in the famous confrontation with Woodfull. When Bradman became so ill in 1934 that his life was despaired of, and King George V asked to be kept regularly informed of developments, Warner alone was allowed by the surgeon, Sir Douglas Shields, to visit him. Bradman was punctilious in replying to the various letters which Warner sent him on his achievements in 1934 and 1938, and he was kind enough to show them to me so that I was able to bring the correspondence together. A typical Warner letter, written in 1934, was:

A line to congratulate you most sincerely on your great batting which brought you 1000 runs before the end of May – a wonderful feat and more wonderful than ever in your case because you have accomplished it in fewer innings than Grace or Hayward or Hallows.

I hope you will go on and prosper for your batting, and I may add your fielding, have given the greatest possible delight to everyone.

While Bradman, in 1930, wrote to him:

What a wonderful game is cricket. There can be no other sport where opponents show such a friendly spirit and where they are willing and anxious to congratulate others on their perform-ances. If my efforts on the cricket fields of England have been satisfactory to your cricket-loving public, then I am amply repaid.

Eight years later, when captain of Australia, he wrote to Warner:

It is my fervent desire during my regime that cricket shall be played in the friendliest possible spirit and I see no reason why that desire should not be fulfilled. We are especially pleased by the pleasing personalities of your young players. It augurs well for the future.

There are no great revelations in the Warner–Bradman corres-pondence but they may be said to represent, on the one hand, a way in which Warner's convictions about cricket and the imperial link were put into practice and, on the other, the readiness of Bradman, when at the height of his fame, to find the time to write to one of the game's elder statesmen. Bradman, too, believed in 'fostering international goodwill through cricket'. The corres-pondence does both men credit.

Another correspondent was the captain of the Indian tourists in 1936, the Maharaj Sir Vijaya Vizianagram. It was no secret at the time that the side was beset with internal problems, highlighted by the sending home on disciplinary grounds of L. Amarnath. A few months afterwards Sir Vijaya wrote to Warner thanking him for his constant help behind the scenes in the difficulties which arose: 'need I say that during the tour you were indeed a pillar of strength to me. Whenever I had a corner to turn I used to fall back upon your strong support. I was a nuisance to you.' In true Indian fashion, he enclosed a present for Agnes of a piece of Benares silk brocade. Rather more unusually, he wrote again to Warner two years later on 27 November 1938 with a desperate plea for help.

He had been asked to give away the prizes at the Benares Hindu University on 18 December:

Much as I wish to say something that is worth saying, I am sorry I won't be able to think of anything really original. I wonder if you can find the time to write out a few lines for me and airmail them to me. You are one of the finest speakers of the day. Your kind help is sure to help me into getting full marks. It is common knowledge that your gift of the gab is phenomenal. Your choice of phrase and extent of diction make many a speaker gape in wondering admiration.

Warner could not resist such flattery and he at once dispatched 'a speech' to Sir Vijaya.

Nearer at home, another correspondent over the years was the old Middlesex captain A. J. Webbe who had introduced Warner to the county at the turn of the century. Webbe felt the time had come to give up the presidency of Middlesex and he persuaded Warner to succeed him in 1936, a post he held until 1946.

On Wednesday 12 May 1937, came the announcement of a knighthood in the Coronation Honours List. There he was, next to Hugh Walpole the novelist and William Wood, senior vice-president of the LMS railway. But it was the cricketer who got all the press attention:

None has devoted himself more whole-heartedly or unselfishly to the game than 'Plum' – the *Morning Post*.

Even if they make him a duke, he will always be 'Plum' in the cricket world – the *Daily Sketch*.

In June he was guest of honour at a dinner at the Savoy to celebrate his knighthood. He chose to speak on being a selector:

In my early days as a selector – and that is going back to 1905 – the England team was picked in about three minutes, after a pleasant luncheon. MacLaren, 'Ranji', Fry, Jessop . . .

Afterwards there might be a jaw – Jessop or Hayward? MacLaren always plumped for Jessop because he said Jessop might throw out Trumper before Trumper had scored!

It was easy in those days. But now, with so much cricket being played and so many players of almost equal merit, we find it necessary to spend hours of the most serious contemplation.

So now you know. Spare a thought for the poor selectors.

They've got nobody to fight their case for an eight-hour day.

During the preliminary work of choosing modern English Test teams, we have come to think almost exclusively in terms of Bradman. I am not sure that is best. I have tried to dissuade the committee from thinking so much about Bradman in their team-choosing deliberations.

The excitement continued in July when he attended the dinner at the Savoy to mark the one hundred and fiftieth anniversary of MCC. He was not one of the speakers at the function and he was critical of those who were, '[they] were not worthy of the occasion and a fearful *faux pas* was committed when the names of Lord Harris and W. G. Grace were not even mentioned'. He was also critical of Allen whose speech mentioned neither of these celebrities (though perhaps it was more Sir Stanley Jackson's place to do so), the recent tour of Australia, nor his opposite number as captain, Bradman. Warner seems to have been slightly unfortunate where anniversaries were concerned. He was not asked to play in 1914 at the centenary of the present Lord's nor to speak in 1937 at this anniversary of MCC. But as a small spectator he had watched WG in 1887 and no one could take the memory away from him.

Another function which Warner attended in 1937 was the reception to meet the first women's Australian team to tour England. He had shown an interest in women's cricket for many years. Women were allowed to play in the nets at Caring House and the official launching of the Women's Cricket Association in 1926 had not only his support but his advice: 'Now do see that you play the game in strict order and decorum.' Sometime after the three 'Tests' of the 1937 series, Warner met Molly Hide, the England captain, and the outcome was a regular feature on women's cricket in *The Cricketer*.

A further invitation in 1937 was to his old school, Rugby. With some surprise he had received a letter in 1936 asking him to allow his nomination as the next vice-president of the Old Rugbeian Society, with automatic succession to the presidency a year later. Although he retained happy memories of his days as a boy at Rugby, he had seldom visited the school. His proposer, Sir John Maffey, afterwards Lord Rugby, wrote, 'I am sure you realise that this is an office which the fates will insist on your filling.'

Warner's nomination was linked to the fact that a new cricket pavilion was to be opened in 1937 (the year of his vice-presidency) and he was invited to speak at the occasion, describing Tom Emmett as his 'headmaster'. He thoroughly enjoyed his day, and was photographed, resplendent in a morning suit, with the headmaster, P. H. B. Lyon, and William Temple, the Archbishop of York and chairman of the governors. Looking over Warner's shoulder through his pince-nez was the Master of Corpus, (Sir) William Spens.

Also in the group was the future Lord Cilcennin, at that time (as J. P. L. Thomas) parliamentary secretary to Anthony Eden who would, in a few months, resign with his political master over Neville Chamberlain's appeasement policy. In his 'bread and butter' letter to Lyon, Warner wrote that he had had 'a most enjoyable day but I felt a bit out of my element among such a learned governing body'.

Thereafter Warner began to pay visits to the school and Lyon remembered him as someone 'who was proud of his Rugby associations, and glad to visit the school from time to time though not an old boy who was forever on the doorstep'. Because Lyon also recalled Warner as 'a man of courtesy', he recollected how stunned Plum was by a certain incident at Rugby in 1941 which we shall recount in Chapter 10.

So came to an end the 1930s. The last summer before the outbreak of war was not a bad one for the 65-year-old Plum Warner. He was freed of the responsibility for choosing the England side. His own 'countrymen', the West Indians, were the tourists. *The Cricketer* was firmly established in the minds of the reading cricket public. He had had, at last, an excellent report from the BBC on his broadcasting and he took an MCC side to Denmark, which included J. G. W. Davies, who would become president of MCC in 1985, almost a hundred years after Plum's own election to membership. The Danish tour was rather less sensational than his experience of management seven years earlier. The sight of the manager scoring 16 out of 18 direct hits at a fun-fair booth and the amazed looks of his players brought the jocular boast that 'all the cricketers of my time threw like that'. Warner, who had captained teams abroad in Queen Victoria's reign, had given these young men, so soon off to fight a war, something pleasant to remember.

10
Wartime Custodian, 1939–45

The Second World War gave some old men a new lease of life. The apothegm is applicable to Churchill, in the grand manner, to the Anglo-Boer War veterans who joined the Home Guard and to Warner who ran Lord's. To suggest that what Churchill did for Britain Warner did for cricket is not a totally absurd comparison. Indeed, there hovers in the back of the biographer's mind some 'slight similarities between the two: both spanned the same 90 years, both believed in the importance of the British Empire, both were men of action and natural leaders who found time to be authors. On totally different planes each was an epitome of his class and generation. The contrasts, of course, abound.

At the outbreak of the war Warner was appointed assistant deputy then deputy secretary[42] at Lord's in the absence on military service of both Rait Kerr and Aird. It was an appointment which he held throughout the war, which made heavy demands upon him and brought a salary of £700 a year. He could hardly be called a 'war profiteer' but the money was extremely useful to someone who had always been dependent on his wife for his standard of living. He remained conscious of her personal wealth and the £4000 or so which his hard work at Lord's during the war earned him was easily eclipsed by one single legacy of over £6000 left to her by an aunt.

Throughout the war, Warner wrote once a week to Esmond who served in the Middle East, North Africa and, in the closing stages, in South-East Asia. The collection of some 200 letters gives a vivid picture of the life of the Warners in wartime and in old age. They follow a similar pattern: the state of the war, family affairs, Warner's own activities and events at Lord's. Money and Agnes's health are constant themes. He managed to get an income tax rebate of £6 through his solicitor and he had paid £22 to those who looked after Esmond's dog, Arkie, when he felt he could not cope with it any longer. He wrote poignantly to Esmond: 'I hated parting with him. Have never liked a dog so much. In the train he made friends with a Canadian soldier, a Petty Officer RN, and two little girls. I had a post-card, he is settling down well. I miss him *terribly*.'

Agnes's life in the 1940s established a pattern for the rest of her days. In physical terms, her heart condition got worse rather than better, and she had a major operation in 1944. When well, she was able to enjoy visits to Wembley, Twickenham and Lord's and to see a Terence Rattigan play. John recalled his mother standing with fortitude on a crowded wartime train journey from the north of England to London. Nevertheless, it was from now onwards that she retired to bed often for days at a time.

A biographer treads sensitive ground in examining family relationships and extrapolates with care. That Agnes was often unwell and in pain goes some way to explaining why she was so often confined to her bed. But perhaps not the whole way. Her bedroom became something of a sanctuary to which she could withdraw from the tensions that could arise in the household. Pelham continued in his devotion to Pearl Allen – but Agnes had long ago learnt to live with that. More pertinently, there was still Miss E.H., her husband's friend from Australian days, around the corner in Gloucester Road. There was also a sense of strain between her husband and her elder son, Esmond, of which she was acutely conscious on the few occasions when the two men were together. For reasons of health and what might almost be called convenience, she gradually made of her bedroom a boudoir where she would entertain her friends, be lively in conversation, place bets on horses and keep up with the latest books and plays.

None of this denies the fun of family occasions. Her sixty-sixth birthday in 1943 was celebrated by a tea-party with the Allens, 'for which', as her husband wrote to Esmond, 'Doris baked a cake and I gave her a pair of shoes'. Warner was not a man given to irony but it was a marginally odd present in the circumstances. His own seventieth birthday a few weeks later was a grander event with a party for 40, including relations and the Allens, Jacksons, Rait Kerrs and his old friend the Eton schoolmaster, C. M. Wells (who wrote a Latin ode for the occasion). Perhaps some of the food parcels they got monthly from South Africa helped to provide the feast. Sir Home Gordon asked him to lunch in Brighton as a birthday celebration and 'to have a whiff of sea air and a most hearty welcome'.

Betty visited whenever she could, sometimes staying a night in the flat to give Doris time off. John, stationed in the Home Counties, and his wife Jean, whom he had married in 1942, came when they could. John's marriage in Kent had been followed, a year later, by news of Esmond's marriage in Italy to Emilia Terzulli, an event which coincided with Esmond's promotion to lieutenant-colonel. His father sent him a cheque for £50 'with fondest love and warmest congratulations on the double event'. Then, as the years went by, came the delight of various grandchildren. For their benefit Warner produced a set of rules for the next generation of young rats. No doubt part of their object was to ensure good behaviour when the rats came to stay but they also continued a family tradition going back to the 'creation' of Agnes as Mother Rat not long after she and Pelham were married. Here, then, are the Rules of the Rat Hole Club:

1 The object of the Rat Hole Club is to provide comfort, shelter and fitness for Young Rats.
2 With this main object in view it is essential to have certain Rules and Regulations which all Young Rats are expected to obey.

The *Essential Rules* are:

(a) No Young Rat to get out of his bed without putting on his dressing gown and slippers – this is important for the health of all Young Rats.
(b) Every Young Rat to help every other Young Rat. This leads to a well organised and happy Rat Hole.
(c) Obedience to every order by the Officers in charge of the Rat Hole to be immediate.
(d) Every Young Rat to be good tempered, easy and pleasant at all times.
(e) It is unnecessary to make any threats, but if Young Rats do not fall in with the Rules punishment of none too pleasant a kind will follow.
(f) Young Rats will bear in mind that the Rat Hole Club has established a great tradition of good order, comfort and happiness, and we expect every Young Rat, without exception, to live up to this tradition.
(g) The Dog Simon is an Honorary Member of the Rat Hole Club and as such is always to be warmly welcomed.

Signed P. F. Warner King of the Rat Hole
Father of all Young Rats.
Doris Smith Lady Commander of the Rat Hole.

In the wider circle of their friends was the marriage of George Jellicoe, who had succeeded to his father's earldom in 1935 – 'this has shaken his mother for it makes her a dowager', Warner wrote, 'he is a gallant fellow with his DSO and MC'. A vignette, soon after Sir Walter Allen died, is portrayed, 'Pearl and I went to Kew, took our lunch with us, the gardens looked wonderful, with a blend of colour and lovely spring flowers. I fed the birds, and fat thrushes fought like tigers over a piece of cake.'

Despite the claims of domesticity, Warner was to be found, as so often in his life, dining with the great and the famous. There were lunches at Claridges' to meet C. R. Attlee, Sir Stafford Cripps and Air Chief Marshal Portal; at the House of Lords, as Lord Lucan's guest to see the introduction of Lord Gowrie to the House. Indeed, at one point, Warner was so frequently a guest at the Upper House that the policeman on duty invited 'M'Lord [to] wrap up on a cold night'.

Warner's 'asides' to Esmond on some of those whom he met call for passing comment:

Brendan Bracken: 'a clever, amusing and attractive fellow. He does not like the Beveridge proposals.'

Eisenhower: 'did all the honours in a very grand manner'.

Beaverbrook: 'can't think why he's been brought back to the Government. I am no admirer of his and everyone I have met dislikes him intensely.'

Warner's letters record the passing of old friends whose funerals he attended and whose obituaries he often wrote for *The Times* or *The Cricketer*, among them Sir Walter Allen, A. C. MacLaren, G. J. V. Weigall, A. J. Webbe and Basil Lubbock, his brother-in-law, and of young friends killed in the war such as G. D. Kemp-Welch, a victim of the Guards Chapel bombing in 1943, who had toured with him to Holland, Kenneth Farnes, ('a fine if moody bowler with a lovely action, arm in the sky, and greatness at his best') and Hedley Verity ('Can you arrange for some flowers on his grave?'). In 1944 his own elder brother, Aucher, died and Warner was proud that he earned a *Times* obituary as a distinguished lawyer and as the first touring West Indian captain. 'So many deaths in the last few years, young and old,' he wrote to Esmond.

In a rather more oblique way the death of one particular young cricketer in the war moved Warner. In 1941 arrangements had been made to celebrate the centenary of the famous match at Rugby between the school and MCC immortalised in *Tom Brown's*

School Days and in which the author, Thomas Hughes, captained the school. Warner, both as the most distinguished Old Rugbeian in cricket circles and as deputy secretary of MCC was closely involved in the occasion and raised the MCC side to play the school on the Close at Rugby exactly one hundred years later to the day. He persuaded the secretary of MCC, Colonel Rait Kerr (another Old Rugbeian), to apply for leave so that he might follow the tradition of his predecessor, Benjamin Aislabie, by playing in the match. Aislabie's great-grandson, Philip Landon, a law don at Trinity College, Oxford was present as a representative of the family. In the original match Aislabie had been caught by one Currie major whose great-nephew came to watch the 1941 match.

However, Warner's day was clouded by an incident, small in itself, which lingered with him as an unfortunate memory. Before the match, *The Times* photographed the two teams and Lancelot Hingley was absent. He had been the outstanding schoolboy cricketer of 1940, captaining Rugby and topping both the batting and bowling averages. His lateness displeased the punctilious Warner who remarked to him, on his arrival, that it was 'not a good example to set to schoolboys'. The young man accepted the rebuke without demur and only at lunch did Warner learn the real reason when P. H. B. Lyon, the headmaster, commented to Warner, 'good of Hingley to get here. He was bombing Dusseldorf eight hours ago.' Warner was full of remorse for his thoughtless remark. Eighteen months later Flight Sergeant Hingley was reported missing, and later presumed dead, in air operations. Lyon recalled Warner mentioning the matter again when he visited Rugby just before Lyon's headmastership ended in 1948. 'The most courteous of men, he still felt upset by it.'

As for the match itself, Warner, by inviting three former England captains to play, in Allen,[43] Wyatt and Holmes, set a somewhat daunting task to the school. Repeating precedent and 'with the usual liberality of young hands' (as Thomas Hughes had written), the school sent their masters into bat and did not do badly, taking 9 wickets before the declaration came at 149. But that was the end of their fortunes, for the pre-war Middlesex and England bowler C. I. J. Smith took 6 for 8 in 8 overs. Wyatt took the remaining 4 for 14 and the boys were out for 31.

It was a brief respite for many of the players from combat duties. Warner's own approach to the war was one of fearlessness as John recalled. 'At one point, no one else was staying in the block of flats except my parents.' Warner's physical courage in the varied circumstances of facing fast bowlers, enduring pain or contemplating air-raids was unquestioned. Inevitably, the strain of wartime life began to tell, as two letters to Esmond in 1944 showed:

We had a nasty raid this morning. The fiercest for two years or more. Fires everywhere. At Lord's a phosperous bomb burnt a house only forty yards from the Pavilion, it burnt like a match. Also a sulphur bomb on the practice ground, near St. John's Wood Station but MCC fire squad had it out quickly. Apparently 60 or 70 machines. MR did not hear alert and as usual very brave as were Betty and Doris, but it got me out of bed. Bitterly cold today but I took MR to England v Scotland at Wembley, but far too cold for us old ones.

We have had the Flying Bombs, a hell of a row, and the bomb shrieking like an express train going through a station at 60 mph. It is a bit nasty and disturbing and at Lord's we played (June 18) in spite of sirens. It is exciting but it does not affect me. What's the good?

He went away for a few days to stay at Eton and then at Rugby while Agnes and Doris went elsewhere. He came back to an empty house and 'Gubby (Allen) came and stayed for a few days when I was alone' and, as two men with no one to cook for them, they were asked out to 'a wonderful dinner of corn on the cob, sole and trifle and lots to drink. We walked home and I got to bed at 11.45 p.m.'

Another letter, in August 1944, is indicative of so many aspects of his life: his wife's health and wealth; his own financial worries; the war; his work at Lord's:

MR is better but must rest. She has arranged your affairs with your bank, and given you £1500 as a wedding present. (A bomb just down some way off.) I am well but very tired and am taking three days off before the big cricket at Lord's next week when England play Australia then the Dominions, then Lord's Schools v Rest, then a Lord's XI v public schools. I had to get up several teams, some in a hurry, lot of writing, telegrams and telephoning. The flying bomb has spoilt the crowds but we expect ten to fifteen thousand. Income Tax is a heavy burden but thanks to my book I am alright with my bank and in credit about £30. Hope to continue to receive royalties, due in December. All clear just gone. Affectionately PFW.

In the event, 16,000 people were present to see Hammond

make a century in England's innings of 226 to which Australia replied with 193. The next day it was L. B. Fishlock's turn for a century as Hammond set the Dominions a target of 258 which they failed to reach by 33 (with 4 wickets in hand). Such one-day games had not yet become limited-overs contests and the match was drawn. Among the schoolboys performing on the next four days of cricket were J. G. Dewes, D. B. Carr and W. H. H. Sutcliffe while Chapman and Robins (with a century) appeared for the Lord's XI.

All this had come at the end of a season in which Warner had produced representative sides throughout the Whit weekend and in June. He had, in 1944, organised 44 matches at Lord's attracting nearly 170,000 people (less than the quarter million of the year before because of the flying bomb scare), and they had raised over £4000 for charity.

Writing in the *Sunday Times*, Elton Ede remarked, 'the thousands who have thronged Lord's have been lucky in their cricket in exchange for their shillings. Games have see-sawed their way to a climax of excitement [but] one-day matches are just a jolly wartime expedient for the full rigour of the game.' It was a view which 20 years later, in the 1960s, was challenged by the emergence of commercially sponsored one-day cricket but it was one with which Warner himself would have agreed. All credit to him, therefore, for doing so much to foster cricket during the war and making such a splendid contribution to national morale.

What happened in that summer of 1944 was similar to the previous four seasons in which Warner was deputy secretary at Lord's. Throughout the war years Lord's was made available for a large variety of matches while MCC's 'out-matches' against the schools continued to be fulfilled. Among sides invited to play at Lord's were the British Empire XI, London Counties, the Services and the Auxiliary Services. Warner took the decision to have a few two-day matches, one of the most spectacular being that between England and the Dominions in 1943, won within moments of time by England by 8 runs.

The raising of teams and organising of fixtures were not his only responsibilities. The various departments of Lord's continued to operate, albeit in skeleton form. From 1940 onwards he virtually 'ran' Lord's with a staff of 30 on big days instead of the usual 140 – 'like holding the line with a company instead of a battalion'. Correspondence was exchanged with members, property maintained (despite bomb damage), squash and tennis courts kept open, the refreshment department operated, wickets and playing area prepared, committee meetings minuted. All this was the ultimate responsibility of the deputy secretary who was accountable to the Committee (of which he himself was a member) and to the Trustees. Nor should the loyalty Warner inspired in his staff be ignored. He successfully achieved a rise in their wages and his courtesy and concern for them was remembered by survivors from those days. The chief clerk, James Cannon, who had started work at Lord's in 1879, wrote to Agnes when he himself retired, recollecting his pleasure at having been at their wedding in 1904 and at serving under her husband, 'a man who has endeared himself to the cricket world even more than dear old W.G.'.

In 1941 Warner negotiated for the RAF to use Lord's for lectures and medical examinations. Some three thousand men came each day, as Warner remarked to Esmond, 'a very good thing financially for the MCC'. One of the lecturers who would march his men up St John's Wood Road to Lord's and then himself lecture on Air Force law was Squadron Leader W. R. Hammond, whose 'living above the shop' meant that he was (in 1944 and 1945) working at Lord's during the week and playing on Saturdays, 'the best bit of news cricketers have had for a long time', commented the *Evening Standard*.

In 1944 Warner was joined by the former Gloucestershire secretary Lieutenant-Colonel H. A. Henson, who had been in-valided out of the army and became his assistant. Together they planned the post-war rebuilding programme, including repair of damaged houses owned by MCC, and held frequent meetings with architects and surveyors.

Only in one area of his work at Lord's did Warner 'get into trouble'. The annual Easter coaching classes were often taken by any members who happened to be in London or even on leave. A notice had appeared in *The Daily Telegraph* for March 1942 announcing that 'Cricket classes are full' but that the dates would be extended if 'sufficient number of applications' were received. 'Cassandra' in the *Daily Mirror* savaged Warner for encouraging 'business as usual' and endorsing the 'public apathy towards the war' by such an unpatriotic gesture. Curiously, it was almost the last piece William Connor ('Cassandra') wrote during the war, for the patriotism which led him to criticise 'public apathy' also led him to volunteer for the army where he produced, in Italy, the forces paper, *Union Jack*. Before he left the paper, he wrote an apology to Warner for 'my stupid and thoughtless blunder' in thinking that half an hour a day for a week for boys of 12 would hurt the war effort. But some damage was done and those who did not know the facts lingered on in their criticism of coaching at Lord's in wartime.

Warner was also involved in the meetings of the Advisory

County Cricket Committee in 1942 and 1943 which considered the future of the game after the war. He used the occasion of the Annual General Meeting of Middlesex in 1942 to give a presidential address in which he argued that there was 'nothing wrong with modern cricket except too many counties and some over-prepared wickets'. Despite the way 'we have been delighted with one-day matches [and] have had some wonderful finishes', they were not the answer to the game in the long term at first-class level. 'Do not be led away by the call for brightening cricket. It is a leisurely, intricate game of skill. We live in an age of speed and people are apt to think that cricket must be speeded up; but my experience is that it is not necessary to have faster scoring to have interesting cricket.' Finally, he urged people to study the Findlay Commission of 1937 which he had strongly supported in *The Cricketer*.

The Advisory Committee appointed a Select Committee under Sir Stanley Jackson to which Warner was appointed (with Rait Kerr) as joint-secretary. It was a large committee with power to invite outside opinion. It met several times between November 1943 and March 1944 and published a 6000-word report, the drafting of which was largely Warner's responsibility as had been the 'servicing' of the committee. In the actual cut-and-thrust of discussion, Warner said little; he was too busy writing the notes.

When the war in Europe was over in May 1945 he set out to get representative sides from the troops who had fought there. 'I think I have got all the "Big" Boys interested,' he wrote to Esmond. He asked General Dempsey, commander of the second Army to lunch with him and this led to troops who had fought in the Normandy campaign playing Warner's XI at Lord's. Dempsey wrote, 'I hope you realise just what it all meant to my people to be playing again at Lord's. We were all most grateful.' Later, a similar approach to General Alexander brought the Central Mediterranean Forces to Lord's.

Then came the visit of Field Marshal Montgomery whom Warner, in the absence of the MCC president, looked after. 'I have never met a man with a greater charm of manner and so nice and gracious to the people. He says he is going to teach young Nazis cricket and he is a great believer in the Boy Scout Movement.' Fry had once had the same idea about the Germans – neither his nor Montgomery's came to anything.

The year 1945 also saw the return to Lord's of the traditional schools matches, the appearance there on seven occasions of the Australian Services (including three 'Victory' matches) and the famous game between England and the Dominions (with centuries by Hammond (2), M. P. Donnelly and K. R. Miller). Warner not only raised the sides but took the decision to invite Constantine to lead the Dominions. 'I was "Colony" while the rest of the team was "Dominion"' was Constantine's way of putting it and his team's success by 45 runs with eight minutes to spare was his final appearance in first-class cricket.

A few days later, Constantine wrote to Warner:

Now that the heat of battle is over I want to thank you very sincerely for the honour and privilege accorded in asking me to lead the Dominion's side. Perhaps you know that the players were very complimentary both before and after the match and in fact, the result achieved was indicative of the spirit in which the game was played. I know that I owe this to you personally and the broad mindedness with which you approach many of these traditionally complicated problems.

   I do not want to miss this opportunity of expressing my thanks and appreciation and to record what in my opinion is a step forward on the road to progress.[44]

It had given Warner particular pleasure to appoint Constantine to the captaincy. His West Indian roots had always meant much to him, especially as he grew older. The West Indian society of the late nineteenth century into which he had been born was one in which Whites managed affairs and Blacks (and Indians) were subordinate. It may be that Warner would no more have questioned such a structuring based on colour than he would one in England based on class. But his instinct to natural courtesy was totally undiminished. As a young man he had had a conversation at Oriel with Cecil Rhodes and displayed an understanding of the negro which penetrated deeper than did that of Rhodes. He was, in the view of all who remembered him, totally without colour prejudice. Quite apart from his relationship with West Indian sides who came to England, his kindliness to the Indian cricketers in 1932 had been noticeable. Other instances would occur in the period after the Second World War. Philip Snow recalled his warmth of welcome to cricketers from Fiji which was similarly extended to the first touring Pakistanis in 1954.

Towards the end of his period as deputy secretary at Lord's, Warner was understandably 'very tired' and there is more than the hint in his letters that he felt 'unrecognised' for his efforts. 'I have never been so busy at Lord's as I am just now. I run all the matches and get up nearly all the teams. I wonder if I shall get a mention.

I doubt it. Anyway, I think I can say that I have done a good job.'
He reflected to Esmond on his prospects of becoming president:

> I lay 10–1 against my ever being President of the MCC. I mean
> that! They so often make a Peer or someone who has done
> *nothing* for cricket and knows nothing about it. I imagine
> Alexander *et al* will be made long before me. I am 71 now so I
> do not expect the honour for a moment. Though many here,
> like you back me for it.

Furthermore, he often felt he was acting as president since
Stanley Christopherson, a busy chairman of the Midland Bank,
'was seldom there'. Among his 'backers' was Home Gordon who
wrote in the summer of 1945, 'may I write next May to congratulate
you on being the next President?'

Warner was a man who needed the plaudits of his fellows. He
prized greatly the letters of congratulation that came to him
throughout his career and it is perhaps an explanation of his
feelings in 1945 that there were very few letters in connection with
his 'war-work'. But then everyone was doing war-work and there
was little time for mutual admiration societies. The upgrading of
his MBE to OBE would have pleased him.

Letters he valued came from Harry Altham, 'You, more than
anyone else, have piloted Lord's through the long and dark
passage', and from Lord Lucan, one of his great friends in the
1940s, 'nobody knows better than I the amount of work it has
entailed for you. In addition to the routine work, you have
arranged matches, and organised so successfully the entertainment of distinguished visitors in the President's box.' As his elder
son wrote to him, 'it is you people associated with the MCC, not
Christopherson'.

His writing, during the war, had been confined to the contributions to *The Cricketer*. He wrote an editorial in the 1940 Spring
Annual indicating that his scheme for distribution to the forces had
had some success – 'The RAF sent a lorry to Wine Office Court to
collect Annuals.' Readers were invited to subscribe both for
themselves and for a copy to be sent to men on active service.
Warner's editorial concluded with a reminder – during the
'phoney' war of 1939–40 – that there was a war on. 'Cricket expects
that its devotees will do their duty, that each of them, of every age
and generation, will move forward in defence of England.'

Soon afterwards, Wine Office Court was abandoned after an
unexploded landmine was found nearby and Langford took *The
Cricketer* to Surbiton where his home, 76 Berrylands, became the

office of a cottage industry run by himself and his wife Meg. Warner, of course, was still the editor and still contributed. No longer (in wartime) a selector of official England sides, he could allow himself the 'political' comments which, in the past, he had had to get others to make for him. 'I write more in it than the reader thinks,' he told his elder son. 'Lots of unsigned pieces are mine too.'

He was pleased to secure £150 of advertising from Pontings in 1944 and to report that the Winter Annual that year sold 6000 copies in two days. He also continued to seek contributors. Among new names were Bernard Darwin, G. B. Buckley (the cricket historian of the game's very early days), Gerald Brodribb, and G. D. Martineau, while in 1944 he rendered a service to his own future biographer whose early contribution in print he published.

All this was transitory compared with the dedicated commitment of the Langfords.[45] Arthur did the day-to-day work, Meg managed the 5000 subscriptions and E. L. Roberts took the copy to the printers in Bermondsey, sometimes passing by Lord's or Malvern Court on the way. Warner did not draw his salary of £600 while he was receiving a larger figure from MCC. Langford's own circumstances were improved by a temporary job with the BBC since *The Cricketer* in wartime barely kept its head above water and, as he said himself, he was working on 'virtually an honorary basis'.

In 1944 Warner wrote to Esmond saying that he wished to retire from Lord's not only because he had 'done his war-work' but also because he wished to 'do a lot of writing'. So far, in this book, we have sometimes taken Warner as an author for granted. Much of his writing in earlier years had been journalism transferred into book-form, as for example his account of the 1903–4 tour, his *Cricket in Many Climes*, and his *Fight for the Ashes in 1926*. The substance of all these books had appeared in periodicals from the *Westminster Gazette* onwards.

This would be less true of his writing in the future, though he was approached by Chatto and Windus in 1942 to gather together some of his recent articles in *The Cricketer* under the title *Cricket Between Two Wars*. It proved a wartime bestseller when published in 1943. James Agate ('a stern critic so his remarks are high praise indeed') called the whole book 'a joy which every young man ought to get somehow' and took Warner out to lunch at the Café Royal for the privilege of having read it! Robertson-Glasgow wrote in *The Field*, 'to pass judgement on a book by Sir Pelham Warner is at once a liberty and an honour'. Nevertheless, he took the liberty. The book had very few shafts of humour for 'the idol may sometimes smile but it must not laugh'; 'Sir Pelham, like many of us, has a relish for rolling the names of the eminent round the palate of acquaintance.'

Warner could not avoid 'bodyline' and a dozen years after the event, he wrote:

> Much confusion has been caused by a very large number of people thinking that bodyline was but a term for leg-theory – a form of bowling which has been in use in this country for fifty years. Bodyline is absolutely and entirely different, and this fact was not at first generally recognised in England nor is it still in some quarters.
>
> One of the strongest arguments against this bowling is that it breeds anger, hatred and malice, with consequent reprisals. The courtesy of combat goes out of the game.

And of Jardine:

> He had many admirable qualities, and was as good a tactician as any captain I have ever seen. He planned and thought and never spared himself and set a fine example of physical fitness. He was absolutely unselfish and would never ask anyone to do anything which he would not do himself.

Robertson-Glasgow called these two passages 'the best thing in the book, fair without evasion; candid without recrimination'. An anonymous review in *Country Life* commented that the bodyline affair was dealt with 'temperately but quite decidedly'. The book sold 6000 copies within a week and Warner received copies in the post for autographing. Hatchards 'tell me scores of people send it to POWs and Chatto and Windus are getting it to Cairo for the 8th Army'.

Success bred success! Whitakers asked him to update his *Book of Cricket* and, when it appeared in 1945 at 9/6 it sold 10,000 copies at once. An invitation came from Harrap's 'to do a book on Lord's'. He wrote to Esmond, 'I can work at it in the winter but it would take a year or two of research and reading. I expect I will say "yes" but I shall make them pay!'

He was also asked to produce volumes on *Oxford v. Cambridge* and *Gentlemen v. Players* and could write, with truth and no false modesty, 'all this will involve a lot of labour. There is a "boom" in the Works of Warner!'

All these activities and plans made him, as he told the BBC, 'a very busy man'. During these years it was not he who was asking to broadcast but the BBC who sought him. It was, indeed, a very different atmosphere from the 1920s and 1930s, as Rex Alston's recollections illustrate:

> It was with some trepidation that I asked for an interview with Sir Pelham to discuss the BBC's plans for broadcasting on cricket. I was first introduced to Henson then met the maestro himself. No-one could have been kinder and more understanding to one who was a novice. He was, of course, enthusiastic about broadcasting war-time cricket, and gave me all the help I needed such as entrée to the dressing-rooms so that I could familiarise myself with the looks and records of players.

Among broadcasts arranged for Warner himself was one on the Foster family in a series, 'The Giants of Sport', broadcast to the Forces. He became on very good terms with the director of outside broadcasting, Michael Standing, who wrote, 'we enjoyed your contribution. It's good to know that we will be able to take advantage of it.' This was followed, after he took part in 'A Question of Sport', with 'quite the best I've ever heard you give in front of a cold, impersonal, microphone, and I'm most grateful for all the trouble you took in the preparation and execution'. For this Standing was rewarded with an invitation to call him 'Plum', while Warner continued to broadcast successfully.

He also found time to give some talks. He spoke at a Warship Week in Hambledon, at numerous RAF stations and was thanked by the Press Club for 'turning out on a horrid February night to gratify our nostalgic desire for cricket talk. It was the kind of speech that only you could have supplied.'

On 8 August 1945 he could with justification 'sign off' from his responsibilities at Lord's. England had played Australia in the fourth victory match when some of the future hopes of post-war Anglo-Australian cricket were playing – A. L. Hassett, Miller, Hutton, Washbrook, Edrich together with the old veteran, Hammond. Agnes had been well enough to come to the match. He had acted as host, in the president's absence, to the new Prime Minister, Attlee. He had found a moment to talk to his old friend of Caring days, Sir Walter Monckton, who had assured him (he told Esmond), 'Attlee's government will be alright, Bevin good as foreign secretary and we have nothing to fear.'

Not frightened by the fear of 'great social revolution' (against which he had once thought cricket was the bulwark), pleased that he had done his bit in the war, happy that none of his family had perished in it, and secure in the thought that he had fresh work to do, Warner at the age of 72 could face the future with equanimity.

11
Elder Statesman, 1945–63

'You have honoured the Harrap imprint' was the exceedingly complimentary letter which Warner received from George Harrap after he had decided to accept the invitation to write a book on Lord's. By 1951 he had completed three more books, all of which sold very well. He was 78 when the last of them appeared. The young Warner of 50 years earlier may be sometimes thought of as a hedonist, pursuing pleasure rather than duty. The old Warner was a stoic in his application to his literary labours. We may contemplate what was the motive for such an outburst of energy. He always welcomed money and would worry more and more about it as the years went by. He enjoyed the craft of writing and, within a surprisingly narrow range of words, had the talents of a narrator. The past appealed to him and he found pleasure in recording it. Just occasionally, his letters reveal doubts and uncertainties about the world of the second half of the twentieth century: history, and more particularly cricket history, became a refuge. Finally, we have a picture of an old man with an ill wife occupying his time when at home during the English winters.

Lord's was produced with immense speed. Shortly after publication, A. J. White, the Harrap house-editor, wrote to him:

> The book is creating an enormous interest. On all sides we hear of people who speak highly of everything to do with *Lord's*. It has been a great privilege to be connected with a production so satisfying. I count this one of the happiest experiences I have had in publishing.

Harrap were well rewarded for their efforts. For reviewers it was the outstanding publication on the 1946 Christmas List and must have solved the 'present' problem for many wives. How many husbands gave it to their wives to 'borrow' later? The *Sunday Times* reviewer with an unconscious pun wrote that 'one simply dipped into the pie and pulled out plums at random'.

It was the first book which Warner's biographer, as a very young writer, reviewed. I turned up the files of the *Scottish Guardian* to read what I had said over forty years ago: 'The key-note of *Lord's* is the characterisation. Sir Pelham has a splendid gift for portraying an individual. This is no mere statistical review but a living record of the past. It must assuredly rank as a classic in its own sphere.' It was a slightly 'priggish' judgement but I see no reason to change my view. Fifteen thousand copies were sold almost at once as was a de luxe edition of 4000. Warner was told that only economy restrictions on paper had prevented a print run of 75,000. His material reward was a little over £1000.

The successful author dragged himself away from the sight of Hatchard's front window filled with copies to holiday in Gibraltar for Christmas. His son-in-law, Harold Henderson, arranged a cruise for him in HMS *Manxman* to get a change of air and to get rid of his catarrh (he even gave up smoking temporarily). Agnes was left at home to face a particularly bitter English winter and Warner's letters to her, all about the people he was meeting, including A. E. W. Mason the novelist, strike a slightly guilty note, and are full of concern, 'do keep doors and windows shut. Don't, I beseech you, try long motor journeys and then get knocked up. I dread your overdoing it.'

He was equally concerned about the news from Sydney with Bradman and Barnes both making double-centuries. 'I anxiously await further news! Bradman again! What scoring. Anyway, Pearl [Allen] will be delighted if we do lose it!' He went for a day to Tangier, bought nylons for his womenfolk back in Austerity Britain and returned all ready to tackle his *Gentlemen v. Players* for Harrap.

Three years later the book was published. With *Lord's*, Harrap had promised 'to produce as good looking a book as the text deserves' and had done so. This time the production was less immediately attractive. The book itself was a statistical record of all these encounters together with an introduction and a page or so of text on each game. The record had been originally compiled up to 1900 by Ashley-Cooper and Warner's version represented the updating of a volume long out of print. To correct Ashley-Cooper, most accurate of researchers, would have been *lèse-majesté*! On publication, *The Times* called its author 'one of cricket's most authoritative historians'. Jessop, in *The Spectator*, described the compilation of the book as a 'stupendous task'.

Warner himself, in 23 appearances between 1897 and 1919, made a best score of 97 in the fixture at Lord's in 1905, commenting that the umpire, J. C. West, 'raised his hand to give me out lbw with an almost grieved look'.

It was a contest with an antiquity far exceeding that of Test matches. Warner believed 'no great lover of cricket would wish to disturb its historic title' as representing gentlemen of leisure playing men who, from the days of Hambledon onwards, received 'payments made to players'. He argued that representative matches of this calibre had 'a quality and atmosphere of their own' and were the best 'training for our encounters with our Commonwealth rivals'. He concluded with the prayer and belief that Gentlemen v. Players should never die out.

His critics have accused him of perpetuating a social anomaly. But Warner simply saw Gentlemen v. Players as a classic of English cricket belonging – even as late as 1949 – to an age when some men could find time to play cricket while drawing no emoluments for so doing. The admiration which so many of the professional cricketers had for him is the best answer to his critics. To one of them, J. B. Hobbs, he dedicated the book. Coincidentally, the last Gentlemen v. Players match, in 1962, was also within the last year of Warner's life.

The trilogy was completed by Warner's autobiography, entitled *Long Innings*. When consulted about the idea Esmond had replied, 'if you do it, it must be no pot-boiler, no hurried affair, but something really good.' He was by now well established in the book trade and was in charge of W. H. Smith's shop in Cairo. He advised his father not to give the book to Harrap who were the wrong sort of publisher for him, 'with a scrappy general list'. Cassell, Hodder or Cape would serve him much better. But Harrap had already extended the invitation and Warner could scarcely look elsewhere. While the ordinary edition was not very impressive, the de luxe one, of which 260 copies were printed and signed by the author, was an attractive volume. Later, he was inclined to think Esmond might have been right, writing to him in 1957, 'I have long thought Harrap lose interest in a cricket book after a short time and have no cricket sense and do not know when and where to advertise. They sell practically none of my books and have not done so for some time.' He contrasts this with 'a windfall of £168 from a Sportsman's Book Club republication of his *England v. Australia, 1911–12*'. His lament is realistically that of most authors who expect their publishers to be forever in the business of selling *their* books!

Long Innings was again well received though some reviewers, for example the *National and English Review*, felt it lacked analysis of how 'a Test Selection Committee actually gets to work'. The book, in the tradition of so much of Warner's work, was narrative and descriptive in style. Its author was rewarded with a private accolade from Neville Cardus:

> I have just finished *Long Innings* and I am impelled to write to you at once to say how much pleasure the book has given me. Its appeal to a lover of cricket was, of course, a natural expectation, but also it has moved me because you showed how the game can be made into a way of life.
>
> It is an inspiration in these darkening days to feel coming through your pages the glow of nature, civilisation and courtesy.

It was Warner's last publication, 'selling almost like a Churchill or a Bryant' he wrote and it brought to an end a writing career which had spanned over half a century and produced nearly twenty books.

The Cricketer, though, would still occupy him and be a vehicle for his writing almost up to the end of his life. After the war it had continued to be run from the home of Arthur Langford who moved from Surbiton to Stoke D'Abernon. Warner had let Langford run the paper very much by himself in the late 1940s, but a letter from Esmond in March 1950 led him again to become more involved. Esmond, with his own very wide experience in the book and periodical trade to back his judgement, wrote, 'forgive my candour, but the paper is now edited without personality, imagination or "shape"; a collection of articles bundled together without being tied up'. Esmond urged his father to play a larger part, direct policy and write editorials. Warner took his son's advice, and agreed that he found Langford 'not always ready to follow the direction I give'. The time had come to alter that 'and get rid of his over-cautious mentality'. Langford, he conceded, was 'a nice chap' but that was that! All this was rather harsh on a man who had written to him so recently, 'My very dear Plum, I do realise how tremendously privileged I have been to be associated with you for nearly 30 years. Even now I cannot realise my good fortune.' Possibly as a result of Esmond's intervention other influences were brought to bear. Warner took professional advice on the paper's advertising policy and sought his old friend Fry's opinion. They exchanged letters on the future of a paper whose later destinies neither of them could be expected to witness. Fry wrote: 'I have been thinking a lot about your *Cricketer*. I am sure that you yourself should do a big match whenever you can. You get more genuine cricket into it and technical interest than anyone I have known.'

Fry resumed contributing and, as Warner wrote to Esmond, 'is tremendously keen about it all and tells us to aim at selling 30,000 copies'. One's first reaction is of genuine admiration for these two near-octogenarians still able to muster this enthusiasm for the success of the magazine. A less kindly thought suggests that *The Cricketer* needed the leadership and ideas of a younger generation.

In 1953 a special meeting was able to pay a dividend for the first time in the paper's 33 years and the Winter Annual sold 14,000 copies. For a few years *The Cricketer* did rather well. Warner treated himself to 400 two-shilling shares whose £40 actual cost was reduced to £10 through a dividend of £30. By 1960 it was again running into economic shoals and facing the challenge of publications designed for a rather less 'establishment' market such as the *Playfair Cricket Monthly*.

At the very end of his life Warner, still drawing £600 a year from *The Cricketer*, passed his shares to his younger son, John. Langford continued to be associated with the paper until 1966. He had never made much money from it but he had had his own reward for, at least, he was as much a romantic as Warner. He had enjoyed his links with the game and with one of its leading personalities. He had found pleasure in dining with Warner at his club, occasionally sitting in his box at Lord's or simply being invited to use his cognomen. And it was Langford's generous obituary of Warner which *Wisden* would publish in due course. Warner could always find a use for a man who loved cricket.

As a respite from his literary efforts, Warner accompanied MCC to the West Indies at the end of 1947. The tour began in Barbados where he stayed as the guest of the governor. He was invited to open the George Challenor Memorial Stand at Kensington Oval and to visit his old school, Harrison College. He was also admitted to the Barbados Bar by the Chief Justice where, in wig and gown, he addressed the assembled barristers and solicitors. He was able to acknowledge the hospitality by giving a dinner party to his principal hosts, 'a small return for the wonderful kindness, at under £9', he wrote to Agnes.

Then came Trinidad, 'here I am in the land of my birth', he told the family. Once again, he stayed in Government House. Nearly fifty years had gone by since his visit with Hawke's team but there were those who still remembered him, 'Mr Pelham, I see you, sir, make a hundred when you come here with De Lord.' The memories crowded in as he called on old friends such as the Challenors, Mrs Edgar Agostini, Rosie Wilson (a cousin), and Sir George Pile – who had captained Barbados in 1884 in a game which young Pelham had watched. He visited his old home and had a trip to Maracas beach. The Mayor of Port of Spain gave him a civic welcome in the Town Hall, the very house his father had died in. 'When I left great crowds cheered me. The name of Warner certainly stands very high in the West Indies.' He went to the church at Belmont built on land given by his father, 'heard prayers for the repose of his soul and put one pound in the plate'.

From Trinidad he went to British Guiana, flying for the first time in his life but not liking it very much and thinking it unnatural. The ladies at the Government House Ball in Georgetown were 'the best dressed in the West Indies and as pretty as their frocks', he wrote and they prevailed on him to dance with them! Finally came Jamaica and by then Warner was ready to go home, writing to Agnes that all the beaches made him think of the idea of taking a house by the sea that summer in England and having all the family to stay. It was a pleasant pipe-dream which came to nothing.

Although he had gone with the MCC party he stayed in different places and he was conscious that 'an old man should not be hovering around'. The cricket itself was unfortunate. Not a single victory was won and the Test series was lost by two games to none. It was the tour in which S. C. Griffith, the reserve wicket-keeper selected because the team could scarcely muster eleven fit men, made a century on Test debut. Illness and injury necessitated the sending out of Hutton to strengthen a side which proved no match for the West Indies. Up to a point Warner bore some responsibility for the weakness of the England team. He had been approached by R. K. Nunes, president of the West Indies Board and the 1928 West Indies captain, to use his influence to get a side out as soon as possible after the war and been assured that the West Indies were not very strong. He took the information at face-value and the team, captained by Allen at the age of 45, was no match for the rising stars of Worrell, Weekes and C. L. Walcott.

Yet in one way Warner's judgement over past years was confirmed. The players rated Allen an outstanding captain showing, as J. T. Ikin recorded, 'leadership of the highest class'. Warner had had no say in choosing the captain but he had backed the same nominee for Australia a dozen years earlier.

One of his letters to Agnes from Trinidad had contained the comment, 'I bet 100–1 I will not be nominated for President of the MCC in 1948 – my instinct tells me so.'[46] So it proved, and it leads us to consider the business of Warner's candidature for that high office. He had been elected a trusteee of MCC after he gave up his deputy secretaryship in 1945 but he regarded that as poor consolation for the presidency which he so much desired. He had, as we saw in the last chapter, sadly dismissed the prospect of it, if not from his mind, at least from the realm of practical politics. He believed that the peers and soldiers would be nominated before him and, on the evidence of the holders of the office between the wars, there were grounds for the argument. There were only four exceptions: Sir Stanley Jackson (a nobleman's son and a man of great public distinction), Sir Kynaston Studd (a Lord Mayor of London), Colonel J. J. Astor (another nobleman's son and a press 'baron') and Stanley Christopherson (a banker).

He did not, however, expect the nomination in 1946 of a general, Sir Ronald Adam, who had *not* been one of the war leaders and whose associations with cricket were fragmentary. It has been suggested that Adam was nominated in order to smooth relations between MCC and the new Labour Government, an argument that seems to have little substance. No crucial issues of politics and sport were on the horizon, and even if they were, Attlee was a cricket enthusiast. Adam proved to be a useful man in the office when he acted with considerable authority and swiftness in arranging with the BBC that Hammond should broadcast to the nation at peak listening time when he returned from the 1946–47 tour. This was to dispel the belief that the tour had been a failure in social terms as much as in cricketing ones.

Adam's successor, Lord Cornwallis, had the impeccable claims of an aristocratic background and the captaincy of Kent, together with a long record of distinguished public service. There followed Lord Gowrie, another old friend of Warner's whose connection with cricket had begun, rather obliquely, when he was Governor of South Australia during the bodyline tour. Since 1840 the presidency, almost without exception, had been in the gift of the outgoing president. In 1949 Gowrie chose to nominate Prince Philip, Duke of Edinburgh, husband of the heir to the throne and a young man who had kept up his interests in cricket and occasionally played.

The Duke's nomination, while generally acceptable, brought a comment from 'Peterborough' in *The Daily Telegraph* voicing opinion on the continued omission of Warner's name. Warner's own post brought a postcard (*en claire*), 'I write to tell you how thoroughly disgusted I am that you were not made president yesterday.' Another postcard drew Warner's attention to the regret expressed as far back as 1918 by Mr Speaker Lowther that Warner had not been nominated. But Lowther's concern carries rather less

19   On duty at the War Office, 1917.   20   Off duty at Caring House, 1917.

21   Middlesex XI, 1920. Back row: H. W. Lee, H. K. Longman, J. Durston, N. Haig, G. T. S. Stevens, C. H. L. Skeet. Front row: J. W. Hearne, F. T. Mann, P. F. Warner, H. R. Murrell, E. Hendren. *(MCC)*

22   PFW in the course of scoring 79 in his last match for Middlesex, 1920.
The Surrey wicket-keeper is H. Strudwick. *(MCC)*

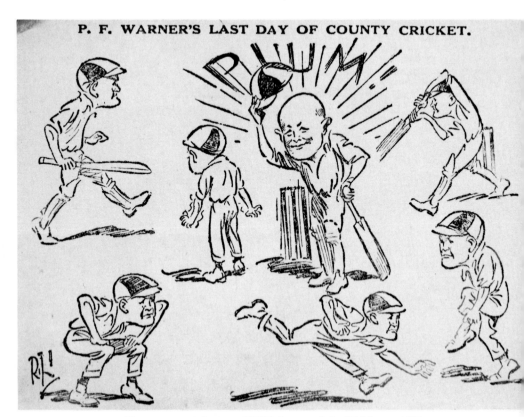

23   A cartoonist's view of PFW's last match for Middlesex, 1920.

24 Portrait at the end of his first-class career, 1920.

25 At The Oval, 1924.

26 Broadcasting the first commentary at Lord's. Middlesex v. Nottinghamshire, 1927.

27 On board ss *Orantes*, bound for Australia 1932–33.

28   An aerial view of the Adelaide Oval during
the third Test, 1932–33. *(Melbourne Age)*

29   W. A. Oldfield hit by a ball from H. Larwood in the third Test at Adelaide,
1932–33. *(Illustrated London News)*

credence in that, when president himself as Viscount Ullswater in 1923, he did not nominate Warner to succeed him. Another wrote to him,

great as is the honour to the Club in the personality of the new president, I am sure that many of us would have wished such a very old friend of Lord's as yourself appointed president. In my ignorance (before I read *The Daily Telegraph* today) I thought you had been president years ago and was horrified to learn that this was not so.

Both his sons wrote to him in commiseration. Esmond criticised 'the system of nomination'. 'If it were done in an ordinary way you would have been president years ago.' John wrote even more strongly:

For as long as I can remember the presidents of MCC have been mediocre people in the cricket world. You have the great glory that if you were made president the whole cricket world would rejoice. The fact that you have not been president does not diminish your fame but only reduces the position of president.

The first hint that he would not be chosen in 1949 had come from Altham, 'if it is not to be this year, let me put this to you: should it not happen, as long as cricket is played, you will be remembered as the man who ought to have been president when the great majority of those who have been are forgotten, and as one who has accepted disappointment with dignity and without rancour'. Shortly afterwards Gowrie himself had discreetly told him that he would not be nominated. Warner was absent from the meeting. Agnes was unwell but possibly she was the diplomatic excuse for an occasion he could not face. We shall never know.

Further speculation, nearly forty years later, is fruitless. Warner was not an aristocrat, a soldier or a business tycoon. He had not much money of his own and, in the opinion of Ronald Aird, his continuing activities in journalism made him unacceptable to some. Most of all, he was the old, familiar and ever-present figure at Lord's; not taken for granted but perhaps undervalued. Except to his close friends, he would have been too proud to let anyone know how much being undervalued hurt him. He needed the prizes that went with fame and duty. For him it was never enough just to serve, however valiantly that service was fulfilled. He had felt that '1932–33' denied him a knighthood at the time. He had written privately (though perhaps not too seriously) that a baronetcy might have come after his war-work at Lord's.

Then, from one of Her Majesty's ships stationed off the coast of Algiers came the letter which he would prize above all others: it was dated on the exact fifty-eighth anniversary of his election to MCC:

> H.M.S. Chequers,
> Algiers.
>
> 15 March 1950.

Dear Sir Pelham,

As you know the term for my Presidency of the M.C.C. is now about to expire and I am writing to you to say that I should like to name you as the next President.

It would give me very great pleasure to do this as I feel sure that the cricket-minded people in the country will agree with my choice.

You have meant so much to cricket for so long and I can think of no one who more readily deserves this honour.

I shall, of course, be away for the meeting but I have asked Lord Gowrie to act for me.

General Browning will be the only other person who knows and perhaps you could let me have your reply through him.

> Yours sincerely,
> Philip.

Sir Pelham, in his reply, wrote:

Sir,

General Browning asked me to see him this morning when he handed me your letter of March 15th from Algiers, naming me as the next President of the M.C.C., and I am very proud and honoured to accept the high distinction you have conferred on me.

I greatly appreciate your gracious reference, 'you have meant so much to cricket for so long and I can think of no one who more readily deserves this honour', and will do my utmost to be worthy of your good opinion.

I fear that at my age I may, perhaps, be failing in energy on occasions, but I love the game and Lord's and everything to do with it, as much as ever, and it will be my never ceasing endeavour to promote the interests of cricket and of the Club.

In April, Altham who had dropped him a hint a year earlier of impending disappointment, could write saying, 'may I, most improperly, admit to having heard the completely satisfying news of your approaching office'.

His nomination at Lord's a few weeks later, on 10 May 1950, was the prelude to hundreds of letters. Warner kept them all and a few convey the feelings of the many:

I must write a letter of congratulation to you on being appointed the presiding genius at Lord's. You have in fact been the presiding genius of the place for more years than I like to think of, and it is eminently right that you should now occupy the seat of the mighty.

Lord Jowitt

I think you must know how delighted I am that you have been appointed the new President of MCC. No one has or will ever deserve the honour as much or be more qualified and fitted for it.

In my six years at Lord's I have never heard a new President get such a wonderful reception or be more universally and sincerely welcomed. It will certainly be a very happy year for the secretariat.

R. Aird, Secretary, MCC

It is the greatest honour that the game of cricket can confer and one which in your case is long over-due.

G. O. Allen

It is a platitude to say that no one has done for cricket what you have done. You found a noble game and made it much nobler.

Frank Pakenham

Although long overdue, over-earned and overlooked, it will give untold pleasure to cricketers all over the world.

A. G. Doggart

If ever a man deserved the highest honour in the cricketing world it was you.

Lord Gowrie

Gowrie's comment suggests that had a royal prince not been in waiting, he himself would have nominated Warner, to whom he had given many confidences over the years.

And so, in the year when the West Indians came to Lord's and won their first Test victory in England, the president of MCC who greeted them was one of their own countrymen. His affection for the islands where much of his ancestry lay was undoubted but an amusing incident during the visit put the bond to the test. The president of MCC was in his bath at Malvern Court after a day at Lord's when his telephone rang. 'Can I speak to Sir Pelham?', asked an unmistakable Trinidadian voice. Warner went to the telephone:

Ah, Sir Pelham, you are the only Trinidadian I know at Lord's. I have not been in England long. I was watching the cricket today and left my raincoat near the sightscreen in the free seats. Could you collect it for me on Monday and leave it at the gate for me to get?

After a mumbled 'damn cheek' to his own household, Warner did this simple thing and was pleased that a 'fellow-countryman' had seen him as such.

With his role as president we can be more dismissive. He attended committee meetings, kept in touch with the Lord's staff and acted as host in the presidential box. These were things he had done for so many years (during the war he had often acted for the president as host to visiting distinguished visitors) that they were second nature to him. In the sense that he knew what was going on and what was expected of him, he was a working president and no mere figurehead. Aird, as secretary, had welcomed his appointment and he was not disappointed. The day after Warner conducted the 1950 AGM, Aird wrote:

I feel I must write to you just to congratulate you on the splendid and charming way you conducted the Annual General Meeting and Dinner yesterday.

It has been wonderful for the Secretariat to have had you as President during the last year and I personally have appreciated it more than I can say.

Aird was particularly appreciative of Warner's presidency as shown in Committee where 'he never took offence if a vote went against him or asked for his objection to be recorded. He accepted Committee decisions without rancour.'

Warner had approached William Findlay just after Christmas with an invitation to succeed him. Findlay hesitated, doubting his abilities or his acceptability to members. But Warner prevailed on him (and what they had once said to each other over the events of

1932–33 – the returning manager and the then secretary – can only be guessed at) and Findlay eventually accepted nomination. He was neither a soldier or a nobleman but, said Warner, 'a servant of the Club who had worked himself to a standstill, realised the importance of cricket as an imperial asset, and radiated a most pleasant atmosphere'. In some senses, Findlay was cast in the image of Warner. Later in the 1950s, the peers and those war leaders whose presidencies Warner had anticipated had their turn.

To all of them, no longer challengers, Warner was courtesy itself. In 1953 the president was the Duke of Beaufort who wrote to Warner at the end of his year saying that it had been made perfect by 'Warner's advice, help and kindness'. In the Duke's absence, Warner had to entertain a group of important Japanese visitors to Lord's. The war had ended only eight years earlier and British public opinion was still sensitive. The Japanese Grand Chamberlain told Warner that he had been shown 'the English character' and Warner's gracious welcome made a tiny contribution towards the restoration of Anglo-Japanese relations. The Duke's successor, the Earl of Rosebery, wrote as soon as he was elected, 'if I am in any difficulties, let me come to you for advice, as you are par excellence, the elder statesman of cricket'. As late as 1960, Sir Hubert Ashton, MP, the president, wrote to thank him for his guidance to him 'at rather a difficult time'. In 1961 his unofficial role as elder statesman guiding successive presidents was rewarded with his election to be the first life vice-president of the Club.

Away from Lord's, he was still very much in demand in the cause of cricket in all sorts of ways. In 1946 an unusual appeal came from the Netherlands, where he had captained MCC in 1928 to celebrate the fiftieth year of cricket at The Hague. During the German occupation Dutch cricket had suffered through lack of opportunity, facilities and equipment and Piet Labouchere approached Warner about its plight. Warner agreed to be president of a 'Save Dutch Cricket' Fund and to use *The Cricketer* as one way of publicising it. Within a few months his campaign had raised enough to buy the Dutch some 200 bats and 100 balls and in the first post-war summer of 1946 internal cricket was resumed with 58 teams taking part in Leagues. Five years later a similar appeal was made to him from Italy. Cricket had been played there very briefly in the 1890s but then abandoned in favour of football. Gianni Manca wrote from Rome to Warner in 1951 to ask for his help in re-establishing the game: 'The question of equipment appears to present no solution locally and it is in this connexion, dear Sir Pelham, that we have decided on turning to you as the only person who could help us through our present predicament.'

Gianni Manca had also asked for 'literature for the indoctrination of our Italian members' and hoped that deferred terms of payment might be allowed for the equipment. Warner replied (he was now over 80) that he had passed the matter over to MCC and wished them well. Some years went by before cricket in Italy was revived with the introduction of the 'Rome Ashes' competition in 1962.

Nearer at home was a visit to Eton College in 1947 to sit on a brains trust when he was momentarily stunned into silence by the boy who asked 'did W.G. ever cheat?' But he obviously gave pleasure as the Provost of Eton, C. A. Elliott, wrote to him to say that even a 'benighted wet-bob such as myself' had enjoyed the evening. The following year was the centenary of Grace's birth and Warner was asked to return to Eton! He also gave an interview to the press on Grace, saying very much the same as he had broadcast 20 years earlier, and adding that the occasional impulsive error by the great man (running out S. P. Jones at The Oval in 1882 when the ball was assumed to be 'dead') had to be balanced against 'a lifetime distinguished by modesty in success, equanimity in failure and a spartan acceptance of hard knocks'.

He was still prepared to turn out on many a winter's evening, for example to Chatham Borough Council in 1948 to speak in one of a series of evening lectures, other speakers including Derek McCullough and S. P. B. Mais. Another occasion was a talk to the Jaeger's Staff Lunch Club.

A more unusual experience was an invitation to Henley Regatta to join the Stewards for lunch and present the prizes. He enjoyed having an escort of two motor cycles from Maidenhead to Henley and John's story of having heard someone say, 'some old bloke, I believe he was a cricketer in his day, gave the prizes away'. 'The old bloke' was still being consulted for his opinions and the *Country and Sporting Publications* who controlled a consortium of magazines and published a lot of cricket material, asked him for a 'confidential criticism of what we are doing and, in particular, of the extensive coverage we are giving to Neville Cardus'. Among dinners, was an invitation in 1949 to Stoke on Trent to speak at the Jubilee Dinner of the North Staffordshire and District League. There were over five hundred guests besides a gallery crowded with unsuccessful applicants. He was much touched to receive a dinner service as a gift. The following year a dinner was given in his honour in the House of Commons. It was the idea of Sir Stanley Holmes, MP, who consulted Attlee, the Prime Minister, and Anthony Eden. 'Both welcomed the suggestion effusively,' Holmes wrote to him. 'No individual cricketer had been so honoured,' Warner told Esmond, describing an occasion at which politicians such as Attlee, Eden, W. S. Morrison, Harold Macmillan and Harold Wilson mingled with cricketers such as Compton, Edrich and D. J. Insole. Aidan Crawley represented both worlds.

Then, in 1951, during the Rugby v. Marlborough match a dinner was arranged by the Old Boys of Whitelaw's House at Rugby to which Warner had gone as 'a somewhat lonely small boy who had never seen snow' nearly seventy years earlier. Rugby was a school, William Temple once wrote, which 'far outdistances all schools in the number of leading posts which its members secure'. Men whose achievements supported the view were gathered around Warner that evening: bishops, deans, generals and colonial administrators. Warner's reply to the toast proposed by Lord Elton was characteristically reminiscent and sentimental, 'an evening of unforgettable memories'. His last effective link with Rugby was in 1955 when he wrote to *The Times* urging supporters to come to Lord's for the centenary match against Marlborough.

Dinners such as these, happy occasions as they were, were all eclipsed by the decision of MCC to hold a dinner in honour of his eightieth birthday. He wrote in great delight to Esmond: 'MCC are paying me a very high, indeed an unprecedented compliment. There has never been a dinner in the Long Room before. I feel quite overwhelmed at the honour done me. Now, of course, you and John *must* be there.'

It was an occasion to which his friends from both the cricket world and outside came and far more than the 200 which could be accommodated wanted to be there. Esmond came across from Brussels and told his father that he 'had made a splendid speech on a difficult wicket as the crowd were restive owing to Fry's egotistical, long and dull innings'.

With the dinner went a cake which Warner himself took round to the Lord's staff the morning after the dinner. Although it belongs, chronologically to three years earlier, this letter is expressive of what the staff felt about him:

MCC Refreshment Department

Dear Sir,
Knowing you the number of years and remembering your wedding day so well as I do, and knowing as I do the years you have done for cricket. There is only one honour fit for one that has done so much for the welfare of cricket and for all those

connected with these grounds. We are all living to see you made President.

Yours faithfully,
G. Portman

Mr Portman and his colleagues were duly gratified in 1950 and played their part in organising the dinner in 1953.

Someone who had only been able to send a telegram of good wishes because he lived so far away was Sir Robert Menzies. Menzies sent a message to Aird asking for it to be read out at the dinner, expressing 'my affectionate greetings to my old friend Plum Warner, one of the immortals of cricket, a very perfect gentle knight'. Late in life Warner had become friendly with the great Australian statesman. During his presidency Warner had entertained Menzies to lunch at the Savoy. The biographer is left with the tantalising remark in Warner's invitation, 'it is important that I should meet you'. Why? Menzies was the Australian Prime Minister and an MCC side was about to go out to Australia, but it is pure conjecture to suggest that as the main reason for their meeting. Two years later, in 1952, Menzies returned the invitation, writing from Canberra to ask Warner to organise on his behalf a small dinner party to which he (Menzies) would like Aird, Allen, Altham, Brown (the England captain of 1950–51), Swanton, Lord Nugent and John Warner to be asked.

So the exchange continued over the years. 'Welcome to England. The president of MCC will be anxious to meet you but don't please forget me,' awaited Menzies at his hotel. 'If Harold Macmillan calls a prime ministers' conference, I will make No. 3 Malvern Court my first port of call,' greeted Warner at his flat.

Warner admired Menzies as a world statesman, 'in England you are regarded with great admiration and affection; great faith and reliance are placed on you', and as a close friend, 'it has been one of the great privileges of my life that I have had the great fortune to know you and to have valued your friendship beyond measure'.

Menzies' letters ranged over the scene of contemporary Australian cricket and a few sentences declare his interest:

I have just picked my team [for England] but will wait to see whether the selectors think as I do.   (1956)

Much as I admire Neil Harvey, I think he will need to develop a somewhat less chancy approach to the turning ball if he is to reach the stature of Clem Hill or Warren Bardsley. But on good wickets he is a joy to behold!   (1957)

Craig has a thoughtful and intelligent mind but one cannot help feeling that a boy of 21 needs to be a positive Bradman to be made captain of Australia.   (1957)

We have regained the Ashes, and on the merits, most properly. Players read too much the sniping efforts of a gaggle of English press commentators.   (1959)

Warner could still keep his end up writing about cricket and among his own comments were:

The West Indies are a very good all round side but our fellows have not done themselves justice so far. No excuses but an XI is a reflection of its leader and I do not feel Hutton is a leader. Was Hawke right?   (1954)

The selectors chose a silly side v. Pakistan in August. I told them three months ago Hutton was no captain. He has no cricket sense.   (1954)[47]

Poor Hutton! In November, he put the Australians in at Brisbane in the first Test, lost by an innings and Warner wrote to Menzies, 'Hutton – a Mutton-Head, always has been. Heaven knows why he put them in.' But Hutton had the last laugh. 'Under his zealous and skilful captaincy, England won the rubber,' wrote Norman Preston in *Wisden* and he deserved credit, 'for the way he conducted himself and his men'. Over Hutton, Warner proved a bad judge.

Warner and Menzies were still corresponding up to the time of Warner's death. The file of letters between the two in the Menzies Papers in the Australian National Library in Canberra is a bulky one. Menzies, busy politician as he was, found in cricket a great relaxation and enjoyed the company of cricketers. The cynics who have suggested that it was good 'vote-catching' in Australia could find little support for their argument in the long letters privately written to a cricket celebrity on the other side of the world. Equally, the cynic might point to the fawning note in Warner's side of the correspondence and he might attract some sympathy for such a view. But it was in Warner's nature to be polite and respectful to great men and his letters to Menzies had the extra dimension of being informative in their area of common interest.

Friends such as Menzies were the more valued as, in the natural order of things, Warner's contemporaries were dying. Scarcely a distinguished cricketer, or a man of distinction who liked cricket, died without Warner contributing as he had done in earlier years a signed notice to *The Times*. The record of a man's career (whether in public life or at the wicket) would already have appeared in the official obituary. Warner's piece a few days later would tell a tale or two, give the reader a glimpse of his subject's abilities, whether as a performer or in committee, and end with an encomium of his character. Perhaps the word 'charm' was overworked and 'good manners' became an imperative but these were the men who responded to Warner himself, and what he said of Kynaston Studd, Stanley Jackson, William Findlay or C. B. Fry was very much what he hoped one day someone would say of him.

Death and old age became a constant theme in many of his letters. He himself became liable to get colds and spent much of the time indoors in winter months. Even in the summer, in a cold spell, he and Agnes both practically 'lived by the television and the wireless', as he wrote in a letter to Alston saying how much pleasure BBC Outside Broadcasts gave to his wife. Family and social occasions became muted. They gathered in the flat in Malvern Court for a small party to celebrate the Coronation. A year later in 1954 Agnes was too ill for anything to be made of their Golden Wedding 'but John came round and we had a bottle of champagne'. This he wrote to Esmond now in Brussels, the loss of whose bookshop in the Cairo riots of 1952 had greatly upset his parents. Warner was worried, too, about John's health and the world of 'speed ... speed ... speed' which took him frequently abroad on business. More and more the grandchildren became important. Visits from Mungo, Michael, Marina, Laura and Sarah were great occasions if (inevitably) a little tiring.

On 1 March 1955, at the age of 78, Agnes died. She had been an invalid off and on for over twenty years. She was capable of making an effort on the big occasion, such as going to a football match, a Test match or, indeed, to a rugby international as late as 1951, but on the whole her active life ended in the middle 1940s. She had made, in the view of her younger son John, 'a happy home' but circumstances had led her and her husband to lead very separate lives. Philip Snow, who knew Warner on and off for the last 15 years of Agnes's life and had visited him at Malvern Court, never even met her.

Despite ill-health, Agnes remained a person of sterling character, often a shrewder judge than her husband, certainly cleverer and less susceptible to charm. As a young woman she could be caustic in her remarks but she had mellowed with the years and it is pleasanter to remember some of the tributes paid to her by friends and acquaintances. Langford wrote: 'I do have the happiest memories of Lady Warner. She always made me so welcome and

I cannot think of a braver woman. I never heard a single grumble from her lips and she must have suffered greatly during the last years of her life.'

Aird wrote of 'her sweetness and kindness' when he had been a young man calling on them at Datchet, and her sympathy to the young was again demonstrated by E. R. T. Holmes:

I first met Lady Warner in 1926 on top of a coach on the Mound during the Varsity match. I had covered myself with inglory by failing to do much at a time when something was expected of me. I was feeling rather low when I was hailed and invited by her to join the party in the coach. In no time at all she raised my drooping spirits and made me realise that to fail in the Varsity match was not really much of a crime.

Warner, after staying with John for a few days, returned to Malvern Court to be looked after by the faithful Doris, 'as always, simply splendid'. His letters to Esmond reflect his agitation about money. 'I am naturally in the red. Meanwhile I live as cheaply as possible, cut down on a lot of things. Doris insists on my giving her ten shillings a week less.' By the end of the year Agnes's affairs had been settled and Warner was left a life interest in the residuary estate giving him an income of about £400 a year, which, with the £600 he received from *The Cricketer*, gave him an overall income of about £1000.

Inevitably, the first Christmas after Agnes's death was a sad one. Esmond and his family were in Brussels, though they telephoned on Christmas Day. Doris went off 'to her people for a couple of days' and Betty came to keep him company. There was a family lunch at John's, though the occasion was even sadder because Warner was deeply worried.

For about twenty years he had been financing Miss E.H. She had never expected marriage but had depended upon him for security. He could no longer meet the demands which she made, to the tune of about £600 a year, the income he received from *The Cricketer*. There had always been the threat of public exposure held over him – Miss E.H. must have realised that simply to inform Agnes would be to tell her nothing she did not know already, except the evidence of how much money was involved. But Agnes's death and the reduction in Warner's circumstances brought matters to a head. John, who was on the spot, advised his father to consult the family solicitor and to put Esmond in the picture. Pelham wrote to Esmond:

[He] has taken over the affair entirely and has had an interview with her which he has dealt with very firmly. He says the matter is entirely in his hands and says 'I am not to worry' which is more easily said than done. It is a sad – very – affair and I am not proud of it. Anyway, no more £ s d is passing. He made it quite clear the 'money is not there'. It has been a fearful strain. I will say no more now. I have been a fool to put it mildly. I have had a life of which Galsworthy could have made a great novel.

Possibly the worrying made him ill and in February 1956 he was admitted to hospital for five weeks. By April he was his old self, thinking about small economies, grateful for a cheque for £20 from Esmond, looking forward to a visit from Esmond and his family, involving himself in the first summer issue of *The Cricketer*, and accepting an invitation to dine at Lord's to meet the Australians.

He continued to be concerned about 'threats of exposure' though the visit of the 1956 Australians raised his spirits a little. Jean, his daughter-in-law, drove him to Lord's, he saw Harvey make a double-century and Aird drove him home. 'I got a great welcome' and he proposed to take Esmond's advice to go out a bit more. He began to notice some of the current cricketers, admiring A. Wharton of Lancashire. But a letter to Esmond, after lots of chat about cricket, concluded:

But what a d... fool and worse I have been. I was 'on form' about the last man to act as I did but you know the background which led up to it but I have tarnished terribly the name of the Warners and if it all came out what a fall that would be, amongst my fellow countrymen, and indeed all over the Cricket World. My remorse is very heavy and my folly is ever present with me. It is a mill-stone around my neck and never absent from my mind.

For the indiscretions of years long past, the sick old man was paying a heavy emotional price. But, at least, the financial price ended, and Miss E.H. was given a lump sum in final settlement and with conditions attached. The affair, in every sense, was over.

A much more cheerful letter went to Esmond in February 1957. He was delighted at some royalties ('a windfall'), had taken Doris to the theatre ('I laughed a lot which did me good'), described himself as 'a different man' and accepted an invitation to stay with his son and daughter-in-law in Brussels in the spring. The visit duly took place – 'a wonderfully happy visit you were so kind and affectionate to me, both of you, and you are wonderful hosts' – and he dined with Piet Labouchere, later the historian of Dutch cricket.

He was back in time for the early season match between MCC and the West Indians, seeing centuries by Walcott, Gary Sobers and D. B. Close. He wrote to Esmond: 'Close played a beautiful innings of the highest class despite being very lame from a fearful crack. Sobers, a tip-top batsman, very hard-hitter, not a chance. WI a fine batting side but their bowling does not look, at present, anything to make us "tremble".'

Warner, deciding for the moment that 'us' was England, and not the West Indies, was proved right and the visitors failed to win a Test, in contrast to their triumphs of 1950. Later in the summer, Esmond and his family came to stay at Malvern Court, Warner's last guests before, in the autumn, he gave up the flat to live in the East India Club in St James's Square. Doris had decided to go and look after her ill sister and Warner, sad at parting with someone who had become a family friend of over thirty years, felt he could not manage without her. The club offered him 'a room for £37 10s a month' and *The Times* 'free every day'.

It was shortly before he moved into the club that the BBC approached him. For the first few years after the war he had broadcast once or twice a year. In 1946 he gave a talk, before MCC sailed for Australia, in which he argued the importance of touring teams going by ship rather than by air though he recognised that such would happen in the future. He took part in interview talks with C. B. Clarke, Ernest Eytle and Constantine earmarked for the West Indies Overseas Service. In the early 1950s the BBC used him to talk about some of the 'greats' of the past such as Barnes, Bardsley and George Gunn. With a touch of his old style, he objected to five guineas as a fee for a four-minute talk on Barnes and got it raised!

By the spring of 1957 Warner was in his eighty-fifth year and Alston and John Snagge both thought it important to have one last great occasion with, as the BBC internal memorandum said, 'the most respected and best loved cricketer of all time'. 'It will be an admirable opportunity to record the voice of Warner, not just for the programme itself but also for the purpose of archives.' Snagge went to 3 Malvern Court with a recorder 'no bigger than a quarter of the size of a cricket bag', had lunch with him and a rather disjointed conversation was recorded. This was intended to be no more than a dummy-run but time went by. In February 1958 Snagge began arrangements to bring Warner to the BBC studios but the old man 'felt too old and feeble in mind'. 'We must leave no stone unturned to get his personal story from him,' minuted Snagge who arranged to send a car for him and fixed a date only to receive the somewhat surprising reply:

Dear John,

Can you change the date as I have been asked to attend the Advisory County Cricket Committee (*aet.* 84!) at Lord's on March 11 . . . You pay me a very great compliment and I shall do my very best.

And so he was brought to the BBC on 14 March 1958 to take part in 'Frankly Speaking', a prerecorded programme, with Snagge, Alston, Ruth Drew (the 'outside' interviewer detached from cricket), Swanton, Compton and Eytle, together with the recorded voices of Rhodes and Hendren. Sir Ian Jacob, the Director-General of the BBC joined them for dinner before the recording.

Ruth Drew asked him what he felt were the consequences of his Spanish blood and he replied, 'I am a great traditionalist in manners, the halo of romance, panache.' To Eytle's question on the qualities of captaincy, he replied, 'good manners and the ability to understand his men'. Hendren remarked that Warner himself as a skipper was 'very strict but very nice with it and a great judge of a player'. Compton took up the point, 'I feel it was Sir Pelham who got me into Lord's.'

In Chapter 6 we noted Warner's first words as a broadcaster. Thirty-three years later (he had come to broadcasting over the age of 50), his last were to be: 'And she went for four. I can feel it on the bat now. I remember that as if it were yesterday.' ("And that's where the New Stand is now," remarked John Snagge.) 'Absolutely, the Stand is there now.'

Warner was taken back to his club and wrote to Sir Ian Jacob:

Thank you for my dinner, and what a good dinner it was. I am very proud and grateful to you for the pleasant evening and you paid me a very great compliment by being present in person. I enjoyed every minute. It was an occasion which I shall never forget.

And in a tribute to the BBC, he added, 'the MCC must do all they can to make the BBC happy and comfortable at Lord's. We can't do without you.' If we may recall that Minute of the 1930s, he had left far behind the image of the 'melancholy personality'. Age had given distinction to what he said.

The broadcast had, of course, coincided with the decision to name the new Stand at Lord's after him. On 7 May, the date of the MCC AGM, at the tea interval in Middlesex's match against Nottinghamshire the president, the Duke of Norfolk, introduced

Warner. He spoke extempore into the microphone and, emotions close to the surface, recalled his first coming to Lord's, though momentarily forgetting the year 1887 which meant so much to him.

Of the new Stand itself there was some criticism. The top tier was allocated to the 'media' so that their view became one from a long-leg or third-man position. In a sense, therefore, the press was back to the position it had had at the turn of the century before Pardon had successfully campaigned in the *Wisden* of 1901 for press facilities end-on. Warner, in his years as a journalist, had a better view than that accorded to his successors sitting in the Warner Stand.

Throughout the summer the 85-year-old was in better spirits, attending meetings at Lord's, lunching with Viscount Portal and going to church at Holy Trinity, Brompton. Little is revealed in his papers of his attitude to religion. He came of a family which had been pillars of the Anglican Church in Trinidad. As an undergraduate he had listened to Cosmo Lang preach in St Mary's, the University Church in Oxford. As a parent, he had seen that his own family went to church. He numbered bishops and lesser ecclesiastics among his friends, deploring the departure of gaiters in the former and delighting in Canon Gillingham among the latter. In later years, he was a fairly regular attendant at Holy Trinity, a 'fashionable' church in South Kensington where Canon Bryan Green remembered him as a man 'with a Faith in his heart and his mind'. Warner commented to Esmond that Green's preaching had 'great enthusiasm, a rare quality'. But his own enthusiasm, displayed so passionately for cricket, was never remotely applied to his religion. He was something more than the conventional Anglican only using the offices of the Church as custom and circumstance demanded, but the 'cathedral' of his life (in a famous phrase) was Lord's.

Three years later, in 1961, his diary showed that he had not entirely lost his zest for life. In February he had the Langfords to lunch at the club, in March he went to a reception at Australia House as the guest of Menzies, in June he sat beside Bradman for a few minutes in the Lord's Test and they talked about 'throwing', in July he went out to lunch on three consecutive days and in October he dined as a guest of the Forty Club, of which he had once been president. Interspersed with a note of these engagements were comments on his health – 'slept well, fit, slept badly, very fit and warm, very feeble, much better'. During the year he left the East India Club to make his home with Elizabeth and her husband Harold at Hamlet House, Hambledon. One of his last letters was to his future biographer. I had sought some information on his recollections of Rugby (see Chapter 2) and not been disappointed. In a four-page reply he had answered my queries with that crystal-clear memory of things long past so often possessed by the old and he ended with the comment, 'I am very feeble and shall not be in London again.'

On Wednesday 30 January 1963, Pelham Francis Warner died at West Lavington in Sussex in his ninetieth year. Out in Australia, Ken Barrington was compiling a century at Adelaide where Warner had captained England almost sixty years earlier. It was not unfitting that he should live in the closing stages of his life at Hambledon where Richard Nyren, like Warner nicknamed 'the general', had come exactly two centuries earlier to play on Broad-Halfpenny Down with William Beldham, John Small and the rest. They had been the first professionals and they had played alongside Sir Horatio Mann and the Duke of Dorset. In John Nyren's view, the bond of cricket among men prevented 'the structure of society from becoming disjointed'. Hambledon's great days were gone by 1787 as the cricketers flocked to London, and the Marylebone Cricket Club was founded. One hundred years on, in 1887, the young Pelham Warner would first visit Lord's and his life's association with the game would echo the thought of the younger Nyren. It was not an ignoble ideal.

12
Plum Warner

'A legendary figure in English cricket' was the heading to the lengthy obituary notice on Sir Pelham Warner in *The Times* of 31 January 1963. *The Daily Telegraph* called him 'the game's greatest ambassador' and the *Sunday Times*, 'an international figure'. In *The Times* on the following day, Ronald Aird wrote that his life of, and devotion to, cricket and especially to Lord's 'was almost an obsession but was completely and utterly sincere' and it was a devotion 'returned in full measure by cricketers all over the world'. There was a private family funeral at Holy Trinity, Brompton and, on a cold but sunny day, his ashes were scattered by his sons in a private ceremony beside the Warner Stand, as near as imagination could encompass to where he had hit his first four at Lord's in 1887.

Warner's talents as a captain exceeded those as a player. He had first won national acclaim when he won the Ashes in 1903–4 against all predictions. But he had learnt the art of leading men in the preceding few years when he took sides to America, New Zealand and Australia. The Australian press also gave him the credit, as a non-playing captain, for England's success in 1911–12. The Middlesex triumph of 1920 was the climax to his years as a leader.

M. A. Noble put him in the same class as the finest captains of his day, 'Patsy' Hendren regarded him as the best captain he had ever known, and C. B. Fry believed that his ability to command the support of a team was 'brilliant' and at the heart of his success. I. A. R. Peebles wrote that 'for a young and nervous bowler to play under his captaincy was an inspiration'. He would 'get the best out of everyone'. Sir George Allen echoed the same thought, 'his enthusiasm and enjoyment inspired the whole team'. That inspirational quality exactly fits. He made his judgements on what seemed right in terms of the nature and temperament of the players rather than on cool calculations and predictions. Such judgements were endorsed by a thorough observation of what was going on and the ability to spot an opponent's strengths and weaknesses, a quality, Jessop believed, which entitled him to be ranked among the very great captains of all time.

Warner, as a batsman – his bowling is no more important to a biographer than the occasional poems written by a novelist – achieved excellence if not greatness by practice, perseverance and perception. W. G. Michell and Tom Emmett at Rugby, Hayward, Fry, MacLaren and R. E. Foster as his contemporaries, all had a hand in it. He was a diligent pupil, a quick learner and equipped with that priceless quality, motivation, without which all teaching and guidance is in vain.

Soon after Warner had left Oxford, Fry wrote of him in *Sporting Sketches* that he could drive effectively on both sides of the wicket and was particularly strong in the area between square leg and mid-on. He had a 'double-edged style'. He could 'cut with the very best' and it seldom cost him his wicket. It was a view confirmed a few years later when, on his return from Australia in 1904, he was featured in *Wisden*'s Five Cricketers of the Year:

> When the sun shines and the ground is hard, he is one of the best batsmen to look at combining a most attractive style with a great variety of strokes. His driving on both sides of the wicket is, for a man of his weight and stature, surprisingly hard and he commands a very pretty and effective cut.

Sydney Pardon wrote in his tribute in the 1921 *Wisden* 'there have been many cricketers far greater', but he was very good at county standard, strong against the fast men, good off the back foot when the ball turned, and thoroughly difficult to get out. It was against such bowlers as Rhodes, Blythe, Lockwood, Hirst, Foster, Kortwright and Richardson that he finished year after year in the top dozen of the English batting averages.

Only at a more representative level, his beloved Gentlemen v. Players or in Tests themselves, did he fall short of the highest standards. His appearances for England at home were intermittent and unspectacular; abroad, the runs mattered less than the leadership. Long after both their cricketing days were over, Warner and Fry corresponded over who should appear in a list of great cricketers between 1894 and 1944 for the new edition of Warner's *Book of Cricket*. Fry wrote: 'I would put you yourself very high on the list to go in first: an excellent starter. You always made a 100 when I was fielding out. I put you alpha plus for guts. I admire a dominating simplicity.' An alpha plus from the man who cornered the market in alphas and Blues at Oxford was praise worth having. Warner, with his 29,000 runs and 60 centuries satisfied the examiners.

When his playing days were over he made a direct impact upon the game as chairman of the selectors for a substantial period between the wars with qualities which, to Allen, were 'brilliant' – 'if too inclined to believe his own opinion, more often than not he was right'. E. H. D. Sewell thought his only weakness lay in his judgement of bowlers. When he retired in 1938 contemporary assessment was of the highest for the results he achieved, his devotion to duty, his identification of talent and his unfailing optimism. 'Devotion' is a word which must occur again and again in an appraisal of Warner and any challenge to his reputation must be sustained not in disputing his devotion to cricket but in some of the implications of that devotion.

He has been seen as the great moralist whose views were expounded in speeches, writing and broadcasts throughout his life. There is nothing wrong with morality so long as its axioms do not find you out. And it is in conflicts of interest, responsibility and judgement that Warner has laid himself open to accusations of being less than thoroughly straightforward. His public and private image could be at variance. An instance of this may be seen in the events surrounding the winning of the Championship in 1920. Warner, in public, did battle in the open against Surrey for a win essential to Middlesex's prospects of the title. Warner, in private, wrote a letter to *The Times* under a pseudonym urging MCC to overturn a possible Lancashire title. Idealism was hotly pursued by Intrigue. Less precisely, the events of 1932–33 make the same point. Set against his pronouncements on fast bowling, written most significantly in his essay on captaincy in the 1920 Badminton volume on cricket, he had nothing to say in Australia. There his silence, one concedes, hid conflicting loyalty to MCC. Only when back in England did his public opinions match his private views.

There were instances, notably in 1926 and 1935, when he was reluctant to accept responsibility in public, when things went wrong, for decisions which he had privately urged. But a more tolerant view may be taken of those occasions (affecting Carr and Wyatt) when he parted company with an England captain in the best interests of the game. Here the conflict lay in a reluctance to speak face to face with a disappointed friend. He preferred instead to write the consoling letter even if it lost much of its credibility when set against those he sent to the man while still in favour.

The conflict between the two sides of Warner may be viewed in another way. He saw a cricket match as a battle involving tactics, strategy and leadership. Sometimes his analogies let him down as, for instance, when he and Field Marshal Montgomery had an exchange in the columns of *The Times* in 1954 on the qualities of leadership and command. But the principle stands: the public Warner engaged the enemy. Yet the private Warner disliked some of the consequences of the fray and was essentially a man of peace. Attrition and Appeasement, as 1932–33 had shown, make strange bedfellows.

His shrinking from confrontation is essential in an understanding of Warner. He had none of the toughness of others, such as Harris and Hawke, who had walked the corridors of power at Lord's. Sir George Allen, who knew him so well, linked it to his desire to like people and the need to be liked, 'he was essentially a kind and soft-hearted man'. Thus the rough-and-tumble of opposition and debate, surprisingly, made no appeal to one who was so persistently and so long in the public eye. He had hoped the problems in Australia would be wafted away from Adelaide on the warm winds to Victor Harbor. Less overtly, he would side-track on problems rather than have the harmony of life disturbed by discord.

Warner knew what qualities he liked and admired in other people. It may be that his affection and admiration were the more easily won if the recipient happened to be a nobleman or a distinguished public servant. He learnt early in life the personal value of such friendships. Indeed, the lesson may have begun very early indeed when the slight and frail schoolboy from the West Indies presented himself at Rugby School. All he could do was play cricket: he figures in no lists of academic or other athletic prowess. In that stern, demanding world of the Victorian public school, he must have had to work effectively to be accepted. When other boys played football, he went for nature walks with his housemaster's wife yet there is no record of bullying or undue unhappiness and in the Rugby of the 1880s he survived. From then on, Warner was a survivor. Lacking the qualities of toughness, hating confrontation, he became someone who achieved his goals by more roundabout ways and, if necessary, by equivocation. He made the 'right' life-long friends at Oxford, men from upper middle-class Victorian backgrounds such as Fry and Leveson Gower; he acquired Lord Hawke as a patron; he married a lady of wealth in the society of Edwardian London; his sons went to Eton. The friends of later years were the distinguished soldiers and sailors such as Roberts and Jellicoe, the peers such as Lucan and the politicians such as Menzies.

That Warner sought and won their acceptance invites the thought on whether or not he was a snob. His weakness for titles and 'handles' may be admitted, but it was offset by his readiness to be interested in all manner of folk. Those who were in his domestic employment, who came under his authority during his deputy-secretaryship, who met him at countless cricket grounds throughout the world, who were his taxi drivers, his bar stewards and his waitresses, found him an interested questioner and a good listener with the patience and equanimity which is a characteristic of royalty. And there was the quality of humility in his insistence on showing his MCC membership card to the attendant every time he entered Lord's, no matter that he was the best-known figure there for so long. He would have been the last man in England (or in Australia) to cry, 'You know who I am: let me in.' If a snob may be defined as someone who is always looking over his shoulder for someone more important to talk to, then Warner was no snob. The novelist W. M. Thackeray wrote that it was impossible, 'in our condition of Society, not to be sometimes a Snob'. Thackeray lived through the first 27 years of Queen Victoria's reign: Warner, the last 27. Only in the sense of the older Victorian's epigram may the word be applied to the younger one.

As H. S. Altham has observed, Warner greeted 'the humblest and most obscure with the same sincere pleasure and interest as the most eminent'. It was as genuine at one level as at the other. And if he had that weakness for the great, it was because, as he once wrote, 'they were men who had seen and done things – governors-general, prime ministers, cabinet ministers, soldiers, sailors, bishops, members of Bench and Bar, diplomats'.

'Men who had seen and done things': did a part of Warner envy them their achievements? In a speech at Valparaiso during his 1926–27 tour of South America he said, 'many would think I may have wasted my life by devoting it to the game of cricket. Perhaps I have.' When he returned home a letter from his Chilean hosts referred to his speech:

Nothing could be further from the truth. Your devotion to the game and your good influence on it can be said to be nothing less than a National Service; you can have no idea what an excellent thing your visit has been for British prestige and for the ideal of sportsmanship.

The same sort of sentiments were expressed wherever Warner

went with touring teams and there can be no doubt that he displayed as a captain the qualities of an ambassador in his representation of England. Only in that sense might one argue that he had wasted his life for he might have made a diplomat.

Part of his diplomacy may be expressed in the link which Warner made between cricket and the imperial ideal. He was so much the right man to take the first MCC side to Australia and to go to South Africa with MCC in 1905–6 to heal the wounds after the Anglo-Boer War. As the personification of cricket and imperialism he had no peer in the first 30 years of the century.

By the 1930s imperialism was beginning to become unfashionable and Warner's ideals would become untenable by later generations. The assumption may be made that he was a reactionary and it has some substance, but the view must be qualified. When he was knighted in 1937, the *Daily Mail* described him as 'neither absurdly old-fashioned nor foolishly and sensationally modern'. He represented the 'best of the old and the new' and he recognised that cricketers were as good as ever they had been. In 1945, when the idea of an experimental knock-out competition was rejected by the Advisory County Cricket Committee he had been one of its advocates. When he was 80 he would not be 'drawn' on comparisons which favoured the past. 'The best batsmen? Bradman, Grace and Hobbs in alphabetical order,' he replied. His advocacy of Gentlemen v. Players was primarily on the grounds that it was a major representative match of top talent and he was a man whom nearly all the professionals from Tom Hayward onwards respected and admired.

Shortly before his death, the distinction between professional and amateur was ended and the occasion for the contest disappeared. Warner would have been sad but for historical rather than social reasons. The professional cricketers in his day were known by their surnames. Warner adhered to the convention and his use of surnames was applied to all whom he knew until friendship and association dictated otherwise. Perhaps he clung too long to the usage when others were adapting themselves to the frequent use of Christian names and he was unduly sensitive to their use by John Arlott as a young and dynamic commentator.

Fry had given Warner's batting an alpha plus for 'guts'. It is not the most elegant word in the English language and it would not be the word one would instinctively link with the name of Warner. But it was used by another admirer who wrote in 1945, 'I do like "guts" and, by God, you have shown it, hard and worrying work all through the Blitz and the doodle-buggery. I daresay there is nothing you can look back on with more justifiable pride than your stewardship at Lord's during this war.'

Warner had prided himself on that stewardship and felt that his efforts were not given sufficient recognition. With pride in himself went sensitivity. He could be easily hurt. His family and closest friends were witness to the annual disappointment of the MCC presidency. Probably from the mid-1920s it became a prospect, as ripples of hope gave way to waves of anguish and then torrents of despair. It provides the most striking example but his sensitivity may also be seen in his relationship with Australian public opinion. There is a sad irony in comparing 1904 and 1912 with 1933. In 1912, the *Melbourne Herald* reported, 'his eyes became blurred with tears as he said he would probably never again undertake a trip to Australia. His name will live as long as the game.' In 1933, the Australian press almost universally attacked him for vacillation and weakness. In some ways the friendship with Menzies and, to a much lesser extent, with Bradman eased the memory of those events but a part of 'bodyline' lingered with him. It was only towards the end of his life that he said, 'I love cricket' with the fervour his son John remembered and which cancelled the cry, 'I hate,' of 30 years earlier. Love and hate are linked emotions. Only those who care enough to love can comprehend hate. Warner was never indifferent to cricket. It was the grand, consuming passion.

Pride and sensitivity were also at the root of his persistent efforts to be acceptable to the BBC. In the 1930s he had been regarded by the Corporation almost as a failure, though, in the end, he acquired a certain status as a venerable figure. I had only spoken to him once so I went to hear the recordings in the BBC Sound Archives at Broadcasting House. His was not a voice compelling authority but rather a soft one, detached and almost apologetic. One could see why those BBC internal memos were so critical. There was a lack of resonance and no variety in pitch or emphasis. His enunciation was clear but not emphatic, his accent that of the educated Englishman of his class and generation without being obtrusively so. No one could call Plum's voice 'plummy' save for the accentuation of the word 'off', which he pronounced 'orff'. You would have either had to like Warner or to like cricket if you wished to listen to him for any length of time. It is strange that a man so much in demand as a public speaker, and, as countless invitations and testimony support, so good at it, should have been infinitely less successful in a medium which depended entirely on the projection of the voice.

However, the microphone bestows no plaudits and those, as we have seen, were essential to Warner. They would come from an after-dinner audience whose warm reception would please him. He enjoyed being appreciated. A chance meeting on a bus with Sir Edward German the composer leaves one wondering who was the more delighted. German wrote a note to say how thrilled he had been to meet and speak to 'my ideal cricketer' and Warner accepted the hero-worship (for such it was) with pleasure. Cricket, as Bill Bowes observed, made him 'somebody who was feted wherever he went'. Yet none of this turned his head. He remained throughout his life a modest man, with a childlike attraction in his enjoyment of fame but without vanity. His cricket talk, Ronald Aird emphasised, 'would be in praise of the performances of others and not of his own'.

The nature of the child in him was also seen in a certain sense of wanting to be spoiled which even some of his family thought more marked in old age. Hard worker as he became with the passing of the years, a part of him always believed the world owed him a living, and it declared a certain naïvety especially noticeable in his attitude to money. Far more meals were bought for him in clubs than he ever bought for other people. Money, or the lack of it, was the Achilles' heel of much of his existence. He always thought he was short of it, kept himself at a distance from his wife's finances, badgered the BBC for more of it, and worried greatly about it. He was, as often as not, on someone's pay-roll, or indeed his own at *The Cricketer* office, but he did not pursue a formal career in the sense that a young man coming down from Oxford, even in the 1890s with nothing behind him financially, might have been expected to do.

When he was about to get married he came very close to a career, or to 'finding a berth', as he told his fiancée. Probably the combination of some success as a writer and Agnes's own financial resources meant that an indifferent business man or lawyer was lost and a distinguished author gained. It was not the least of his services to cricket that Warner wrote fluently with a technical understanding, a sense of history and an accumulated folklore. Writing was one of the great consolations of his old age and three substantial books, written when he was over 70, crowned a lifetime of literary endeavour. As Alexander Pope observed, 'true ease in writing comes from art, not chance'. Warner, finding he could write, had persevered in learning his craft and by 1914 was, next to Fry, the most distinguished player commenting on cricket.

His delight in writing and his interest in people came together in the vast correspondence he maintained. Throughout his life he would send notes of congratulation or commiseration besides being the recipient of them himself. All of these he kept and many suggest that his friends seemed to know what was expected of them. During both world wars he wrote to those who had lost loved ones. Often his letters would evoke a lengthy reply, and perhaps an outpouring of grief. Sometimes he felt a second letter might bring a little help and he wrote again. Among random congratulations were those to Edrich in South Africa on getting the double-century, so vital to his career, in 1939, and to Compton in India, keeping him in the picture of cricket at Lord's during the war. Postcards followed Cowdrey to Perth, Brisbane and Melbourne during the 1954–55 tour. He had a gracious way of accepting compliments. To a letter of congratulation on the publication of his *Long Innings* in 1951, he replied, 'I shall keep and treasure your letter and hand it on as an heirloom. I am delighted to know you like my book so much', and, to a young collector, 'I am proud to know that you consider my book worthy of a place in your library.' His prodigious memory, not just for cricket matches, meant that he would remember a correspondence when he met the correspondent for the first time. Typical of this was the experience of J. D. Coldham, the cricket historian. As a young serviceman in India he had sent in his first 'modest contribution' to *The Cricketer*. At a Cricket Society dinner in 1949, Sir Pelham at once knew all about the man to whom he was introduced.

Letter writing was one expression of his kindness and concern. Both institutions and individuals benefited from these virtues. It was he who ensured that the Liberal Jewish Community might worship in a building at Lord's after their synagogue was destroyed in the war, and he was pleased to be able to attend the reconsecration of a new synagogue in 1951. His talks on cricket could raise money for a swimming pool in Muswell Hill; or a Spitfire in National Savings week; cheer up patients in Mount Vernon Hospital; or bring some colour into the drabness of a prison.

His kindness to particular individuals may be illustrated by his help to Philip Snow, the distinguished historian of Fiji cricket and founder of the Fiji Cricket Association, when he came home on leave to England in 1951. Warner, the reigning president of MCC, secured him honorary membership and invited him to play for an XI he was raising. When, shortly afterwards, Snow decided to stay in England and apply for the bursarship of Rugby School, Warner strongly supported his application and took some personal pride in its success. Snow, in due course, was able to invite Warner to meet his own brother, C. P. Snow, an opportunity Warner accepted 'with alacrity'. It was a meeting of mutual enjoyment for the future Lord Snow was a great cricket enthusiast (and something of a cricket philosopher) and Warner was pleased to meet a novelist of distinction.

Almost to the end of his life, he delighted in meeting people. Ronald Aird regarded him as 'a first-choice for a luncheon or dinner party because he would always draw out the best in other people by finding out their interests'. In the valedictory broadcast which the BBC arranged in 1958, John Snagge said of him that he refused to think ill of anyone, whatever he had heard about them. It was a quality – Swanton has called it 'an amiable characteristic' – which occasionally led him into making errors of judgement in the face of less emotional and more rational advice. But it was a quality which was not necessarily translated into his private correspondence. Of a solicitor whom the family had occasion to use, he wrote 'a very bad executor, very indifferent, slow and lazy as hell, too self-centred and selfish'. Less harshly, someone else was adjudged to be 'a rogue, but very brave in the war'.

Warner by no means moved only in a man's world despite the image of days spent in the masculine exclusiveness of Lord's or some London club. Women found him an attractive personality and he responded to them on their own terms. They were never asked to be the silent recipients of his views on cricket and, in that sense, they did not find him dull and boring. If they were both 'pretty' and able to 'bowl well' this was an undoubted bonus in their favour, as he had noted in the young Mrs Whitehead in those pre-1914 occasions at Caring.

In his pre-1914 tours to Australia and South Africa he had always been accompanied by Agnes. It was her great contribution to the marriage that she became a convert to cricket from the start. The telegrams of match results sent to his fiancée had left her in no doubt about what she was letting herself in for! As the years went by, she acquired a judgement of players and their potential which made her opinions worth seeking, as her husband and others acknowledged. Warner paid her a tribute in his autobiography when he wrote that she was a 'really good judge of the game, with a flair for spotting true ability'.

Agnes did not accompany Warner when he went as manager of the 1932–33 tour. As we have seen, he wrote to her frequently and he missed her company. One of the consolations in his unhappiness on that tour was the ladies whom he met on board ship and in Australian households. On the principle, perhaps, that attack was the best form of defence, Warner dutifully reported to Agnes on the physical charms of those with whom he dined and danced.

The name of Miss E. H., whom he had also met there, was an omission as significant as was her later impact on his life. There had indeed been several women who had mattered to Warner over the years but convention, circumstances and choice dictated that the marriage to Agnes was never at any risk. She remained the partner of his life for over half a century for whom he deeply cared and he was genuinely grieved at her death. There was always an outward harmony in their relationship, for Warner, as in so many other aspects of his life, shrank from conflict. But the deep affection of the earlier years was not sustained and in the closing ones the harmony was one of mutual companionship.

His relationship with his children was a close one and he enjoyed the youth of each one of them. Later, as they grew up, there was some tension in the family, primarily because of differences of opinion between the two brothers, but it was broadly contained. Pelham kept his links with all three, seeing Betty and John frequently, and writing abroad to Esmond with the same regularity in old age as he had done during the war. He welcomed the partners they each made in marriage. His Italian daughter-in-law, arriving alone in a strange land from an alien country (with whom peace had only recently been made), never forgot the warmth of the welcome she received when presenting herself for the first time without even her husband's support. Grandchildren were a joy, and welcome visitors at the flat in Malvern Court. Their recollections are of the happiest. No picture of his household is complete without mentioning his life-long devotion to dogs – often mentioned in *The Cricketer* – to one of whom he awarded 'an England blazer' for fielding at Caring.

One of his great friends, the Winchester schoolmaster, cricket historian and future president of MCC, Harry Altham wrote to him: 'When the time comes, many, many years hence, I hope, for your services to cricket to be assessed in history, I do not believe there will be found anyone in its long two centuries to whom a greater debt will be owed.'

These words were written in 1945, the same year in which I met the subject of this biography for the only time. The circumstances do not matter: suffice to say that the Central Mediterranean Forces were playing a Lord's XI at Lord's. I was taken into the pavilion and introduced to Sir Pelham and greeted with warmth and friendliness. His delight in finding that it was my first visit there brought a personal conducted tour. Next day England would play the Dominions and the deputy secretary carried the administrative responsibilities of the occasion but they could wait. I had experienced his 'charm', as had – and would – so many others over so long. I would know what other people meant when they used that word so frequently about him.

So, 40 years on, I find myself, as his biographer, committed to an assessment of Altham's judgement. If its validity is upheld, it is done so at a price. One ignores the contribution of W. G. Grace not only to the evolution of the game but also as an eminent Victorian. One sets aside the statistical domination of Sir Donald Bradman and the extension of that achievement which made him a folk-hero in Australia's social history. One turns away from the great administrators and 'grandees' such as Lord Harris and Lord Hawke.

The case for Warner must stand apart from all these men. His playing career belonged to a single period in the game's history rather than to the half-century and more claimed by Grace. No argument can be founded on figures remotely compatible with those of Bradman. Nor can there be serious advocacy for him as one of the game's leading administrators (despite his sterling work in the Second World War), still less as one of its financiers.

Yet Altham was a man of independent scholarship and a distinguished cricket historian. His opinion must command intellectual respect. What services, then, did Warner render to cricket which led Altham to place him above all others? He was a man who brought to the game a commitment in time, knowledge, judgement, affection and dedication which the circumstances of his life and generation permitted and which is unlikely ever to be paralleled. As John Arlott has said, no man ever saw so much first-class cricket in a lifetime. No man ever will. Lord's, that place so special to him, claimed his love and devotion for over seventy-five years. He was a cricketer who made himself good enough to hold his own among those more naturally talented than he. He was a born leader of men and proved one of the outstanding captains in the game's history. His readiness to identify and encourage young cricketers paved the way for several distinguished careers.

When he no longer played the first-class game, cricket continued to benefit collectively for a further 40 years from his wisdom as a selector, his lucidity as a writer, his perseverance as a broadcaster, his urbanity as a chairman and his ubiquity as an observer. Yet all was accomplished in the face of adversity for there was a frailty as well. His body was often ill and racked with pain and his mind shrank from contending with the ugliness of dispute. Robustness and masculine assertiveness found no reflection on the countenance of that smooth, white, even epicene face.

This frail Plum Warner survived the years. He had been the

youthful captain in Victorian times who would win the Ashes twice before 1914. He would become, between the wars, the man of many parts. As the doyen figure at Lord's, his energies, counsels and presence brought a fitting closure to a way of life which had claimed his loyalties for so many decades.

The Warner Family

The Warners were originally East Anglian folk who had come to England during the Saxon invasions of the eighth and ninth centuries. After the Norman Conquest they held the Manor of Warners in the parish of Great Waltham in Essex from the de Bohuns, Earls of Hereford. In deference to their Norman over-lords, they became, for a spell, known as Le Warner. Curiously, the line of the Warners would one day unite with that of the de Bohuns in the marriage of Thomas Warner to Jane Walrond in the seventeenth century. In the vellum roll of the family's claim to Arms there is a picture of John, Lord of the Manor in the reign of Edward III, equipped to serve his feudal lord in battle.

In the late fourteenth century, Robert, a younger son of another John Le Warner, moved into the neighbouring county of Suffolk and through him the descent of Pelham continues to be traced. Two generations later his grandson, Francis, established the family in the Old Hall at Parham near Woodbridge where the most famous of the early Warners, Thomas, was born about 1575. Hitherto, the family had been prominent only at local level: justices of the peace serving the Tudors and seeing that the dictates of ministers such as Thomas Cromwell and William Cecil had an impact in the county of Suffolk. In those troublesome times, to serve the sovereign on the perimeter of government might be safer than to be at its centre, as one Warner cousin discovered. Sir Edward was Lieutenant of the Tower of London until committed to the custody of his own Tower by Mary I.

Yet Thomas was to paint the family fame on a larger canvas. He was 13 when the news of the Spanish Armada's defeat was signalled by beacons through England. Even in far-eastern Suffolk the tales of the West Country sailors, such as Drake, must have reached his ears and fired his imagination. The end of the war with Spain in 1604 brought an English challenge to Spain's monopoly of land in the New World and among the earliest of adventurers overseas was Thomas himself. He went first with Sir Walter Raleigh on his ill-fated search for gold in Guiana. Back home in Suffolk, he sought backers for an expedition to an island he had spotted on the return voyage. With his wife and son and 14 others he sailed from Woodbridge in 1623 for the tiny West Indian island of St Kitt's. Soon others joined and four years later he had been sufficiently successful as a planter and an administrator to be able

222

to sail home to be knighted by Charles I, to be granted the first letters patent under the royal seal given to any colonial governor and to be made sole Governor of the island for life.

Success brought rivalry and he was forced to share the island with the French. Nevertheless, by 1639 he estimated the annual duties derived from the island to be the enormous sum of £12,000 and soon he was establishing 'daughter' colonies at Nevis, Antigua and Montserrat. He died in 1648, as Governor of all these Leeward Islands and Lieutenant-Governor of all the other English West Indian colonies, second in importance only to Robert Rich, Earl of Warwick and governor-in-chief of all the plantations in America. Of the great migration from which sprang the British Empire and, in due course, the United States, Warner had been a pioneer. More particularly, he had pointed the way for the movement of the men and women of East Anglia, possibly 50 per cent of the total immigrants, to the New World.

So began a West Indian connection in which the Warner family were to figure prominently for 300 years. Thomas's son, Philip, was Governor of Antigua in the late seventeenth century. His career was briefly interrupted by imprisonment in the Tower of London on charges of having murdered a group of Caribs led by 'Indian Warner', a natural son of Sir Thomas. He was acquitted on the grounds that his opponents 'were killed in fair fight' and he ended his days as Speaker of the Barbados House of Assembly.

Philip's son was another Thomas and it was his marriage to Jane Walrond which had brought together the two families whose relationship in the Middle Ages was, as we have seen, one of feudal lord and tenant. We may turn aside for the moment from tracing the descent of the Warner male line to glance at the ancestry of Jane Walrond. It is through her that Pelham Warner may trace a direct ancestry back to the Castilian Spanish kings and to Ferdinand III canonised for his zeal as a crusader. In 1254, Ferdinand's daughter, Eleanor, married Edward I, King of England. Their daughter married Humphrey de Bohun, Earl of Hereford and feudal lord of John Le Warner. The next generation married into another Anglo-Norman family, the Courtenays, Earls of Devon and the direct descendant from the West Country strand was this Jane Walrond.

By the eighteenth century, the family links of the Warners in the West Indies were well established. The economy of the islands, albeit based on a slave society, had proved a prosperous one in sugar and tobacco and the Warner fortunes flourished. With wealth went responsibility: families such as the Warners would be expected to play their part in administering government and ensuring an English legal system in the colonial empire. Thomas's son, Ashton, became Attorney-General of the Leeward Islands. But links with the mother-country were never severed and Anglo-West-Indian families such as the Warners would be found serving in Parliament or educating their sons in England where they might carve independent careers for themselves. Such a career had Joseph Warner, the second son of Ashton. While his elder brother stayed in Antigua to look after the family estates, Joseph went to England in 1720 to be educated at Westminster School and to be apprenticed to the Barber-Surgeons Company. When he was 28 he accompanied, as a surgeon, the forces of the Duke of Cumberland sent to Scotland to put down the Jacobite Rebellion in 1745. Five years later he was elected a Fellow of the Royal Society and he became the first member elected to the Royal College of Surgeons. To contemporaries he was a greater man than John Hunter though it is Hunter's name which posterity knows. Joseph's publications provide an insight into the techniques of the surgery in an age before antiseptics or anaesthetics were available. He died in London in 1801, a wealthy man, who had derived a substantial income both from his practice and from his share of his father's estates. Joseph outlived his son William whose own son, Edward, went to live in the West Indies and who would become the father of Charles and the grandfather of Pelham Warner (see Chapter 1).

The Warner Family Tree

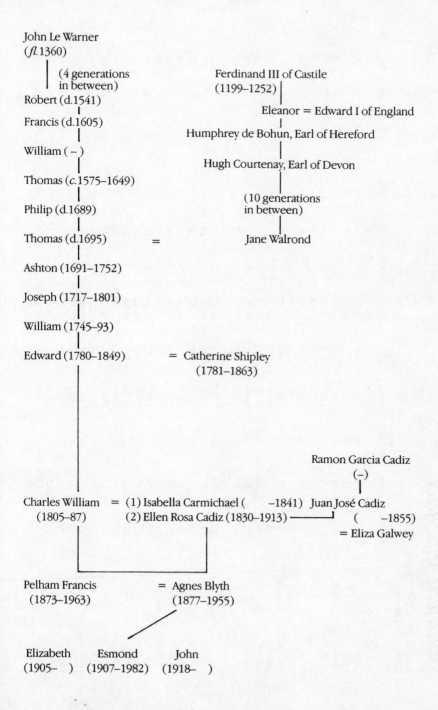

John Le Warner
(*fl.*1360)

| (4 generations in between)

Robert (d.1541)

Francis (d.1605)

William (–)

Thomas (*c.*1575–1649)

Philip (d.1689)

Thomas (d.1695)   =   Jane Walrond

Ashton (1691–1752)

Joseph (1717–1801)

William (1745–93)

Edward (1780–1849)   = Catherine Shipley
(1781–1863)

Ferdinand III of Castile
(1199–1252)

Eleanor = Edward I of England

Humphrey de Bohun, Earl of Hereford

Hugh Courtenay, Earl of Devon

(10 generations in between)

Ramon Garcia Cadiz
(–)

Charles William   =   (1) Isabella Carmichael (–1841) Juan José Cadiz
(1805–87)   (2) Ellen Rosa Cadiz (1830–1913) ———⌐ (–1855)
                                                              = Eliza Galwey

Pelham Francis   = Agnes Blyth
(1873–1963)   (1877–1955)

Elizabeth   Esmond   John
(1905–)   (1907–1982) (1918–)

Statistical Appendix

SIR PELHAM WARNER (1894–1929)
First-class career

Year		Matches	Inns	Times not out	Runs	Highest score	Ave.	100s	50s	Catches	Overs	Mdns	Runs	Wkts	Ave.
1894		4	8	2	133	50	22.17	—	1	2	3	0	18	0	—
1895		16	28	0	658	90	23.50	—	4	10	2	2	0	0	—
1896		12	21	0	562	77	26.76	—	5	7	63.5	16	151	6	25.16
1896–7	W. Indies	7	13	3	407	113*	40.70	1	1	1	26	5	89	2	44.50
1897		22	40	1	1137	176	29.15	2	4	12					
1897	America	2	4	0	62	51	15.50	—	1	1	3	0	10	0	—
1898		18	30	3	848	88	31.40	—	4	9					
1898	America	2	4	0	63	25	15.75	—	—	—					
1898–9	S. Africa	5	8	1	214	132*	30.57	1	—	1					
1899		23	42	3	1140	150	29.23	2	5	5	8	1	31	0	—
1900		23	39	1	1727	170	45.44	5	9	5	5.4	2	22	0	—
1901		22	39	2	1680	197*	45.40	3	11	6	20	6	63	1	63.00
1902		16	28	1	832	139	30.81	3	3	4	16	3	63	1	63.00
1902–3	Australia N. Zealand	10	16	2	771	211	55.07	2	2	7	1	1	0	0	—
1903		21	33	4	1141	149	39.34	3	4	10					
1903–4	Australia	14	24	1	694	79	30.17	—	6	5	10	3	28	0	—
1904		22	39	5	1390	163	40.88	3	5	7	2.4	1	5	1	5.00
1905		19	35	0	1537	204	43.91	3	9	6	12.1	3	40	2	20.00
1905–6	S. Africa	12	22	3	314	56	16.52	—	2	3	8	1	36	1	36.00
1906		17	33	2	1299	137	41.90	2	10	9	8	1	30	1	30.00
1907		27	47	6	1891	149	46.12	5	13	5					
1908		29	45	5	1822	120	45.55	5	10	7					
1909		25	44	6	1333	127*	35.07	3	8	8					
1910		27	44	4	1646	150*	41.15	5	7	17	3	0	13	0	—
1911		31	51	5	2123	244	46.15	5	15	13	0.1	0	1	0	—
1911–12	Australia	1	1	0	151	151	151.00	1	—	—					
1912		13	20	4	533	130	33.31	3	1	1					
1913		20	31	2	1072	125	36.96	3	4	9					
1914		15	22	3	446	79	23.47	1	1	3					
1919		15	23	2	481	101	22.90	1	3	6					
1920		23	33	4	804	139	27.72	1	3	4	2	0	8	0	—
1926–7	S. America	4	6	0	109	46	18.16	—	—	—					
1929		1	2	0	8	8	4.00	—	—	—	11	0	28	0	—
TTN		518	875	75	29028	244	36.28	60	150	183	205.3	45	636	15	42.40

Middlesex (1894–1920)

	Matches	Inns	Times not out	Runs	Highest score	Ave.	100s	50s	Catches	Overs	Mdns	Runs	Wkts	Ave.
1894	2	4	2	53	29*	26.50	–	–	1					
1895	7	12	0	116	27	9.66	–	–	3					
1896	4	7	0	200	74	28.57	–	2	1					
1897	16	29	0	916	176	31.58	1	4	10	8	2	24	0	–
1898	17	28	3	817	88	32.68	–	4	8					
1899	19	34	3	1014	150	32.70	2	5	4	6	1	28	0	–
1900	18	30	0	1335	170	44.50	5	5	4	2	1	4	0	–
1901	17	30	2	1382	197*	49.35	3	10	4	3	3	0	0	–
1902	13	24	1	661	139	28.73	2	2	3	13	2	51	0	–
1903	16	24	2	899	149	40.86	3	2	8					
1904	18	31	3	1077	163	38.46	2	4	5	2.4	1	5	1	5.00
1905	14	27	0	1077	166	39.88	2	6	3	10.1	2	35	2	17.50
1906	14	27	1	1013	137	38.96	2	7	8	8	1	30	1	30.00
1907	20	35	4	1392	149	44.90	1	12	4					
1908	18	26	2	1298	120	54.80	5	6	4					
1909	18	31	5	905	127*	34.80	3	4	6					
1910	21	32	4	1248	150*	44.57	4	5	16	3	0	13	0	–
1911	22	35	3	1346	121	42.06	4	9	11					
1912	8	14	4	336	130	33.60	2	–	1					
1913	17	26	4	987	125	41.12	3	4	8					
1914	13	18	2	398	79	26.53	–	1	2					
1919	11	16	2	271	101*	19.35	1	1	5	2	0	8	0	–
1920	22	31	4	766	139	28.37	1	3	4					
TOTAL	345	571	50	19507	197*	37.44	46	96	123	57.5	13	198	4	49.50
COUNTY CHAMPIONSHIP	329	545	45	18565	197*	37.13	43	92	114	52.5	12	172	4	43.00
OTHER MATCHES	16	26	5	942	127*	44.85	3	4	9	5	1	26	0	–

Summary (1894–1929)

	Matches	Inns	Times not out	Runs	Highest score	Ave.	100s	50s	Catches	Overs	Mdns	Runs	Wkts	Ave.
England (Tests in England)	3	4	0	77	39	19.25	–	–	–					
England XI	2	3	0	22	16	7.33	–	–	2					
Gentlemen	23	46	1	1248	97	27.73	–	10	7	20	3	87	1	87.00
Gents of England	3	5	0	138	85	27.60	–	1	3	2	1	5	0	–
Londesborough's XI	1	2	0	100	60	50.00	–	1	1					
MCC	38	69	8	2406	204	39.44	4	14	8	30	3	79	2	39.50
MCC Australian Team	3	4	1	180	126	60.00	1	–	1					
Middlesex	345	571	50	19507	197*	37.44	46	96	123	57.5	13	198	4	49.50
Oxford University	18	32	1	966	90	30.18	–	8	13	5	2	18	0	–
Rest of England	10	14	1	891	244	68.53	4	2	4	3	1	12	1	12.00
South	4	7	2	210	88	42.00	–	2	1	3	1	10	0	–
The Rest	1	2	0	85	53	42.50	–	1	–	0.1	0	1	0	–
Thornton's XI	3	5	0	107	40	21.40	–	–	–	0.4	0	8	0	–
Tours abroad (incl. Tests)	57	98	10	2785	211	31.64	5	12	18	82.5	21	215	7	30.71
Warner's XI	4	8	2	219	60*	36.50	–	2	1	1	0	3	0	–
Webbe's XI	3	5	0	87	51	17.40	–	1	1					
TOTAL	518	875	75	29028	244	36.28	60	150	183	205.3	45	636	15	42.40

Test Matches

	Matches	Inns	Times not out	Runs	Highest score	Ave.	100s	50s	Catches
v. Australia	7	13	1	287	79	23.91	–	2	2
v. South Africa	8	15	1	335	132*	23.92	1	1	1
TOTAL	15	28	2	622	132*	23.92	1	3	3
Home	3	4	0	77	39	19.25	–	–	–
Abroad	12	24	2	545	132*	24.77	1	3	3

Runs at Lord's

	Matches	Inns	Times not out	Runs	Highest score	Ave.	100s	50s
for Middlesex	179	288	27	10886	197*	41.70	28	58
for MCC	32	57	7	2018	204	40.36	3	13
for Gentlemen	11	22	0	656	97	29.81	0	5
for Oxford University	3	5	0	95	42	19.00	0	0
for Other Teams	10	14	2	558	126	46.50	1	3
	225	386	3?		204		32	79

Centuries in first-class cricket (60)

Score	Team	v.	Opponent	Venue	Season
113*	Lord Hawke's XI	v.	Barbados	Bridgetown	1896-7
176	Middlesex	v.	Nottinghamshire	Leeds	1897
108*	MCC	v.	Yorkshire	Lord's	1897
132*	England	v.	South Africa	Johannesburg	1898-9
150	Middlesex	v.	Yorkshire	Lord's	1899
114	Middlesex	v.	Somerset	Taunton	1899
170	Middlesex	v.	Essex	Lord's	1900
146	Middlesex	v.	Lancashire	Lord's	1900
134	Middlesex	v.	Nottinghamshire	Nottingham	1900
114	Middlesex	v.	Sussex	Lord's	1900
100	Middlesex	v.	Surrey	Lord's	1900
197*	Middlesex	v.	Somerset	Lord's	1901
112	Middlesex	v.	Sussex	Brighton	1901
103	Middlesex	v.	Essex	Leyton	1901
139	Middlesex	v.	Sussex	Eastbourne	1902
109	Middlesex	v.	Gloucestershire	Bristol	1902
107	MCC	v.	Cambridge Univ.	Lord's	1902
211	Lord Hawke's XI	v.	Otago	Dunedin	1902-3
125	Lord Hawke's XI	v.	New Zealand	Wellington	1902-3
149	Middlesex	v.	Gloucestershire	Lord's	1903
135	Middlesex	v.	Somerset	Leeds	1903
115	Middlesex	v.	Rest of England	Oval	1903
163	Middlesex	v.	Nottinghamshire	Nottingham	1904
145	MCC	v.	Yorkshire	Scarborough	1904
106	Middlesex	v.	Surrey	Oval	1904
204	MCC	v.	Sussex	Lord's	1905
166	Middlesex	v.	Lancashire	Lord's	1905
152	Middlesex	v.	Essex	Lord's	1905
137	Middlesex	v.	Sussex	Lord's	1906
122	Middlesex	v.	Kent	Tonbridge	1906
116	England XI	v.	Nottinghamshire	Oval	1907
113*	Middlesex	v.	Surrey	Oval	1907
149	Middlesex	v.	Essex	Leyton	1908
120	Middlesex	v.	Essex	Lord's	1908
117	Middlesex	v.	Hampshire	Lord's	1908
110	Middlesex	v.	Somerset	Taunton	1908
105	Middlesex	v.	Hampshire	Bournemouth	1908
104*	Middlesex	v.	Australians	Lord's	1909
127*	Middlesex	v.	Surrey	Oval	1909
106*	Middlesex	v.	Surrey	Lord's	1909
102	Middlesex	v.	Warwickshire	Worcester	1910
150*	Middlesex	v.	Hampshire	Lord's	1910
145*	Middlesex	v.	Surrey	Lord's	1910
137	Middlesex	v.	Kent	Lord's	1910
126	Rest of England	v.	Essex	Oval	1910
101*	Middlesex	v.	Warwickshire	Lord's	1911
244	England	v.	Surrey	Lord's	1911
121	Middlesex	v.	Nottinghamshire	Lord's	1911
118	Middlesex	v.	Essex	Leyton	1911
114	Middlesex	v.	Kent	Lord's	1911
109	MCC	v.	South Australia	Adelaide	1911-12
151	Middlesex	v.	Sussex	Lord's	1912
130	Middlesex	v.	Rest of England	Lord's	1912
126	MCC Australian Team	v.	Rest of England	Lord's	1912
105*	Middlesex	v.	Lancashire	Lord's	1912
125	MCC	v.	Essex	Oval	1913
115	Middlesex	v.	Surrey	Lord's	1913
100	Middlesex	v.	Warwickshire	Oval	1913
101*	Middlesex	v.	Australian Imp. Forces	Lord's	1919
139	Middlesex	v.	Sussex	Lord's	1920

Centuries in minor cricket – on tours

Score	Team	v.	Opponent	Venue	Season
119	Lord Hawke's XI	v.	Queen's Park CC	Trinidad	1896-7
156	Lord Hawke's XI	v.	St Vincent	St Vincent	1896-7
110	Lord Hawke's XI	v.	Antigua	St John's	1896-7
125	MCC	v.	XVIII of Western Transvaal	Potchefstroom	1905-6
128	MCC	v.	Middelburg & District	Middelburg	1905-6

Wicket Partnerships over 150

Score		Wkt		Partner	Team		Opponent		Venue	Year
169	for	2nd	with	F. G. J. Ford	Middlesex	v.	Nottinghamshire	–	Nottingham	1898
167	for	3rd	with	H. W. Kaye	Middlesex	v.	Essex	–	Lord's	1900
200	for	1st	with	H. B. Hayman	Middlesex	v.	Gloucestershire	–	Lord's	1901
218	for	1st	with	J. Douglas	Middlesex	v.	Lancashire	–	Lord's	1901
233	for	1st	with	C. J. Burnup	MCC	v.	Cambridge Univ.	–	Lord's	1902
158	for	2nd	with	G. W. Beldam	Middlesex	v.	Rest of England	–	Oval	1903
248	for	1st	with	L. J. Moon	Middlesex	v.	Gloucester	–	Lord's	1903
306	for	1st	with	J. Douglas	Middlesex	v.	Nottinghamshire	–	Nottingham	1904
161	for	1st	with	J. H. Stogdon	Middlesex	v.	Essex	–	Lord's	1904
195	for	1st	with	E. A. Beldam	Middlesex	v.	Surrey	–	Oval	1904
189	for	1st	with	R. H. Spooner	Gentlemen	v.	Players	–	Lord's	1905
182	for	3rd	with	C. A. L. Payne	Middlesex	v.	Kent	–	Tonbridge	1906
222	for	2nd	with	J. T. Tyldesley	England	v.	Nottingham	–	Oval	1907
187	for	1st	with	T. Hayward	South	v.	North	–	Oval	1908
158	for	1st	with	L. J. Moon	Middlesex	v.	Hampshire	–	Bournemouth	1908
161	for	1st	with	L. J. Moon	Middlesex	v.	Nottinghamshire	–	Nottingham	1908
151	for	2nd	with	F. A. Tarrant	Middlesex	v.	Somerset	–	Taunton	1908
212	for	1st	with	L. J. Moon	Middlesex	v.	Sussex	–	Lord's	1908
203	for	1st	with	F. A. Tarrant	Middlesex	v.	Hampshire	–	Lord's	1908
180	for	1st	with	F. A. Tarrant	Middlesex	v.	Sussex	–	Eastbourne	1910
155	for	7th	with	R. Anton	Middlesex	v.	Worcestershire	–	Worcester	1910
167	for	2nd	with	G. Gunn	MCC	v.	South Australia	–	Adelaide	1911/12
157	for	5th	with	F. R. Foster	England	v.	Warwickshire	–	Oval	1911
234	for	5th	with	C. B. Fry	Gentlemen	v.	Players	–	Oval	1911
208	for	3rd	with	R. H. Spooner	Middlesex	v.	Worcestershire	–	Worcester	1911
155	for	4th	with	E. S. Littlejohn	Middlesex	v.	Essex	–	Leyton	1911
171	for	1st	with	F. A. Tarrant	MCC Australian Team	v.	Rest of England	–	Lord's	1912
193	for	5th	with	F. E. Woolley	Middlesex	v.	Sussex	–	Eastbourne	1913
206	for	3rd	with	J. W. Hearne	Middlesex	v.	Warwickshire	–	Lord's	1913
150	for	5th	with	E. H. Hendren	Middlesex	v.	Warwickshire	–	Lord's	1913
165	for	1st	with	H. W. Lee	Middlesex	v.	Sussex	–	Lord's	1920
241	for	1st	with	H. W. Lee	Middlesex	v.	Hampshire	–	Lord's	1920
157	for	4th	with	E. H. Hendren	Middlesex	v.	Sussex	–	Lord's	1920
172	for	4th	with	E. H. Hendren	Middlesex	v.	Kent	–	Lord's	1920

Notes

1 Pelham Warner could recall his father describing to him the excitement when the news of Waterloo came through.

2 From now on, he was 'Plum' to his associates and Warner (or 'Plum' Warner) to everyone else. Pelham, which his family used, appeared more generally when he was knighted. He belonged to a generation which preferred the use of surnames and, in general, he will henceforth be styled 'Warner' throughout this book.

3 The connection between cricket and colonial development is not implausible. Hawke knew Alfred Lyttleton who was a political colleague of Chamberlain's and who succeeded him as Colonial Secretary in 1903.

4 Several papers both in England and South Africa called the matches Test matches though *Wisden* avoided the phrase. In retrospect, Test status was accorded. Warner therefore made a century on his Test debut.

5 Still (1987) a record by English players.

6 It had been abolished in England in 1900.

7 The speed of the London postal service calls for comment. Warner wrote his letter at 6.30 p.m. It bore a 9.30 p.m. postmark and was delivered next morning in time for Agnes to send a message of acceptance to the lunch invitation.

8 C. R. Browne was the first West Indian to be elected an honorary life member of MCC.

9 Illness kept Jones out of three of the five Tests, the side being led by F. L. Fane, an Essex amateur and a close friend of the Warner family.

10 No. 15 Tedworth Square, having survived the bombing which destroyed many neighbouring houses in 1940–41 fell victim to the development planners in the 1970s – despite the protest of conservationists who argued its case as a Victorian building and as the home of four well-known people: Sir Henry Dickens, Mrs Lily Langtry, Sir Pelham Warner and Mrs Patrick Campbell. Today a block of flats stands on the site.

11 Its value and status may be estimated by the price it commanded when sold in 1985 for £285,000 freehold.

12 But which Cumberbatch (a well-known West-Indian name) one does not know.

13 I am indebted to Mr Peter Bowden for checking references for me in the Maidstone Library.

14 Despite the new family nomenclature of 'rat'.

15 Unexpectedly, the immediate eventuality was saving the Princess Royal and her family when the ss *Delhi* sank.

16 Another family nickname – used especially by the children to him as they grew older.

17 Now just a modest occasion compared with the pre-war 'training camps'.

18 During the Surrey innings, both Hendren and Durston left the field at teatime in order to play football for Brentford in the Third Division (South) in the evening. One must make the assumption that both captains had agreed to this and that an arrangement existed between Middlesex and Brentford. Fender would have had little objections to Middlesex being

deprived of two strong players but Warner must have been distressed at the possible implications.

19   Many of which he included in an Appendix to his *My Cricketing Life* (1920).

20   E. W. Swanton, *Gubby Allen – Man of Cricket*, 1985.

21   Subsequently published in book form in 1926 and many times reprinted, with E. W. Swanton later a co-author.

22   To be fair to Warner the book was very well reviewed. *The Times* called it the product 'of a thoughtful and mellow mind'.

23   The Reverend R. H. Hodgson whose country vicarage was in Hampshire.

24   I am grateful to Mr Sinfield for discussing this with me.

25   As late as 1982–83, the same title was used by Chris Harte in a book published by the Glenalvon Press, Adelaide.

26   Agnes was also asked to check that MCC had paid £250 into his bank account at Lloyds.

27   Author's italics.

28   Or possibly unavailable while negotiations took place over his role as a writer.

29   See E. W. Swanton, *Gubby Allen – Man of Cricket*, pp. 118–25.

30   I have included the texts of the draft cables since this is the first time, so far as I am aware, that they have been published. The cables which were actually exchanged have appeared in various books though sometimes abridged. They are printed in full in *Wisden* for 1934.

31   The italics are Warner's own.

32   Brown would be captain 1950–51.

33   Fifty-one years later New Zealand would defeat England by an innings at Christchurch, and win the series for the first time.

34   Reuter's particular agent, Gilbert Mant, knew a great deal about cricket. He happened to be an Australian. For that reason more than any other he felt he had to be extremely objective in what he said. When, some years later, he wished to publish a book on the bodyline issue, Reuter's suggested it was not in keeping with their policy.

35   There is an interesting article in *The Cricketer*, 6 May 1933 on the broadcasting arrangements used in the 1932–33 series.

36   A convenient arrangement in an age before air travel had become established by which a member country nominated someone in England to act on its behalf.

37   Soon after the Second World War it was Lotbinière who recognised the potential talents of Brian Johnston as a broadcaster.

38   See Gerald Pawle, *R. E. S. Wyatt* (1985), pp. 168–9.

39   The visit of E. R. T. Holmes' side in 1935–36 to New Zealand and Australia.

40   E. W. Swanton, *Gubby Allen*, p. 212.

41   Gerald Howat, *Walter Hammond* (1984), pp. 146–7.

42   At first the former secretary, W. Findlay, was appointed deputy secretary coming up to Lord's once a week but in 1941 Warner took over completely.

43   Allen, although he had last captained England in 1936–37, would do so again in the West Indies in 1947–48.

44   This letter is the more interesting as Constantine was a very infrequent correspondent, as I found to my loss when I wrote his biography.

45   *Arthur Langford: A Memoir* (1977), a limited edition of 50 by Irving Rosenwater is a well-deserved tribute. See also *The Cricketer*, May 1981.

46 Three years earlier he had considered the odds 10–1 against.
47 *Wisden*, 1955, 'England did not field their full strength, the selectors deciding that the opportunity of Test match experience should be given to some of the players chosen to tour Australia a few weeks later.' Pakistan beat England, and shared the rubber.

A Note on Sources

Manuscript

The Papers of Sir Pelham Warner (in the possession of members of the Warner family).

The 'scrapbooks' (1896–1904) of Sir Pelham Warner in the Library of MCC.

The Warner files at the Written Archive Centre of the BBC.

The Minutes and letter files of MCC.

The Gowrie Papers (MS 2852 Series 2) in the National Library of Australia at Canberra.

The Menzies Papers (MS 4936) in the National Library of Australia at Canberra.

Miscellaneous papers in the Library of the Melbourne CC, and in La Trobe Library in Melbourne.

Newspapers

Sir Pelham Warner's career is covered extensively in papers throughout the English-speaking world. Australian papers are of particular interest for his early years there as a player as well as in the period 1932–33. The principal sources for these papers were the British Museum Newspaper section at Colindale, The Bodleian Library, Oxford and the Australian National Library, Canberra.

Books and Journals

Wisden's Cricketers' Almanack is an essential source from the issue of 1890 onwards. The more important references, other than to matches themselves, are listed in the *Index to Wisden, 1864–1984* (ed. Derek Barnard). The issues of 1904, 1921 and 1964 make particular mention of Warner. To give a list of the cricket books in the twentieth century in which he is named would be comparable to offering a list of books on the Second World War in which there is a reference to Sir Winston Churchill. *The Cricketer*, from its foundation by himself in 1921, is the principal cricket journal but there are substantial references to him, in his early years, in *Cricket* (which ceased publication in 1914) and C. B. Fry's *Magazine of Sports* (1904–11).

Sir Pelham Warner's own output was considerable. He wrote, at various times, for the *Westminster Gazette*, the *Morning Post*, *The Daily Telegraph*, *The Times*, *The Field*. Some of the material therein found its way, in more permanent form, into his books, the full list of which is as follows:

Cricket in Many Climes, 1900
Cricket Across the Seas, 1903
How We Recovered the Ashes, 1904
MCC in South Africa, 1906
Book of Cricket, 1911
England v. Australia (1911–12), 1912
Imperial Cricket (ed.), 1912

Cricket Reminiscences, 1920
Cricket (ed.), 1920
My Cricketing Life, 1921
Fight for the Ashes in 1926, 1926
The Story of the Ashes, 1926
Oxford v. Cambridge at the Wicket
    (with F. S. Ashley-Cooper), 1926
Fight for the Ashes in 1930, 1930
Cricket Between Two Wars, 1942
Lord's, 1787–1945, 1946
Gentlemen v. Players, 1806–1949, 1950
Long Innings, 1951

While no full biography of him has been written, there have been a few short contributions:

F. S. Ashley-Cooper, *P. F. Warner's Cricket Record, 1888–1919*, undated.
L. Meynell, *'Plum' Warner*, 1951.
R. Mason, *'Plum Warner's Last Season (1920)*, 1970.

Index